ROUTLEDGE LIBRARY EDITIONS: EDUCATION

EDUCATION

EDUCATION
Capitalist and Socialist

BERYL PRING

Volume 193

LONDON AND NEW YORK

First published in 1937

This edition first published in 2012
by Routledge
2 Park Square, Milton Park, Abingdon, Oxfordshire OX14 4RN

Simultaneously published in the USA and Canada
by Routledge
711 Third Avenue, New York, NY 10017

First issued in paperback 2014

Routledge is an imprint of the Taylor and Francis Group, an informa company

© 1937 Methuen & Co. Ltd.

All rights reserved. No part of this book may be reprinted or reproduced or utilised in any form or by any electronic, mechanical, or other means, now known or hereafter invented, including photocopying and recording, or in any information storage or retrieval system, without permission in writing from the publishers.

Trademark notice: Product or corporate names may be trademarks or registered trademarks, and are used only for identification and explanation without intent to infringe.

British Library Cataloguing in Publication Data
A catalogue record for this book is available from the British Library

ISBN 13: 978-0-415-50587-1 (Volume 193)
ISBN 13: 978-0-415-75299-2 (pbk)

Publisher's Note
The publisher has gone to great lengths to ensure the quality of this reprint but points out that some imperfections in the original copies may be apparent.

Disclaimer
The publisher has made every effort to trace copyright holders and would welcome correspondence from those they have been unable to trace.

EDUCATION
Capitalist and Socialist

by

BERYL PRING

METHUEN & CO. LTD. LONDON
36 Essex Street, Strand, W.C.2

First published in 1937

PRINTED IN GREAT BRITAIN

TO MY HUSBAND
DOUGLAS HARDING

PREFACE

THE complexion of British politics is likely for a great many years to be coloured by the relatively high standard of living of the English working class. The middle classes also in post-war England have never experienced any degree of insecurity and financial loss comparable to that which affected the political thinking of the Germans, unfortunately in the direction of fascism. It is urgently necessary that the propaganda of the labour and socialist movement be reconsidered in the light of this very obvious fact. At the moment, the working-class core of the Labour Party is held together by the appeal of trade unionism and its ability to give a certain security to the workers under capitalism, particularly when prosperous, and has not yet really considered the possibility of fundamental social change. The propaganda of the more intellectual section of the socialist movement has naturally been considerably influenced by foreign writers and speakers of the left. That propaganda takes its stand on the economic issue, arguing that capitalism inevitably exploits the working class in the interests of private profit. Such an idea has been realized as a fact of personal experience only by a small proportion of the working class, and by very few of the middle class.

It is essential to the progress of the socialist movement in this country, that at least part of the middle class and of those who aspire to its ranks be won over. The numerical strength of the middle class is such that it is necessary to obtain some support from them, but that support is not likely to be forthcoming without a change in socialist propaganda, unless the whole economic position of Great Britain is worsened by fresh crises or by war. Large numbers of the middle classes are professional people, who are sufficiently far advanced intellectually to be interested in the status and national importance of their work, apart from the private pecuniary profit to be gained by their practice of it. These people cannot be interested in the socialist theory through fear of economic insecurity, but the socialist need not therefore despair of inducing their attention. There is increasingly apparent among professional people a realization of the relations of their work to the surrounding social conditions, and further, a sense of frustration that those conditions are at present a hindrance to their efforts for social betterment; economic restrictions on the national exchequer affect their outlook, even though their own security remains assured. Doctors know the futility of the medical art in the face of continued poverty and undernourishment; architects helplessly see the face of England marred by the builder speculating for private profit; lawyers are aware that differences in income nullify the supposed equality before the law.

The teachers form a large proportion of the professional middle class; they are in contact with all classes in the schools and they hold the key to all social change, because they are in charge of the fundamental force of society, the mentality of the nation. They, too, know frustration in their work, the constant battle to overcome unsuitable conditions, poor equipment, ugly buildings, and overcrowded classes, the farce of training children for intelligent citizenship in a world which so often offers them the alternative of unemployment and dull, unimaginative work, the slow rot of malnutrition. Nevertheless, the teachers as a body cling to the dogma to which they have been trained, that education is a profession beyond and above the vulgarity of politics. It has been my object in writing this book to develop the thesis that politics, in the sense of the government of our whole social structure, holds the key to the resolution of modern educational problems; that the teacher will be relieved of his present sense of frustration only through government, and ultimately, socialist action. The invasions of the first National Government into the sacred territory of education did something to bring the teacher out of his splendid isolation; it is to be hoped that he will consider still further the general political and economic implications of such action.

My thanks are due to many who have given me help and encouragement, and principally to Mr. J. F. Horrabin, to whom I owe a debt of gratitude. I would like also to thank Mr. Lionel Elvin for his interest and assistance, my brother, Kenneth Pring, J. L. Gray and Pearl Moshinsky for permission to quote from their investigation into the ability of London schoolchildren and its relation to opportunity, and lastly many friends who have taken a great deal of trouble to supply me with material.

December 1936

CONTENTS

	PAGE
PREFACE	vii

PART ONE
CAPITALIST EDUCATION

CHAPTER
1. INTRODUCTION   3
2. INEQUALITY OF OPPORTUNITY   20
3. BIAS IN CAPITALIST EDUCATION   58
4. THE FAILURE OF CAPITALIST EDUCATION   103

PART TWO
SOCIALIST EDUCATION

5. IMMEDIATE AMELIORATIVE MEASURES   127
6. THE MACHINERY OF SOCIALIST EDUCATION   157
7. SOCIALIST TREATMENT OF SPECIAL EDUCATIONAL INSTITUTIONS   173
8. THE AIMS AND METHODS OF SOCIALIST EDUCATION   207
   INDEX   275

PART ONE
CAPITALIST EDUCATION

CHAPTER ONE
INTRODUCTION

THIS book is an attempt to work out the relation between education and the reconstruction of society that is proposed by socialists; consequently I am more concerned with the relation of these two things than with either apart from the other. This being so, and since I do not wish to preface my book by two others, I have had to assume much about the nature of both education and socialism that to many people will be unproven. Nevertheless, I have thought the relationship between these two things to be sufficiently important and interesting to make these assumptions permissible, provided they were clearly stated. In the first place I assume that socialism will be able to provide a form of society that is economically and psychologically preferable to that of capitalism. I assume that a socialist state will be able to make a great increase in the national expenditure on education, although the economic arguments for this claim are outside the scope of this book. Since education deals with the human mind in its individual development and in its relations to others, I have naturally been more concerned with the psychologically and sociologically important aspects of socialism. There is more agreement between socialists of varying points of view on these aspects of socialism than on the more purely economic, and therefore I have thought it unnecessary to outline my own particular brand of socialist theory. Education is a matter that socialists will have to consider in connection with their long-term policy, rather than with the immediate reforms of society; since socialists disagree more about the manner of transition from capitalism to socialism than about the broad outlines of the future socialist state, I have considered this another reason for allowing the socialist reader to fill in my arguments where I have deliberately left them vague, with the details of his own theory of political method. I have qualified the suggestions made in Chapters Five and Six for the reconstruction of some of the present educational machinery, by saying that, if the transition to socialism is so violent as to sweep away that machinery, then the socialist state must build entirely anew. The ideas of the last two chapters are referring to the state of society that all socialists may be taken as aiming at for the distant future. But for the purposes of Chapters Five and Six, I have assumed the possibility of a transition to socialism by means of legislation.

One opinion, however, I have stated strongly since it is directly connected with my subject, and indeed might be called the thesis of the book; I have set out to prove to the best of my ability that education, like all other forms of social activity, is tinged by the economic structure of society. For this reason I have spent nearly half the book in an analysis of contemporary education in its environment of capitalist society. Education and the economic forms of society have infinite repercussions on each other, but it seems to me that in the present state of European civilization, the political and economic reconstruction must precede the educational. The rest of the book must support me in that statement. That our economic systems of production and distribution are in need of reconstruction, readers of a great variety of political opinions will agree in allowing me to assume;

that our educational systems are in equal need of reform is something I hope to prove.

Many people are unwilling to accept the idea of the close relationship between the state and education, and of the next step in educational progress being through state control, because such control seems to be an encroachment on individual liberty. The problem of the reconciliation of individual liberty with the organization of community life is, however, fundamental to any consideration of the future of education. One of the most cherished freedoms of the individual has always been the right to train his children to follow in his footsteps. One of the most successful ways of preserving a social system has been by the influence that can be exercised on the growing generation of future citizens in the schools. A child must be trained as an individual who has his own particular gifts to develop and as a social being who has to recognize the existence and the rights of his fellows. The state, which is the administrative machine of the community, has every right to be interested in the training of its constituent individuals. As socialism stands for the extension of state control, it is necessary, in order to appease the extreme individualist, to show that that extension does not necessarily curtail individual liberty. In capitalist society to-day we can observe a mentality that assumes a wide divergence between the claims of the individual and of the community, an attitude indicative of social dislocation; one of the signs of health in a society is the approximation of the good of the individual to that of the community. To-day on the one hand there is the widespread conception of the state as above the laws of the individual, and existing on a different moral plane. On the other hand there is an interest, amounting sometimes to hysteria, in the doings and personalities of certain individuals. Both are best exemplified in the fascist countries, where the welfare of 'the corporate state' is reckoned before that of its constituent citizens, and where the superman, the great individual, the Leader, is also made of predominant importance.

The community is often spoken of as being a personality, a greater individual than the men that compose it in their intricate and complex relations, a whole, working to its own ends and moved by its own emotions. Whether or not it is necessary to accept this fascist conception of the state, it seems to be beyond dispute that the world and its fortunes depend on the working of communal motives. It is becoming more and more difficult for the individual, whatever his creative genius, his magnetic personality, or his perseverance, to do anything to control the stream of political and economic development, unless he has behind him the confidence of society. The politician has perforce to do business with the public, however much of his activity he would like to keep hidden. The problem of socialists, in the present capitalist world, would be reduced to the simplicity of inventing tactics, ways and means of achievement, if the mass of the people in a country were aware of, and antagonized by, the appropriation of the economic power by the few. The sinister and depressing aspect of their problem is that the capitalist has been able to link the motive power of the mass of the people he controls, onto the purpose of driving the economic machine that causes them so much misery. The majority of the people of Europe, and undoubtedly of England, do not desire to put an end to the capitalist system. Political democracy has not achieved its logical result in the rule of the working class, who form the majority of the voters. The most disconcerting feature of the Hitler régime in Germany is not perhaps the barbarism of its attack on its enemies, but the mass support and enthusiasm given to Hitler by the German nation.

Yet despite the importance of communal interests and motives in determining the course of world affairs under both socialist and capitalist governments, the mentality of the people of this country reveals the fact that they are not yet thinking in terms of the community. There is a strong desire among different types of people to find some individual or some organization which they feel to be above and beyond them, and on which they can rest the responsibility of dealing with the economic and psychological problems of their society. The strong man who has the appearance of controlling the destinies of nations on his own initiative is welcomed with the relief usually felt by the common man as he hands over a difficult task to his superior officer; the man in the ranks is willing to run the risk of being led into any dangers, rather than be compelled to take command of the situation himself. This relief accounts for the joyful acceptance of such men as Hitler and Roosevelt, the luxurious abandonment of responsibility with which their countries set them on pedestals and waited breathlessly for the word of the oracle; nor, unfortunately, will the inevitable failure of these mighty beings necessarily disillusion their supporters concerning the power of the individual in modern society, but only concerning that of these particular individuals. Of all the palpable puppets that formed the last National Government, Mr. Hore-Belisha alone made any appeal to the imagination, since in his small corner he attempted a feeble manifestation of personal power. Mr. Eden rose to power on a wave of popularity for much the same reasons. The phenomenal interest shown in T. E. Lawrence, at the time of his death, was due, not to the remarkable genius of his writings, but to the colourful circumstances which made possible his romantic Arabian adventure—one of the few incidents in the war which, while achieving little or nothing ultimately, gave glamour to individual heroism, and stands out with obvious charm against a background where immense and ruthless forces of economic necessity drowned the personal courage of the soldiers in a sea of mud, or smashed it to bits with machine-guns. English newspaper readers do not find their matter written in terms of community and mankind, but the headlines go to this statesman, that record-breaker, to the criminal, the sportsman, and the society belle. In the religious sphere, what is Buchmanism but the counterpart of this political irresponsibility, the wish to be folded in the arms of a power which produces guidance with the comfortable regularity and infallibility of a calculating machine? Not the least of the tasks of the socialist state will be to inculcate the idea of communal responsibility, the necessity of active participation on the part of every individual in matters of state, the impossibility of shifting onto the shoulders of one man or of a few the tasks of managing a nation. It may be possible now successfully to run a communal service, such as a library or a road, by the simple restriction of the individual with certain rules and regulations. But the management of a whole nation and all branches of its life on socialist lines, demands a more positive conception of the individual's ultimate responsibility for the acts of the community.

Some have conceived of the community as a new type

of individual, emerging from the aggregation of separate human beings in various complex relations. Even if this is so, the community cannot demand the unreasoning devotion of its elements, and especially if the good of the individual is not incorporated in the welfare of the community which he serves. The Hegelian theory of state is a conception that in some developments has merely pandered to the extremes of fascism; Prussianism, and its modern descendant Nazidom, are clear examples of how unelevated may be the morality of the state supreme. It is a common observation, and one that is of peculiar interest to the educationalist, that the mass emotions of men are at a far more primitive level than those of the normal individual. The communities of the world, which together form the creature, mankind, are at the moment in paramount danger of destroying themselves in war, unless men can by intellectual control of their environment sublimate the still primitive emotions of man in society. For, though war may be ultimately due to economic causes, and is often engineered for individual profit, it can only be prolonged and carried through to its devastating conclusion by arousing nationalist hysteria in the mass of people involved. In these situations a high standard of morality among individuals is ineffective in restraining the communal excesses. Though the community is generally successful in restraining the anti-social behaviour of the individual, when the community itself acts, it frequently outrages the private moralities of its members. This is partly because mass emotion is easily whipped into hysteria, and the presence of numbers of his fellows in a high state of excitement often deprives a man of his reason. But the individual, owing to the prevalence of irresponsibility, has not yet learned to apply his highest standards of behaviour to the community of which he is a part, or even to all the spheres of his own activity. This may clearly be seen in the various associations of men for specific purposes. An individual contains within himself sufficient interests to link him to many associations, but an association exists solely to organize the same interests in different individuals. Thus a man may belong to many associations, one for the satisfaction of his religious instincts, an association which probably professes a high standard of morality, one to provide for his leisure hours, athletic or aesthetic, and one where he earns his living, an association for making money. He will be an unusual man if he attempts to put into this last any part of himself other than his desire for financial security. Should he attempt to infuse the money-making concern with the ideas gathered in the association for religious purposes, he will doubtless meet with contempt and fierce opposition from his fellow members. It is a courageous man who will try to generalize his behaviour in a world divided into neat and water-tight compartments.

Herein lie the dangers of modern community-life; the individual who with his fellows constitutes the community has not yet learnt to feel any real responsibility for the communal activities, nor to impose on his various associations his highest standards of conduct. The strength of communal emotions, combined with the lack of intellectual control by the mass, allows the few to manipulate the many to their advantage. This exploitation is actually an extraordinary fact, were we not so used to it that we accept it without question. It means that by an admixture of economic pressure with manifold suggestions to the communal motive force, men may be persuaded to continue living in an economic society that is unjust to them. It is suggested to them that it is their duty to accept their inferior economic status and their lack of opportunity to rise above their circumstances, and instead of being roused to indignation by this denial of their birthright, they glow with righteous satisfaction in the sacrifice. Against this colossus of unreasoning mass emotion the pigmy, education, is sent forth with no better weapon than a torch.

It seems on the first sight that the schools can provide the obvious means to counterbalance this force of mass suggestion, and such is the opinion of many educationalists to-day. The Marxist, however, who has accepted the interpretation of history and political forms by reference to economic factors, finds it hard to have any patience with such a liberal humanist view of education. While education may sometimes give to an individual the realization of the power of the working class and of the insidious control wielded over it by the owners, as often as not it is the ally of the capitalist against the worker to whom he has allowed a smattering of his own cultural inheritance. It is necessary that there should be a clear understanding of the relationship between educational and socialist aims; it is too facile on the one hand to dismiss a political demand for educational extension as a lapse into humanitarian liberalism; on the other hand it is too sanguine to hope that a transition to a socialist society will be achieved by the gradual permeation of culture and knowledge through the contemporary forms of educational institutions, among all the individuals in a community. No real socialist can feel assured that the present educational system in England is bringing a socialist state appreciably nearer. Education is not to-day providing citizens trained to live in a community, nor is it injecting an anti-toxin to the mass of commercial and capitalist suggestion that stands for many people in the place of culture. Indeed, it is probably true that it is blurring the sharp outlines of class that the Marxist considers necessary to successful proletarian revolution, a fact that is not lost on the ruling class. The following quotation from Dr. Cyril Norwood shows the typical public-school attitude to educational extension as a safety-valve: 'Incomplete as it is, elementary education has been a steadily civilizing agency. It has, I think, been the main influence which has prevented Bolshevism, Communism, and the theories of revolt and destruction from obtaining any real hold on the people of this country.... It was just the fact that there had been enough social conscience, enough love of one's neighbour, in this country to have provided public education for a couple of generations, and to open the gates to political power to all, and that there were enough therefore who could read and think, that saved this country from a ruin to which it went near.'[1] Admittedly the Marxist thesis is most pointedly illustrated by the Russian example, and the illiteracy of the mass of the Russians under the Tsar was one factor among more obvious economic causes that made the revolution a success. An illiterate peasantry and proletariat cannot be flattered into submission to its exploiters by the brightly coloured lies of newspapers, and, fortunately for the Bolsheviks, the cinema as a universal entertainment in Russia is their own invention. Force is all that will persuade the illiterate, and force and economic oppression bring an inevitable reaction and the sins of generations of oppressors are repaid in kind. Equally, of course, the

[1] *The English Tradition of Education.* Cyril Norwood.

Russians had the inestimable advantage of a clear field when the Soviet educational system was created. There were few engrained traditions, or multiple minute perversions, unconsciously accepted and imbibed by teacher and taught.

Thus it is that the Marxist thesis and socialist plans of action, in this country and on the continent, have been much befogged by the existence of universal elementary education, which, though riddled with class-bias, does tend to blur the sharp lines of class division. Our major universities certainly cannot be said to be free from snobbery, but the fact that the working-class scholar, once arrived there, does enjoy equality of educational opportunity with the aristocrat mitigates contempt and intolerance. The British ruling class can be beaten by none in the art of letting slip a crumb in order to keep the loaf. Is it not a source of continuous disgust to the proletarian voter to watch the surrender of his leaders to cultured flattery and social charm? The British workman has acquired a sufficiently high standard of living, compared with that of the workers on the continent, to quench his revolutionary ardour. Nevertheless, an extension of educational advantages is a change to be worked for, on the grounds that a capitalist education is better than none at all, in the same way as the trade unions are right to wring from the capitalist an increase in wages, though a starving proletariat is probably nearer to communist revolution than one that is well-fed.

There are a large number of people in this country who have a genuine appreciation of the ideals of education and a disinterested desire to extend its advantages. Generally speaking, the teachers are highly principled, and stand with many professional workers, such as the doctors, in being little influenced in the quality of their service by the sum of their pecuniary reward, and often keenly interested in the science and practice of their craft for its own sake. They are right as to the importance of education, and socialists would do well to consider whether their educational policy will satisfy these specialists, for the educationalist would be a very valuable ally in the socialist cause. Socialist theorists would be wise to consider the particular claims of the educationalist on society, and to work out the relation of their Marxist thesis to education, however much easier their task would be if the working class of this country were illiterate. For it is my belief that a synthesis is possible and I shall attempt to show that the socialist state of the future will provide for those things that the intelligent educated person thinks valuable, art, science, and philosophy, the development of personality, individual freedom of criticism, and the scientific attitude to the problem of truth: in fact, all the things that have been claimed for education. To satisfy the educationalist that changes are necessary in the present system, it must also be demonstrated that the contemporary educational institutions in England are alive with class-bias and that their tradition works subtly and inevitably for the stabilization of the *status quo*, for the preservation of capitalist privilege, even where those institutions contain disinterested, sometimes socialist, members of the teaching profession. To keep alive the struggle for socialism in this country, it is necessary to combat the capitalist with his own methods in every field of social activity. Socialist critics of contemporary society should both disclose the capitalist influence latent in our educational system, and take advantage of what educational opportunity exists for the working class to awaken their realization of their real strength. It must always be remembered that the weapons of fascism are unreasoning, that the socialist arguments are eminently reasonable, that, though education, in the restricted sense of the three Rs, gives the capitalist unlimited possibilities of ingenious propaganda, an introduction to logical methods of thought is also one to the possibility of detecting the falsities of that propaganda, and that incidentally the English poets provide an excellent introduction to revolutionary literature.[1]

In the following chapters, I intend to analyse the system of education prevalent in England to-day, with the purpose of revealing its close connections with the economic system of capitalist ownership, and the class-bias inherent in it; and to make clear the immediate ambulance measures that may remove the faults of administration, though not of spirit, through which that bias is allowed to filter. I shall also attempt to judge the degree of failure in the present capitalist system in providing what I consider from a purely educational point of view a satisfactory training, and to describe the place to be taken in the fully-fledged socialist state by education. I do not intend to preface that analysis with a detailed statement of my personal views on the aims of education, as no one has yet achieved a definition that altogether satisfies anyone

[1] Undoubtedly Lady Bracknell would have put the blame for the excesses of the French Revolution down to the inflammable doctrines of Voltaire and Rousseau rather than to the poverty of the peasants. ' The whole theory of modern education is radically unsound. Fortunately in England, at any rate, education produces no effect whatsoever. If it did, it would prove a serious danger to the upper classes, and probably lead to acts of violence in Grosvenor Square.'—*The Importance of Being Earnest*, Oscar Wilde, Act 1.

but himself. My own particular version would merely provide a target for the snipers among educational theorists, and is unimportant in this connection; the main lines of my opinion on this subject will be sufficiently clear from my criticism of capitalist education. I shall also have something to say on the possible transference of the more generally accepted aims of education into the socialist state.

But before coming to the meat of the matter, it is important to say again that, in putting forward this plea for a more fundamental understanding of the relationship between political and economic systems and education, I am not in any way suggesting that it is possible to achieve socialism in this country by the gradual spread of educational advantages. As the Soviet writer on education says: 'We are not supporters of the thesis that an existing society can be changed through the school. To make the school the embryo of a future socialistic order is impossible, for the simple reason that the school cannot be independent of its environment.'[1] Nor is it desirable that the school should feel itself bound to react against society, for a healthy school atmosphere is dependent on close co-operation with the wider community around it, and a broad similarity of principle between the two. It is becoming more and more obvious that gradualism is outmoded, that chipping bits off the capitalist structure is no way to build the socialist state, and that the crumbs thrown to the working class from the capitalist table are from the rich man's loaf and must in the long run be regarded as dope. We meet here the problem that arises in regard to all social services. In opposition the Labour Party has an easy time pointing out that the

[1] *The New Education in the Soviet Republic*, Pinkevitch.

capitalists provide a faulty and biassed education; when, however, in time of prosperity they extend the amenities of education, Labour must either accept a concession that will lessen the force of their arguments, or risk denying to those who most need it an education that is preferable at its worst to none at all. It is impossible for a capitalist system of education to further a socialist revolution, except by way of reaction. But a clearer understanding of the cultural weapons in the hands of their enemies would enable socialists to make a stronger appeal to a literate nation.

The tight hold that can be maintained on educational influences may be surmised, when we consider the tyranny that is exercised over the cultural life of the mass of the people, in spheres that are not strictly educational nor under direct state control. A society that condemns a vast number of people to live in sordid, dirty, and unromantic surroundings, must, for the sake of its very existence, provide also a dream world into which its citizens can escape from depressing realities. An extrovert in a slum will often put his energies into altering these conditions. It therefore pays the capitalist, though his actions are rarely consciously propelled by such motives, to use the universal psychological tendency to introversion and to pander to the desire for a dream world by providing luscious cinemas, showy films, and novels fantastically absurd. Print and elementary education have also made possible the cheap and nasty state of advertisement in this country. Where there is capitalist competition, there will also be advertisement. One of the most refreshing things about modern Moscow is the cleanliness of its walls, free from the placards of rival merchants in tooth-paste, cigarettes, and beer, appealing to their public through fear, snobbery, or pornography. Many illuminating indictments of this state of advertisement will be found in *Culture and Environment* by Messrs. Leavis and Thompson, though it is difficult to understand how the authors can seriously imagine that such an environment can be successfully counterbalanced by a few enlightened teachers of literature in the capitalist schools. One could enlarge considerably on this aspect of capitalist civilization, with particular reference to *Middletown* by Robert and Sylvia Lynd, where there are many choice examples of the poverty of contemporary taste. Finally, of course, there is the capitalist Press; it is almost with despair that the socialist attempts to deal with the mind moulded if not manufactured by our daily newspapers, and regards with envy the Soviet Press which, as the Webbs say, 'contains absolutely no "police-court news" and no reports of divorce cases; nothing about fashions in dress; no stories of sex or murder or suicide or accidents; and no gossiping personalities about the private lives of royalties, or millionaires, or national celebrities.'[1] The present reverence for print, the inability to criticize, the credulous sensation-seeking, have enabled the capitalist to make the Press of this country unreliable as to fact, if not always by perversion, then by omission, psychologically lurid and unhealthy, and culturally contemptible.

To-day, money can buy the mental integrity of a nation; a civilization that throws up the type of bestseller novel that the circulating library thrives on, that encourages the sale of trash in large quantities, is obviously not producing a high level of critical taste. Mrs. Leavis in her book *Fiction and the Reading Public* paints a dismal picture of a trash-fed nation, and even

[1] *Soviet Communism*, Sidney and Beatrice Webb, 1935, p. 912.

though her taste is irritatingly exclusive, nevertheless her main diagnosis cannot be disputed. It is not the least damning indictment of capitalism that its last stages tend to produce an effete and debased culture, in which the genius, like D. H. Lawrence, cannot grow in a healthy, vital environment, but must use his strength in battling with false gods who would demand his art as a sacrifice. Other evidences of this impoverished cultural tradition can be found in the worthlessness of a great part of the entertainment provided by the B.B.C. and the theatres. If we consider the constant suggestion provided by the news-reels in the cinema, the apparently unlimited flow of money that is poured out on all forms of propaganda, from pageantry to posters, it is not surprising that the British capitalist has found it unnecessary so far to indulge in the more blatant forms of fascism, when his predominance can be maintained by subtler means. It is obvious from the capitalist practice that the control of the cultural springs of a nation will be as ultimately necessary to the persistence of a socialist state, as control of the means of production and distribution. But as for the moment of change, it is no more use to wait for the working class of this country to react against the insidious cultural pressure of capitalism, than it would have been for Lenin to wait for the Russian peasantry to understand the more difficult chapters of *Das Kapital*. The pressure of economic and political conditions will produce the right moment for change, and the leaders may realize its implications, though their followers may not. This book is not attempting to challenge that position, but to describe in detail another aspect of the capitalist stranglehold and to suggest some methods of dealing with education under the socialist state.

CHAPTER TWO

INEQUALITY OF OPPORTUNITY[1]

IN proving a connection between present education and its capitalist environment, we may start with the simple case of inequality, as it is inherent in capitalist society and socialism aims at eliminating it. It says much for the force of suggestion in propaganda, that the opinion is often seriously maintained, that every child in England has an equal chance of a satisfactory and prolonged education, whereas, in fact, education provides a glaring instance of inequality in our society. If education is power, if it holds the key to interesting and profitable work, if it provides for the lasting and positive enjoyment of leisure, if it is in any way desirable—then capitalist society stands at once accused of withholding some part of the product of civilization from a large number of its citizens. It is an unscientific generalization that maintains that the son of a working-class man has the same chances in education as the rich man's son. In isolated cases this may be so, but the fundamental truth remains that the educational system to-day in England is based on class divisions and gives unfair advantage to the children of the rich. No one can deny that a working-class child,

[1] The inequality of opportunity in present English education cannot be better illustrated than by the following diagrams, taken from two articles by J. L. Gray, M.A., and Pearl Moshinsky, B.Sc.(Econ.), which appeared in the April and July numbers of *The Sociological Review*, 1935. These diagrams are obtained from the figures given as a result of an investigation in the London schools, which I shall have occasion to refer to later in the text.

This diagram (p. 154 of the April number) shows the comparative opportunities of those pupils who have ability who are receiving free education in elementary or secondary schools, and of those, in various types of schools, whose parents pay fees. The second diagram shows the comparison with relation to the occupation of the parents (p. 317 of the July number).

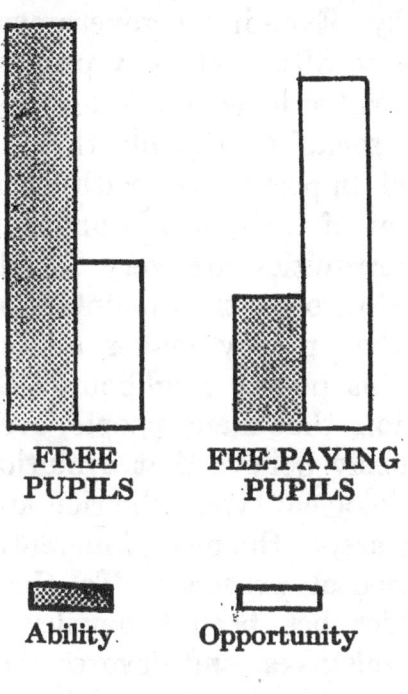

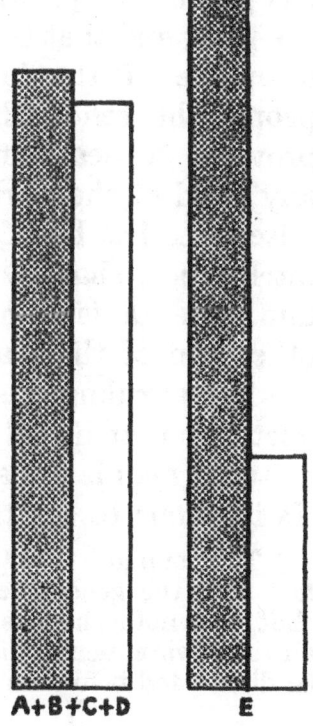

A. Employing and Directive Classes.
B. Professional Occupations.
C. Minor Professional and other highly skilled occupations.
D. Clerical and Commercial Employees.
E. Manual Workers.

unless he wins a scholarship, cannot prolong his education after he is fourteen plus, whereas a young man whose father has ample money to spend on his education, can continue it until he has reached the age of twenty-two or more at the university. Even if the government raises the school-leaving age to fifteen, as they propose to do in 1939, the disparity will still remain. Education to-day virtually denies the socialist principle that all men have a right to equal opportunities with their fellows, to a full development of their talents and personalities. Educational opportunities are very largely parcelled out on the basis of income, thus maintaining the capitalist assumption that money makes a man of a different species from his poorer neighbours.[1] So deeply engrained is this notion, that many people, even among educationalists, seriously believe that evolution has produced two distinct biological types, the rich and the poor, and that the latter are, in the mass, inherently incapable of the higher mental processes. To these people the scholarship ladder has been benevolently provided to deal with any mistakes, and ensures that any child of the working class, who by some biological mischance has been gifted with the normal upper-class intelligence, shall receive the education that is due to him. Class-division has, of course, taken its toll at the other end of the scale also, by putting the culture of the liberal ruling-class education in danger of becoming effete and artificially restricted, a danger which the cultured man is too apt to rejoice in rather than deplore. 'Is it unfair to say that the British devotees of culture

[1] This opinion is superficially supported by the undoubted fact that the general level of intelligence among working-class children is not as high as among other classes. There are, however, all the environmental disadvantages both in school and home to be discounted before an hereditary inferiority can be proven.

INEQUALITY OF OPPORTUNITY

not only accept as inevitable the exclusion of the masses from the realms of gold, in which they themselves find so much virtuous enjoyment, but also secretly rejoice at their own exclusive possession of something in which the common lump of men cannot share?"[1] Thus the Webbs criticize modern English culture in comparison with that of Soviet Russia.

It is obvious to all but the politically primitive that there is great injustice being done to the vast majority of working-class children. Eighty per cent of the children in this country come under the code governing elementary schools and 5 per cent only of those are in selective 'central' schools. A very small number of these children ever find their way out of these schools; thus in the school year 1925–6, 8·85 per cent of the children, aged ten to eleven, in public elementary schools entered secondary schools. The chances are considerable that vastly more than that number would profit by further education, or, at any rate, are unfitted, at the present school-leaving age of fourteen, for the responsibilities of adult life. The present system of reducing the length of education as we go down the scale of income, is not only unjust but a great waste of valuable material. In the book *Schools of England*, by Dover Wilson, on page 98, there is a chart of the various types of education provided in England to-day; the most striking thing about that chart is a large black patch marked ALTOGETHER NEGLECTED which represents over 400,000 children aged fourteen to sixteen. In the investigation into the ability of nearly 10,000 London schoolchildren between the ages of nine and twelve and a half, in various types of schools, carried out by J. L. Gray, M.A., and Pearl Moshinsky, B.Sc.(Econ.), they

[1] *Soviet Communism*, p. 924.

discovered wide maladjustments between the ability and opportunity of the free and fee-paying pupils. They estimated by means of intelligence tests the numbers of children of high ability in various groups; of the total with high ability, judged by the higher of the two standards they used, the free pupils provide 81·9 per cent, and the fee-paying pupils 18·1 per cent. Those who go, or will go, to central schools provide 25·5 per cent of those with high ability. The authors have the following comment on these figures: 'We are far from suggesting that the inferiority of the mean intelligence of the children of the relatively poor does not create a problem which calls for immediate investigation. For the present discussion the relevant fact is that on their observed performance alone the comparatively poor very greatly preponderate in the production of individuals of high ability. . . . It will not fail to be observed that in the single case of children whose educational future is limited to the central school there are many more superior individuals than in the entire group of fee-paying pupils.'[1] They found 6·6 per cent of the children of elementary school origin had opportunity of free places in secondary schools. While not suggesting that the child of less ability cannot benefit from higher education, the authors point out the following converse maladjustment to be deduced from their figures: 'In the whole school population more than 50 per cent of the able pupils are without the opportunity of higher education. While only three per thousand of free pupils in secondary schools fall below the selected level of ability, the corresponding figure for the entire group of fee-paying pupils (all of whom, nevertheless, enjoy the opportunity of a higher education) is nearly 50 per cent.

[1] Op. cit., April number, p. 151.

In other words, taking children of equally high ability, seven fee-paying pupils will receive a higher education for every one free pupil. Conversely, if we consider children who fall below the selected level of ability, for every one free pupil who is afforded the opportunity of a higher education, there are one hundred and sixty-two fee-paying pupils who enjoy the same advantages.'[1]

Modern psychologists, who, whatever their shortcomings, deserve a hearing from those who devise an educational system, while not necessarily denying that generations of unhealthy physical and mental background may ultimately affect the hereditary birthright of a child, maintain that there is nothing inherently inferior in the product of working-class stock. They lay great stress on the possibilities of influence from environment. When we consider that capitalism has made the general cultural background of the mass of people cheap and nasty, that it has placed the great majority of children in homes which emit poor taste and ignorance, to say nothing of filthy slum-dwellings where physical health is also undermined, we may be justly indignant that it is exactly those children who most need the intelligent and artistic environment of a good school, whom capitalism considers to have had all the education they can usefully experience at fourteen. In allowing the school-leaving age to remain at fourteen, or even at fifteen when that age limit is made a farce by exemptions, the government of England shows itself biassed against the claims of the working class to equality in educational opportunity. In educational theory there is nothing whatsoever to be said for this age as terminal of education; it does not need a psychologist to know that at that age a child is in the first

[1] Op. cit., April number, p. 160.

stages of adolescence, and will in any environment have difficulty in adjusting his new powers of thought and added emotional depths to the world around him. He needs freedom from pecuniary responsibility, from the rigid routine of office hours, or the aimlessness of unemployment. He needs exercise and physical training; he can at this age learn to sublimate his instincts if the right intellectual fields are there for his discovery, and lay the foundations of a lasting delight in knowledge and art. He is far too young to decide what trade he wants to follow, even if economic circumstances allow him any choice. Even with nothing better offered than capitalist education, it is preferable for a child of fourteen to be under the influence of people who have some knowledge of psychology and some educational ideals, than to be exploited by an employer who regards him as an instrument for making money. The opinion of educationalists in this matter has been so strong, that it has induced other capitalist countries to conduct their state education on far more equable lines. For instance, in America, the paradise of the capitalist, secondary education is free and the vast majority of children from all classes go to the same state schools, until the age of seventeen to eighteen.

That, in England, the inequality of age-limit is not the result of a plan nicely balanced to accommodate differences in talent, but the direct outcome of the class-system, can be demonstrated by the history of elementary education. We owe most of the impetus that roused an interest in elementary education to the churches, a fact which many people, reviewing the later history of educational legislation, will deplore. Education at the Renaissance, though often of a high standard, was designed in the first place for the courtly;

it embraced the genteel quite quickly, and in the nineteenth century, the prosperous also made their claims; and it is their claims that are still being met to-day. The churches have, however, always maintained a theoretical equality of soul between rich and poor. It was the Society for the Promotion of Christian Religion, not having, in the eighteenth century, to go among the heathen to find the darkness of ignorance, which set up the first free charity schools, with the intent of teaching the poor to read the Bible and answer the catechism, with salvation rather than education as the primary object. Sunday schools began to spread rapidly at the end of the eighteenth century, and attempted to develop what was left of the mentality of the victims of the Industrial Revolution. Even such small beginnings were regarded with suspicion, and a Mrs. Trimmer, in 1805, reviewing the laudable efforts of Mr. Lankester to save the souls of the English working class, remarked that her aim was to make the workers' children merely 'so far civilized as not to be disgusting'.[1]

The efforts of Bell and Lankester, vitiated by a religious controversy, finally drove the government to get a committee report, and in 1833 to make a grant for elementary education, to be disbursed by the private societies of these educationalists, the National Society for the Education of the Poor in the Principles of the Church of England, and the British and Foreign Schools Society. Since that date the history of government intervention in elementary education has been one of shifty irresponsibility, driven by popular demand to concede the minimum it thought necessary to placate the clamorous. The government has always preferred to regard education as a charge upon the exchequer rather

[1] Quoted in *Working-class Education*, by W. and F. Horrabin.

than a national asset. The commercialization of education could not be better illustrated than by the Lowe system of Payment by Results, whereby from 1862 to 1897 government grants became dependent on a percentage of proficiency among the pupils in each school in the three Rs, a commercialization of examination results which is now to a large extent enforced by the employer, though abandoned by the state. The attempt in 1918 by the Fisher Education Bill to provide compulsory attendance at a part-time continuation school for all children to the age of eighteen has never succeeded. Local authorities are not inclined unless unusually enterprising to make out schemes for educational development which the Board of Education are very likely to turn down on the score of expense. The school-leaving age remains at fourteen and it is legally permissible to employ a child of twelve out of school hours. The National or conservative government, having finally been driven by election promises into raising this limit, are putting off the change until 1939 and making it practically ineffective by the method of exemptions. Thus they have been forced into this reform by circumstances, in the same way as building grants and the abolition of fees was wrung from them in former battles.

As usual in the nineteenth century, the capitalist, following the principles of *laissez-faire* and leaving the initiative in public services to humanitarian individuals, was reluctant to take over the organization of public education as a state service. Though as early as 1839, when a Privy Council Committee was set up to superintend parliamentary grants, it was suggested that it should also consider all educational matters, this second clause was dropped, and it was not until 1899 that the various central authorities were coalesced into the Board of Education in its present form. Great forward strides were possible after the war; there was a willingness among the people to attempt a repair of four years' slaughter by an enlightened educational policy. That spirit of progress was allowed to evaporate and during the life of the last National Government we saw a reversal of all progressive educational ideas by the policy put forward in the notorious circular 1421 and its companion documents. A comparison of the Hadow Report of 1926, which is a remarkable claim for secondary education for all, with that circular is illuminating. The report recommended not the mere improvement of the later stages of elementary education, but an absorption of that form into a system of secondary schools. The circular went so far as to retrace some of the steps made even before the war in educational progress. As a result of its recommendations the expenditure of the Treasury on education was cut down by about £6,000,000 a year; scales of staffing and teachers' salaries were reduced, and a means test imposed on the parents of scholarship holders in secondary schools. It was made abundantly clear that the government still viewed education as an expense that was parallel to any other luxury; battleships are a necessity to the state, but not education. This policy condemned still more children to the fourteen limit, for many parents, having considered the expense of the 'extras' in the way of fares, uniform, and equipment, differ from the government as to their capacity for supporting a child at a secondary school. The mean and niggardly parsimony of the government cannot be better illustrated than by the fact that during the Great Economy book prizes were replaced by certificates, ornamented scraps of paper. It sounds a small point but for a book-loving child it is often his only way of starting a personal library; and yet the authorities could afford to give away scores of worthless and hideous jubilee mugs. The more conscious motive is, of course, obedience to the fantastic economics that recommend restriction of output and petty economies as cures for a surplus; though there are signs that the capitalist is sometimes half-conscious of the class enmity that lies behind such action, a fear that a working-class child in a secondary school should receive an education equal, if not superior, to that of the public-school man. Circular 1421 amongst much talk of saving the country's money, also states that improvements in education involving additional expenditure must cease, 'since the standard of education, elementary and secondary, that is being given to the child of poor parents is already in very many cases superior to that which the middle-class parent is providing for his own child'. In fact, if the middle-class parent in the interests of snobbery chooses to send his child to an atrocious private or 'public' school, where he is taught little in the way of useful knowledge, but imbued with many conventions and prejudices, including a conviction of his innate superiority to his fellow men, then the working-class child must not be provided with an education even up to this standard.

The inequality between working-class and bourgeois education is not, of course, confined to the age-limit. The circular 1421 did far more damage than is obvious from its most spectacular clauses. The teachers' salary cuts have been restored, but scales of staffing are still down and it is still the policy of many local authorities not to replace a teacher who is leaving but to divide his work among the remaining members of the staff.

The policy of the first National Government was also to discourage local authorities in reorganization and re-building, which, of course, principally affects elementary schools. That policy will be only slowly reversed as it will take initiative and enterprise in high places before local authorities will take up again the detailed work of technical improvement in which they have been discouraged. In these matters it is far easier to slow down the rate of progression than to get up speed again.[1] Great inequalities of equipment exist; and all psychologists are agreed that the equipment of schools, the educational environment, makes a deep if unrealized impression on children. For reasons of health so much floor-space and so much good air are required for children at school. Is it not also important that the room should be pleasant, the furniture in good taste, and the decoration stimulating to the imagination? There should be good pictures in class-rooms and corridors; a child is less likely than an adult to spend many months with a picture and never look at it. The old educationalists who considered that no normal child could possibly wish to learn, took no trouble to make his school surroundings at all pleasant and, the subjects taught not usually extending far beyond Latin and Greek syntax, they were certainly logical in beating their pupils into learning it. We are now more apt to consider a child abnormal if there is nothing in the modern varied curricula that he does not like, and our object in teaching should be to share a skill or knowledge that is a source of happiness to its owner. Nor is

[1] 'The Board of Education report for 1934 shows the number of schools existing as unfit for use, at 1,244. In the year only 72 of these schools were removed from the black list. At that rate it will be 1952 before such schools disappear altogether.'—*Daily Herald*, August 22, 1935.

it true to say that the working-class child will not learn to respect and care for beautiful possessions; is it the working class alone that has turned our countryside into a happy hunting-ground for flower-ravagers and paper-scatterers? The desk at which I am writing is in the library of one of the older universities, the flower of capitalist learning; the desk is covered with ink and scratches; many and many an ardent seeker after knowledge has carved his name with a pen-knife or scribbled it in ink; the desk number and notice are covered with ribald and futile remarks and drawings, such as you might expect to find in a very adolescent rough note-book. In the county school in which I taught, one with a very large percentage of children from elementary schools, the desks are in light wood, well-made, and in a good pattern; ink is sand-papered off them, they are ardently polished, and no one considers it necessary to obtain a dubious immortality by ill-using good furniture with a pen-knife. Elementary schools vary a great deal in equipment, but on the whole they do not have the best in artistic surroundings; we have become so used to the idea that our sense of the fit and proper would be somewhat outraged if we found an elementary school as well equipped and decorated in such good taste as a secondary school. Though much improvement has been made in this way there are numbers of elementary schools, particularly in the country, which are drably decorated, ill-lit, and poorly furnished, such as can provide no stimulus to the imagination, nor even encourage habits of care for furniture and buildings. It may be said that some boys' public schools are as bad; this is owing to the hang-over of the nineteenth-century tradition that education can be little more than dreary at the best of times. Where the state provides education, it reserves the best for the fee-payer's child in secondary schools.

Equipment is, however, not merely a matter of background; material must be used or it is valueless. The scientist must have his laboratory, the artist his studio, the carpenter his tools. Educationalists lay more and more stress on the value of children handling things themselves, attempting creation and experiment. As a teacher of literature I should have liked to let loose the children I taught, not in a wilderness of books, but into an ordered well-stocked library, arranged for various stages of development. Many teachers have maintained that subjects should be connected with special rooms. The former headmaster of the Cambridge Perse school, Dr. Rouse, believed that Latin should be taught on the direct method, and that there should be a special room where only Latin should be spoken, so that the language should become ingrained by association. Does even the best elementary school provide sufficient room for such a scheme, or even for studios and carpenters' shops? In how many elementary schools is it not the case that the children sing, do gymnastics, and eat in the same hall? And if it be objected that the studies mentioned here are advanced and do not come under the usual scheme of elementary education, we may inquire in reply by what right is any child debarred from the chance of benefiting by such studies, and turned out at fourteen, supposedly educated, with no glimpse of the endless possibilities of knowledge and skill that would be opened out by a study of these subjects? In any case, a child is never too young to try its hand at singing, drawing, and all kinds of handwork, and it is in the very early stages of history and geography teaching that a special room

D

with pictures, maps, and models is most needed. With regard to playgrounds do the elementary schools have the same chance? The playing fields of Eton and the poor piece of asphalte that surrounds an elementary school in a slum district provide a glaring instance of inequality. However poor in equipment is the public school in some respects, it is rarely stinted in the satisfaction of its athletic requirements; public and new secondary schools consider it almost a necessity to have a swimming-bath, and who has not seen the children of an elementary school on a hot and dusty day, trail down to the council's public baths? Is swimming an advanced study?[1]

Inequality does not stop here. For even without much space and material, in a darkly built, rather frowsy town school, an imaginative well-trained teacher with a reasonably small class can do a very great deal to replace the maps, models, and instruments he would like to have. All educationalists know that a child's interest in a subject cannot usually be stimulated without individual attention from the teacher, and that the teaching of any subject suffers if the problem of

---

[1] The following table illustrates the inequality in equipment and building between elementary and secondary schools.

School Maintenance	Average Cost per Head per Annum
Secondary School	£35
Central School	£20
Senior (Elementary) School	£15

School Building, 1929–1932	Average Cost per Child
Secondary School	£103
Elementary School	£35 14s.

These figures are taken from the Board of Education reports for 1933.

discipline and order cannot be forgotten.[1] In 1932 in elementary schools 7,900 classes had more than fifty children in them; there were 52,000 classes with forty to 'fifty children, and a large proportion of these had over forty-five. In secondary schools the limit is thirty-five and there are rarely more than thirty. In the select schools, where very high fees are paid, it is not unusual to find a class of ten children, and there are rarely more than twenty. Add to these facts the inequality in training of teachers. To my mind it is not sufficient for a teacher to be a lover of children; that should go without saying; he should also be in love with his subject or his craft. For teaching should be a sharing of a mutually interesting study, in which the teacher gives his greater experience in exchange for new enthusiasm. What numbers of difficulties could be overcome if boredom could be eliminated from school-life! All the petty personal hatreds and irritations would

[1] Cf. an interesting article in *The New Statesman and Nation* for November 28, 1936, signed by A. Pindar. The writer had considerable experience of Senior Elementary Schools, in which, of course, are the residue left after the selective examinations for the central and secondary schools have taken place. He considers that the appallingly low level of intellectual attainment that he encountered and the preponderance of disciplinary problems were fundamentally due to over-crowding. ' I taught recently in a senior school in a newly built Western suburb. The school was equipped with large classrooms, an admirable swimming-bath, a large sports ground, extensive gardens, science and music rooms, playgrounds, and assembly halls. The place was a den of iniquity. It was in this school that several boys of twelve in my huge class were unable to write their own names. One class had "broken" five masters and the life of the man then in charge was a calvary.' There are, of course, senior elementary schools with a really practical bias in the curriculum and a genuinely sympathetic and 'free' discipline, which mitigate the deficiency of personal contact due to over-large classes. Such achievements, usually dependent on very forceful personality, are no reason for allowing such conditions to persist.

disappear, for what does it matter if children are restless and teachers nervy, if their relationship is not a pitched battle of personalities but a partnership for a mutual, objective interest?

Now, though a great many public schools, particularly boys', still consider the names of a public school and university satisfactory substitutes in their staff for a training in the teaching profession, such teachers, though knowing little of psychology and educational theory, have yet had leisure to specialize in the study of the subject most congenial to them. The elementary teacher has seldom had such an opportunity; there are some even without any post-school training. In 1931 there were 30,632 uncertificated teachers in elementary schools; such teachers are, of course, cheaper and do not have to come under the certificated scale of salaries. The majority of elementary teachers, however, do a two-year training course, general study running concurrently with professional training. Thus in addition to the so-called professional studies, such as the Principles and Practice of Teaching, Hygiene, Voice-Production, etc., the two-year student is expected to study at least four other subjects. It is not to be expected that he could study them in any detail or know the pleasures of a really specialized knowledge of any one subject, and it will be unlikely that he will avoid studying something that has few attractions for him. When he comes to work in a school he will have to teach several subjects to the same children and will not vary much in the ages with which he comes in contact. The secondary teacher, if lucky, will teach only his own subject which he has studied for a degree at a university. The National Government's reduction of staffing scales has led to the demand for specialists willing to assist in teaching other subjects in lower forms, so that it is not uncommon for a secondary school advertisement to ask for a specialist with two or even three subsidiary subjects and an interest in games. But, despite this retrograde tendency in the secondary schools, there is still inequality here and the elementary school teacher must often find himself having to teach forty to fifty children something that has little interest for himself, and without proper materials to help him. It is astonishing how much excellent teaching is done in elementary schools in spite of these obstacles, nor is it to be wondered at that occasionally methods of teaching under such conditions are apt to approximate to those of the parade ground. I have even heard of instructions given in a botany lesson for the dismemberment of a violet by numbers thus: 'Violets up, one, two, three. Pull off the sepals, one, two, three etc.' There are a great many teachers out of work and yet the classes contain far too many children. 'Economania' prevents their being used to their mutual advantage.

Curricula are usually a reflection of the school's provision in the way of staff. A school that provides for specialized and varied interests must be more fully staffed than one that allows little or no choice of study. The elementary school does its best, providing roughly per week two and a half hours for religious instruction, ten or more for the three R's, five for history, geography, singing, and drawing, five for science and practical work of all kinds from needlework to drawing, and one and a half to physical training. This is all that is really necessary in the first stages of education, though one might criticize the proportions, but such a curriculum bears hardly on the older children in an elementary school. In any case, it is they in particular who require the stimulus of new studies and fresh equipment as that of the company of their most gifted fellows has been removed. At the age of eleven-plus the best scholars have been weeded out by examination to go to the secondary and central schools. It is bad for a school to have a continual drain of its best brains, just as it is bad for a subject, such as geography, to be alternative to Latin, which, owing to antiquated convention, always claims the 'possibles' for the universities, leaving the other subject with the less intelligent remainder. Those who remain in the elementary schools have the initial disadvantage of feeling themselves left-overs; there is then nothing in the curriculum that will stimulate fresh interest in a new start, and while secondary school children are exploring the possibilities of laboratories, studios, and stage, there is little to keep these children from boredom. It is not surprising that they are glad to go at fourteen, and where the age-limit to fifteen is optional, many parents consider their children to be wasting their time in taking advantage of it. There can be no comparison between the range of subjects, the qualifications of the staff teaching them, and the conditions under which they are taught, in state secondary and elementary schools.

We have been considering inequalities between elementary and secondary education, due mainly to administrative and economic causes. The types of inequality discussed refer mainly to the county day secondary school, under direct control of the local authority, as compared to the public elementary school, though many of the points of comparison refer also to the 'public' schools. There are, however, many other types of educational institution in England to-day, and it remains to be shown what chance the working class have of benefiting by them and what opportunities they afford to the children of the middle and upper classes.[1]

Education of the very young necessarily lays great stress on physical environment, and it is at this stage that the working-class child has a crying need for a counter-influence to his home. Anyone who works in clinics in a slum area knows the tragic frequency with which the healthy new-born baby becomes a puny under-sized child through lack of hygienic surroundings, fresh air, and good food. It was partly in order to fill the gap between the clinic and school medical inspections, a gap sometimes of three years, that the movement for nursery schools was begun. Compulsory school attendance begins at five years, in the infant departments of the elementary schools. In March 1932, fifty-five nursery schools only had been provided and recognized by the Board of Education, and twenty-five of those had been initiated by voluntary bodies. No one will deny that it is physically better for children to be in an open-air nursery school, than to run about the slum streets of a city, until they are old enough to go to the elementary schools. Educationally, also, such policy is sound; modern psychology is at last impelling us to take into consideration the fact, which the Jesuits discovered long ago, that the marks impressed on the young in the earlier years of infancy are well-nigh indelible. The foundations of character, of aesthetic appreciation, and

[1] In their investigation of London schoolchildren and the relation of their ability and educational opportunity to parental occupation, J. L. Gray and Pearl Moshinsky found that among the 1,718 children in private and preparatory schools, there was only one child of an unskilled manual worker, and he was being educated at the expense of his father's employer. Cf. op. cit., p. 298 of the July number.

of physical strength are laid in those years before seven. Yet for the vast majority of young children there is no educational provision; there is no money in most homes for early education. So important is this aspect of inequality that I should be inclined to rank it above the injustices at the other end of the age-scale, for by the opening of adolescence much of the damage is done, and can never be repaired.

The methods of nursery-school education are as yet in the experimental stage, but sufficient research has been carried out to allow for considerable expansion in this direction. The report of the Consultative Committee to the Board of Education on Infant and Nursery Schools (1933) considers 'that the nursery school is a desirable adjunct to the national system of education; and that in districts where the housing and general economic conditions are seriously below the average, a nursery school should, if possible, be provided. The nursery school should be designed primarily for those children who by reason of unsuitable environment require careful attention to their physical welfare and need to spend longer hours at school and to be provided with meals.' The report also comes to the conclusion that nursery schools are educationally desirable for all classes. Yet the report gave the figure of these schools as fifty-five in 1932 for the whole working class, whereas money can buy the best Montessori or Froebel education for young children. It is ironic that these methods and materials should have become so definitely the prerogative of the rich when their originators had no thought of class division. Madame Montessori did her work among mentally-deficient slum children, and the pioneer of nursery schools in England worked in Deptford. The well-to-do parent can train his child at home or, if he think fit, send it to a Froebel kindergarten department or Montessori school; such departments are frequently attached to girls' schools, which, even if they admit elementary scholars later, do not do so at this early stage. There is little choice for the working-class child, except between a dingy respectability indoors and a life of sordid excitement and dirt in the streets.[1]

Of the state elementary and secondary schools enough has already been said. The working-class child has far less chance of reaching the state secondary school than the child of parents willing and able to pay fees, for the latter does not have to take a competitive examination. For young children of moneyed parents there are a number of schools outside the state system altogether and in which, characteristically of our nation, most people consider English education to consist. The normal procedure for this type of education is to divide the school-life into the preparatory and public-school stages. Boys who do not go to a state secondary school at eleven, usually continue at a preparatory school until they are

[1] The annual report of the Board of Education for 1934 shows an increase of one nursery school for that year; there are now 0·25 per cent of the children under five attending recognized nursery schools, with the total of such schools at 62.—Cf. *Daily Herald*, August 22, 1935.

The Board of Education circular, 1444 (January 1936), has a section urging a much-needed expansion of nursery schools, but owing to the present administrative machinery, initiative depends on Local Authorities, and the recommendations state that where possible the cheaper method of converting existing infant departments of elementary schools should be followed, rather than building new premises. The following statement is in itself a revelation of the unwillingness of the central authority to encourage expenditure. 'The present cost of provision and upkeep of nursery schools is not generally extravagant, but there is little doubt that the high cost in individual cases has acted as a serious deterrent to a more rapid increase in the number of nursery schools.'

thirteen or fourteen. Some public schools run separate preparatory departments, but it is most socially desirable to attend a different preparatory school. Both preparatory and public schools are usually boarding-schools, and the amount of state supervision varies considerably; all schools wishing to qualify for a grant from the Board of Education must, of course, accept a certain number of scholars from the elementary schools; 25 per cent is the recognized lowest number, though in some schools a lower percentage is allowed. Other schools desire to be recognized as efficient by the Board of Education and to be inspected, without taking the grant, as the efficiency certificate is a valuable qualification. Other schools are jealous of their independence and dislike any interference. The public schools, of course, provide an education until the age of eighteen, when boys pass to the universities or to other training institutions.

Girls' schools are roughly of two kinds, those which attempt to ape the traditional boys' public schools, and those which have developed on their own lines. The first kind follow the usual forms of preparatory and public schools, and the latter are usually day-schools, sometimes embracing all stages of education from kindergarten to sixth-form, and often of a high standard of educational efficiency. It is fortunate for girls that there have been some educationalists anxious to strike out on new lines for them and not content with mere copies of the traditions of boys' education. Adequate education for girls is, of course, a fairly recent development, the result of the feminist struggle of the late nineteenth century. So bitter was that struggle that the successful Amazons in the early stages of women's education determined to have everything that was given to men, good, bad, or indifferent, forgetting that there was a mass of false psychology and dried-up tradition in the boys' public schools. Whatever there is to be said for a traditional school there is no virtue at all in an imitation of one, just as it would be a mistake to build a woman's college at Oxford or Cambridge in pseudo-Gothic. Thus there is the altogether unfortunate development of the ladies' college, genteel, cast-iron, a cram factory for knowledge, besides the more suitable type of education found often in the schools of the Girls' Public Day School Trust, though that is also somewhat too firmly embedded in the academic tradition to suit the needs of all the pupils. It is probably also owing to the fact that the social ban on day-schools is not so formidable in girls' education as in boys', that the county secondary school for girls, directly under county or municipal authority, is frequently more efficient and better qualified than its masculine counterpart. The same thing accounts for the story of the headmaster of a county day co-educational school in London, who at first determined to choose his staff solely according to qualifications and not to sex, but soon discovered that his staff would be totally feminine unless he kept an artificial balance. And in Russia if you ask what proportion of men and women are on a school staff they frequently cannot tell you, as there is no longer inequality between the sexes.[1] A new start in education allows the women to cease to strain after things that are given a false importance by being considered masculine privileges.

Besides these older types there are numbers of experimental schools, in all stages of revolt against the tradition

[1] 'Let me emphasize again that there is complete equality between the sexes, so that sex plays no part in deciding appointments.'—*Changing Man*, Beatrice King, Chap. 15, p. 221.

of English education. These, of course, unless like Bedales, the pioneer co-educational school, they have already staked their claim to part of that tradition, depend for their existence on the interest of a sufficient number of parents in advanced educational theory. Finally there are the dregs of education, the small private schools, usually rather struggling financially and very inefficient; they are often for small children before the age of the preparatory school stage, and frequently run by maiden ladies who have a house of their own too big for them, but no knowledge of psychology, or hygiene, or, indeed, anything of importance in education; this is the sediment always present in private enterprise, and one sometimes feels that slum streets are a less harmful environment. And presumably somewhere in this wild undergrowth that passes for an educational system in England, are a few remnants of the academy for the daughters of gentlemen, still dabbling inefficiently in music and French.

There is also in the English educational system a characteristically tangled growth, known as technical education. Part of it caters for children before the leaving-school age, and the rest comes within the sphere of adult and part-time education. The institutions in which technical education is delivered are usually composite and purely evening work is often housed in elementary schools. There is a general poverty of equipment and lack of co-ordination and central control; the system of technical education, if it can be dignified by that name, shows the effects of its haphazard growth in the attempt to make good some of the deficiencies of working-class education, and the supposed inferiority of vocational training. There are six different types of Junior technical education, full- and part-time, and four Senior. (Cf. *Technical Education*, a pamphlet by Barbara Drake and Tobias Weaver. The New Fabian Research Bureau, pp. 7–8.) The inferior status under which technical education labours is mainly due to the unwillingness of the academic tradition of the ruling class to concede anything to the working-class demand. This is particularly obvious at the higher senior stages; for instance, it is not thought necessary to provide any training colleges for technical teachers. The N.F.R.B. pamphlet states that the mechanics' institutes 'have never gained an intellectual prestige equal to that of a university' (p. 32). 'Some institutions are given or loaned plant and apparatus by engineering and other firms, but, on the commercial side particularly, there is a shortage. Library facilities in the schools are deplorable' (p. 13). By the means of these technical schools, the working-class child may obtain a certain degree of higher education of the less academic type. But, with the possible exception of the full-time junior technical schools, the equipment and prestige of these institutions reflect the general disadvantages under which working-class education labours. The full-time junior schools, being restricted in numbers by the needs of the local industries, are often of a high standard; academicism has passed them over and there are no examinations. Unfortunately, there are only 194 such schools in the country with a total of 22,158 pupils. Technical education modifies only slightly the fundamental inequality of the present English educational system.

The English university system shows perhaps even more clearly than the secondary schools the class divisions in education, and the unfortunate mingling of tradition and social snobbery. Oxford and Cambridge hold their unique position owing to their great age and ancient endowments. In many ways they show the advantages of tradition in education, in that their endowments allow of very fine equipment and the atmosphere of these university towns can be a great benefit to scholars. The buildings are mostly ancient and have the traditions of generations of learning; libraries and museums are numerous and well-stocked. There is always sufficient money from endowments for the addition of equipment necessary for new branches of learning, as, for instance, the many modern sciences. The mediaeval intention in founding these universities might still make of them fine places, if they were institutions where 'poor scholars' might be maintained for their devotion to learning, where class differences disappeared, and where there was a commonwealth of scholarship. But these universities have become connected with the structure of social privilege, as are the public schools, and it is often an advantage to have a degree from Oxford or Cambridge, when obtaining employment, not because the standard of scholarship is necessarily higher—it is in some subjects even lower—than that of the newer universities, but simply because their names carry a flavour of better social standing. The system of privilege has ruined Oxford and Cambridge; for whereas it is possible for some working-class students to reach these universities by the scholarship ladder, it is also possible for a great many fools and non-intellectual youths, out for a 'good time', to get there, because their fathers were there before them, or because they can afford the exorbitant fees.[1] Unfor-

[1] 'There are no rules regulating the time by which a student must be in, or whether a woman student may take tea or dinner with a member of the opposite sex in his rooms, or vice versa. The students were incredulous that such rules exist in English universities. Amusements such as painting the town red on any

tunately there are far too many young people in these universities who have the money to use them as a vast hotel and amusement park; and there are many others, oppressed by fears of the future, who spend too much time cramming for the degree which alone will get them a job. Between the two, real education is apt to get squeezed out.

The newer universities do not so often have the system of colleges that are boarding-houses as well as units for teaching, and so there is not the same opportunity for detachment from the life of the surrounding town; the hot-house atmosphere of social privilege, the distinction between town and gown, is not so easily maintained in the newer type, which is part of the reason why the ruling-class tradition in education has clung to the boarding-school system in its secondary schools and universities. There is the same class sliding-scale within the university system as there is within capitalist education generally; although it is possible for the working man to get to Oxford or Cambridge, it becomes increasingly easy for him to obtain something approximating to a university education as the institutions fall off in social prestige. There are, however, far too few fully-fledged universities to meet the needs of the working class; Wales and Scotland are better equipped in this way than England. There are, nevertheless, institutions of a semi-university character, often with a technical bias, in most large towns; there are colleges for two-year elementary teachers' courses,

and every occasion, smashing lamp-posts, or knocking off policemen's helmets, simply do not appeal to Soviet students. They regard them as suitable antics for ten- or twelve-year-olds. As for the spectacle of a grown man chasing adult students round the town for some childish offence, it is simply incomprehensible to them.'—*Changing Man*, Beatrice King, Chap. 14, p. 181.

secretarial, journalistic, and typing schools, and many part-time evening institutions, where it is possible to pick up a smattering of more general study, but which are poor makeshifts for what a university education can and should be. Finally, there are a mass of evening classes, extension lectures, and various spasmodic forms of adult study which have little or no connection with any formal educational institution, and which spring up frequently from the initiative, benevolent or resentful, of some individual. Such efforts bear witness to the insistent demand for education and the skill with which the ruling class have been able virtually to retain for their special benefit certain exclusive institutions. The question of adult education can be given more consideration when we are dealing with the workers' attempts to claim some of the benefits of higher education.

As a system it is fairly obvious to any observer that English education has little claim to that name at all. The chaos, of course, has the usual advantage of the English way of managing affairs; it preserves what is good in tradition, along with a great deal of what is bad, and leaves room for the spirited experiments of enlightened individuals. It allows also, of course, for much inefficiency, and great waste by overlapping. Almost any small town has far too many schools. There are usually five or six preparatory schools or departments as well as the elementary schools. There may be a central school, with an age-limit of sixteen years and a technical bias. Then come the two normal county secondary schools for boys and girls, or one co-educational one; there is usually a high school for girls and an imitation public school for boys, besides two or three struggling private schools, usually for girls. A large number of the boys of the town will be sent away to public schools, and a much smaller percentage of the girls. The working-class child in this town will, of course, most probably stay in the elementary school until fourteen and unless he goes to evening classes, which a day's work will not encourage him to do, his education is over. He may, however, win a scholarship to the central school where he will stay until fifteen or sixteen, receive the beginnings of some vocational training, and possibly, if he obtains employment when he leaves, will find his way into the minor ranks of the black-coated workers, or become a skilled workman. If he has had the luck to develop his brain to examination standard by the age of eleven, he may win a scholarship to the secondary school or even to the local public school. Even at a secondary day-school he is only bound to stay till he is sixteen, and his parents having made sacrifices to pay for the 'extras', may easily expect him to leave at that age and help the family finances. The majority of scholars from elementary schools in a state secondary school never reach the sixth-form stage. The elementary scholar will probably have gained a General School Certificate by the age of sixteen, and in an employer's eye will consequently be equipped for office work. If he is at the county secondary school he may, however, stay another two years, take a Higher School Certificate, and even proceed to a two-year training course to become an elementary teacher. A state secondary school may send a few boys to a London university or to one of the northern ones, although these few are not necessarily elementary scholars. It is rare for a county secondary school to send a boy or a girl with a scholarship to Oxford or Cambridge. The elementary scholar will have more chance of that if he has gone to the local public school, for their tradition would be closer to that of the older universities; but he will be in a far smaller minority in this school, subject most probably to snobbish prejudice from boys and masters, and having to compete with others whose homes offer opportunity and quiet for study and some pretences at least at culture. It is an unusual mind and character that can surmount these difficulties, and it is a mistake to consider that only the very unusual are in need of higher education. The working-class child has no chance of sitting for the scholarship examination for one of the big public schools which provide the greater number of students who go to the universities, unless one of these schools happens to be in his district, and then the examination often requires a specialized training, based on later demands for classical study, that he is not likely to have acquired. Even if he does win a scholarship to one of these schools, he comes under the inevitable prejudice against day-boys.

It is not surprising that very few working-class students find their way to the normal college at Oxford or Cambridge. The scholarship ladder is slippery and has several rungs missing. A man with money can, however, buy his children education of what type he desires. One of the advantages of the English system for the rich man is that he can choose what education he prefers for his children. He may be a fool and send his girl to a ladies' college, where she will be crammed with knowledge and subjected to the monstrous type of discipline that constitutes it a punishable offence to walk on the wrong side of a line in a corridor; and his boy to a poor minor public school, with second-rate equipment and a staff usually suffering from gross ignorance of psychology and ill-concealed boredom. On the other hand, if he is intelligent, he will consider what type of knowledge, discipline, and educational ideal is suited to his children's particular characters, and will buy the right education for them. The 'difficult' child of rich parents may be placed in a school which is designed to enable him to accept his surroundings and achieve some kind of objective interest which will reconcile him to his environment. A 'problem child' of the working class goes automatically into an elementary school, and whether cursed with genius or mental deficiency, usually ends in Borstal, which, though possibly tolerable in these so-called enlightened days, is hardly socially propitious in after-life. Even if sent to bad schools, the rich man's children are at least exempt from dull employment at an early age, and if they have to earn their livings when older, the name of a school which is socially satisfactory, though not necessarily efficient, will assist in acquiring work that is reasonably paid and more or less congenial. There are no doubt men with brilliant degrees wandering about with nothing to do and little chance of employment; such a fact only suggests how desperate must be the state of unemployment lower down the educational scale. Social prestige as well as money still counts for something in the educational world and the schools at the top of the social scale suffer from acute snobbishness. A boy is tacitly admitted to his father's public school and college; and a woman's college at the older universities, though competition has made entrance largely a matter of scholarship, requires to know what is the profession of a candidate's father and what is her religious denomination, the latter being in this case also a matter of social prestige. A remarkable precentage of the women who find their way into these universities have distinguished parents, which may, of course, merely be due to the superior stock.

It is owing to the hopeless inadequacy of this system to provide the common man with the first glimmerings of cultural education that there has arisen the long series of attempts to give the working classes some opportunities for higher study, attempts which have been sometimes the result of the demands of the working class itself, and sometimes initiated by benevolent or socialist individuals reacting against the injustices of the present system. It will be worth while considering in a later section what is the psychological effect of reaction and rebellion on such institutions as experimental schools and adult working-class education. This development has often been connected with the desire of many intelligent middle-class people, to continue their education, to keep fresh their cultural interests by discussion, or to acquire a new skill. Consequently, as in all working-class movements, there has been an infiltration of purely liberal or non-political interest, which has been partly responsible for the somewhat academic tendencies of the present types of adult education. The movements for adult, as for elementary education, in the early nineteenth century, were mainly religious and connected with the Sunday Schools. The Mechanics' Institutes, which were the result of the next stage of development, grew out of Birkbeck's work at Glasgow and had as a predominant aim the instruction of the workers not only in the technique but in the principles of the sciences that were rapidly changing industrial life. These institutes were the product of the new importance given to science in contemporary life and thought. However, their working-class connections were short-lived; the workers objected to the atmosphere of fees, best clothes and middle-class leisure; they suspected ulterior motives on the part of the employers. The workers' struggle for predominance in these institutes, a struggle led mainly by Hodgekin, ended in defeat; with the collapse of the Grand National Consolidated Union, and of the Chartist movement, there was no holding out against the middle-class backwash and all pretences of working-class control of these institutes disappeared. Birkbeck College still continues, but its traditions have been middle-class for a long time. The educational movement initiated by the group of enlightened humanitarians, including Maurice, Kingsley, and Ruskin, was in some ways a reaction against the Birkbeck tradition, for these men were deeply appreciative of the value of humane, as opposed to purely scientific and vocational education, and determined that working men should share what they considered the most valuable fruit of university scholarship. In 1854 they set up the London Working Men's College, but their work there depended too much on their own striking personalities to lead to the creation of any very lasting, wide-spread organization. Their influence has, however, undoubtedly had something to do with the formation of working-class colleges, such as Ruskin itself at Oxford, and with the remarkable success of the Workers' Educational Association.

The Horrabins, speaking of this movement in their excellent little book on working-class education, say, quite rightly, of Maurice that 'he and the group who worked with him, wanted, he declared, "to make our teaching a bond of intercourse with the men we taught". His social aim therefore like Lovett's, was essentially one of co-operation, between the different classes; and in such co-operation, inaugurated from above and not below, there is inevitably more than a tinge of patronage. Workers are quick to feel and resent any such tinge. The Working Men's College still survives. But throughout its whole career always less than 50 per cent of its students have been working men' (p. 29). I have given this quotation in full because it illustrates very clearly the metamorphosis that overtakes all educational efforts made by the genuine educational humanitarian to extend the higher types of education down to the working class. It illustrates what so many admirable educationalists, and also a great many working men and women will not understand, that the development of working-class education must evolve out of the needs and theories of the working class itself. Class divisions, not necessarily emanating from particular individuals, but inevitably creating suspicion and dissension, destroy or pervert the educational efforts, directed towards the working class, of the most benign and idealistic liberals. The working class must accept that situation, and, without necessarily refusing what advantages can be obtained from capitalist education and the extension system in particular, should attempt the creation of their own educational institutions. Such institutions need not try to keep up the pretence of non-political impartiality which cloaks most of the insidious influence of capitalist education. The ideal method of introducing children to controversial subject matters is to allow them to witness, and to take part in, vigorous disagreement and discussion between opponents balanced in numbers and ability, not vapidly to avoid all such subjects. In adult education the facts of society and environment are too pressing to be ignored, and an artificial balance between two points of view, capitalist and socialist, need not be maintained, where society has already decided that the pupils of an adult working-class school shall be exploited. All attempts at extension have never yet really permeated the mass of the working class, and all genuinely working-class movements have been socialist; which means that when the working class are sufficiently class conscious to demand what has been denied them in education, they are also conscious of their general exploitation by the capitalist class. Both the workers and the educationalists may as well make up their minds to that fact and accept genuine working-class education as part of the struggle for socialism.

In the light of these ideas it is easy to sum up the character of existing adult educational institutions. There are continuation schools for boys and girls who have left school at fourteen, and though attended by a very small proportion of school-leavers of that age, they can be noted simply as providing some further knowledge or technical skill on the lines of general capitalist education. The Workers' Educational Association, with its administrative companion, the University Extension Movement, deals with the bulk of adult education. Being the result of humanitarian liberalism as well as working-class demand, it also smacks of patronage and includes many students who are not working class. It has, despite a left-wing group, an air of unreality about its proceedings and academic discussions, though Marxist individuals can effectively use its organization for the expression of their own ideas. It must, of course, be afforded a good deal of respect compared with the blatant attempts of the last National Government to introduce fascism under the cloak of education, in the labour camps of their notorious Employment Bill; its students are at least voluntary.

The National Council of Labour Colleges provides a really genuine working-class point of view; this organization was formed out of the Plebs League with the definite aim of creating something different from the humane education of all extension movements. It looks upon its students, not as men and women free to enter into a heritage of undiscovered knowledge and art, but as victims of a social order which denies their everyday life the natural endowment of such culture. It therefore, refusing to blink at the realities of the economic situation, determines to use education, and in particular the study of economics and social and political history, to further the emancipation of the working class in a socialist state.

Something must be said here concerning the part education may play in the actual achievement of socialism; it will also be my main comment on adult education. To illustrate my principal remarks in the next chapter on class bias in education, I shall draw most of my examples from that of children, their minds being the most receptive and the mischief consequently the greatest among them. In the final chapters I shall take it for granted, without much discussion of possible ways and means, that socialism can be achieved, in discussing the place and form of education in a socialist society. I have already stated in the first chapter that I consider it impossible to achieve the logical conclusion of democracy, that is the rule of the working class, by the gradual permeation of general culture: in short, by the methods of the extension movement. To the Marxist there can be no doubt that education, as every other aspect of environment, is influenced by the economic formation of society, that is in the present case, capitalism. To extend education in England to-day is to extend capitalist education. I do not for that reason deny that the Labour Party is right in demanding the extension of educational opportunity to the working class, for I firmly believe that in a great many individual cases capitalist education is better than none, and that an enlightened cultured product of capitalist society, one who has skimmed the cream of its advantages, is frequently a more civilized individual than an illiterate poverty-stricken peasant. But I do maintain that, although the spread of the present form of education will improve the condition of many individuals, it will get us no appreciable distance further towards the achievement of socialism. It should be the object of adult working-class education to keep sharp the lines of class division, to expose continuously the strain of bias and propaganda latent in the present educational system. By all means allow individuals to make use of such institutions as the Workers' Educational Association, but the working class, in an organization such as the National Council of Labour Colleges, should make it clear that such educational institutions blur the division between class and class, and for the sake of the final achievement of socialism, that division must be kept plain. Owing to the economic history of Great Britain, it is unlikely that, for a long time, the working class will be driven into the extremes of poverty that produce revolution by desperation and starvation. It is all the more important, therefore, that through a working-class educational movement as many workers as possible should become aware of the dialectic process, so that, when the moment comes for revolutionary change, bloody or otherwise, it shall not be passed over and opportunities missed.

CHAPTER THREE

BIAS IN CAPITALIST EDUCATION

IN reviewing the existing educational institutions in England to day, I have been attempting to show merely that different types exist for different classes of society, that the division is only blurred not eliminated by the scholarship ladder, and that the resultant inequality is parallel to the general inequality of income in capitalist society. The quality, however, as well as the quantity of education is affected by the form of society within which it exists. It cannot be denied that there is a connection between the state and education. The ancient Greeks, the Jesuits, and the Russian communists, all in different ways, are examples of leaders who have realized the importance of education in preserving the existing form of society or dogma. 'It is generally taken for granted that the state has the right to determine the kind of education to be given to its citizens. So far back as Aristotle we find it laid down as a principle that politics is architectonic to education, by which is meant that since the politician—or rather, let us say, the statesman—has to use the material worked up by the educator, he, as statesman, is entitled to say what that material shall be. In other words the educator must take his orders from the statesman.'[1] Thus we cannot fairly blame education in capitalist society for being capitalist; but since capitalists have held it against socialist education that it will be socialist, and have made exaggerated claims of impartiality

[1] *Educational Theories*, by Sir John Adams, 1927, p. 73.

and freedom from state interference for their own education, we may in fairness track down some of the capitalist bias and propaganda in the present schools.

One has to be more alert in scenting the elusive quality of capitalist influence in English schools than in many continental educational systems. The English are among the most subtle purveyors of propaganda and produce it often without consciousness of class motives, sheltering under a supreme contempt of the more blatant continental forms and of the more strident English newspapers who adopt them. It is in *Stalky and Co.*, a book which is an excellent revelation of a certain type of capitalist mentality, that there occurs the immortal picture of the Jelly-bellied Flag-flapper; the English like their patriotism discreet. Our pretence at educational impartiality is about as true and as politically convenient to the capitalist as our pretence at liberty. This, of course, has its immediate effect on educational policy and theory, and in my attempt to prove capitalist bias in the present schools, I know I shall be arousing genuine indignation in the breasts of many highly-principled teachers who would consider a political bias in their teaching a disgrace to their profession. They would be the first to agree with all that has been said in the last chapter concerning the injustices to the working-class child through inequalities in opportunity. They are even sometimes loud-voiced in demand for universal free education. They are also usually the first to object that a socialist government would poison the wells of education with vicious and perverted propaganda. I have a great respect for their ideals and for their attempts at integrity; I am also convinced that those ideals are impracticable in the present order of society, and that a very considerable bias exists in education to-day towards the maintenance of the *status quo*.

A very interesting example of this typically English state of mind, this attempt to practise an ideal without considering its practicality in relation to society, is afforded by the effect of the Great War on educational thinking in this country. The genuine belief that the world had been made safe for democracy by four years' wholesale murder, was accompanied, amongst the more enlightened, by a recognition of the fact that the success of a political democracy depends on the educational level of its members. Woodrow Wilson was quoted with satisfaction as declaring: 'that no more vital truth was ever uttered than that freedom and free institutions cannot long be maintained by any people who do not understand the nature of their own government.' The interest in education in the first years after the war was wide-spread, and produced a crop of books on the teaching of history and civics, but had little real effect unfortunately in improving educational conditions. But when we read these books we find in all of them the same complacency that accepted the war as an unpleasant duty in which our quarrel was God's quarrel. It was easy to harangue against the Prussian spirit as exemplified by the Kaiser's proclamation on education, which is quoted in *Essays in the Politics of Education* by F. Clarke (1916). 'I have for a long time been occupied with the thought of making use of the schools in their separate grades for combating the spread of socialistic and communistic ideas. The prime object of the schools will ever be to lay the foundations for a sound comprehension of both civic and social relations, by cherishing reverence to God and love for the fatherland. . . . Moreover the schools must show by statistics how considerably and constantly in this country the wages and conditions of the labouring classes have improved under this monarchical protection.' It was easy to show the connection between Prussian militarism and this predetermination of the results of statistics. Yet the author of *A Defence of Classical Education* (1916) heads his first chapter by the following quotation from *The Round Table*: 'The war has indeed revealed grave shortcomings of detail in English education; but on the whole it has been a vindication of its essential soundness. It has proved us a nation not only sound and strong in character but far more adaptable, both in soldiering and industry, than either we or our enemies suspected. The grave defect of our national education is that there is not enough of it.' If the Germans had won the war this is doubtless what they would have said, despite the Prussian educational ideal of the school as a forcing ground for unquestioning patriots. The educational writers of this time do not stop to consider that a bias towards militarism in English schools may also have had something to do with the outbreak of war, and that a conviction of the sanctity of one's cause is always part of the ammunition of war.

However, there was also a considerable movement at this time towards providing some more definite instruction in civic duties and individual responsibilities to the state. Mr. Showan in his book *Citizenship and the School* expresses a wish to increase civic education in order to ensure that 'the most is made of our opportunity to induce respect for time-honoured institutions, and to encourage patriotism and the community-spirit'. There was the usual technical bicker as to whether this type of instruction should be a separate school subject or merely part of the normal history teaching. The unreality of the controversy is clear as it always resolves into the cliché that all subjects if properly taught provide training in civics, and that history teaching in particular should always be linked up with social facts that are within the child's every-day experience, the policeman, his parents' vote, the upkeep of roads, and local administration, a principle that anyone with some psychological knowledge knows to be the only way of introducing a subject to a child so that its interest will be caught. There was no attempt to face the problem of what is good or bad in tradition, what in social institutions should be honoured, and what should be superseded. Thus Miss Sophie Bryant in *Moral and Religious Education* (1920) can write: 'All school children should understand something of the great ideal which is in process of being realized in the Federation of Free States which is called the British Empire' (p.100). The idea that England can do nothing wrong, and that this country has had a special call to put into practice the ideals bred from the aftermath of war, continued to be implied in schools. A recent ridiculous incident which actually reached the House of Commons was comic in its details, and revealed the fact that to the majority of people in this country patriotic propaganda is not propaganda at all, but truth elevated above the realms of controversy. An inspector rebuked a schoolmistress for teaching her children the unqualified statement that England was the best country in the world. She was obviously guilty of the most flagrant nationalist propaganda, but it was the inspector who came under official displeasure until it was revealed that he was a respectable Tory, when the incident was allowed to die down. The only comfort the socialist can gain from this incident is that even a conservative inspector has sometimes more understanding of the meaning of education than the public-school man at Westminster. Good-hearted liberals might ponder the official attitude thus revealed, when next they inveigh against the devastating effects of fascism on the integrity of culture and education.

We are on the whole free from the organized attempt by the government to dictate what political theory shall be taught in schools. Even our present government would think twice before it issued instructions to teachers, on the German model, to impress their pupils with the advantages of capitalism and deliberately to pervert the ideas of socialist thinkers. That is one of the advantages that educational chaos has over a system; parts of it can wriggle out of effective state control when not in agreement with the prevailing atmosphere of the state schools. It is in fact unnecessary for the government to do anything so crude. Certain psychological traits in man are exploited by the forms and traditions of modern English education, to implant a deep-rooted dislike of social change. The instinct to preserve what has been evolved by past generations and to reverence tradition is strong, very possibly stronger, than the instinct to destroy, which is usually bred out of a desperate need of self-preservation. The English have a hearty respect for such feelings and there are many things in the tradition of English life that one would be sorry to see disappear; the most revolutionary of us would hardly feel justified in throwing a bomb into King's College Chapel, or even into the new Stratford Theatre, because they had harboured different aspects of capitalist culture. One cannot but be impressed by the oath of the Greek schoolboy: 'I will not disgrace my sacred weapons, nor desert the comrade who is placed by my side. I will fight for things holy and things profane, whether I am alone or with others. I will hand on my fatherland greater and better than I found it. I will hearken to the magistrates and obey the existing laws and those hereafter established by the people. I will not consent unto any that destroys or disobeys the constitution, but will prevent him; whether I am alone or with others. I will honour the temples and the religion which my forefathers established.' To hold fast to that which is good, and to be prepared to sacrifice life for the preservation of what civilization men have been able to wring from their environment, is no mean thing. Many who died in the last war fought in that spirit; it was not the spirit that was wrong but the mockery of that enthusiasm by the circumstances of mass murder, of capitalist ambition and nationalist hate. You cannot go through Lenin's tomb in Moscow without realizing that the seeds of a great tradition are already within the Soviet state, and that the Russian determination to preserve what has been won from the darkness of capitalism evinces the same spirit that prompted the Greek youth to defend his city home against the besieging hordes.

The saddening and exasperating thing to the socialist is, of course, what can be realized at one glance at the Greek boy's oath, that to the vast majority of those who reverence tradition, its preservation is incompatible with change. Socialist thinkers have a mighty task to perform in making people realize that not only is change inevitable, but it provides the sole means of obtaining any continuity of spirit in any institution. An institution will either be transformed or decay; there is no standing still. 'We fail to understand the mechanism of our social universe and in consequence maintain our established customs for fear that our social world may come tumbling about our ears. And the terrible thing is that perhaps the opposite result is taking place. We may perish just because we fear the new and do not know how to change.'[1] A tradition to be vital must be fluid. An attempt to preserve intact the order of things as they are is to necessitate a sudden break and the disappearance of all continuity and tradition for some time. This is a concept that modern man seems to find difficult to grasp; earlier times took it for granted though they deplored it.

It is, of course, simpler to envisage things in fixity unless you have the mind of a Shelley, who always seemed to think in terms of movement. Change, to be intelligently conducted, needs imagination, forethought, and reason. To see the nature of what exists, to find it good, to seek to preserve it, is not a bad thing. To understand the nature of what exists so that the good may be sifted from the bad, to envisage the trend of change which will preserve the good and destroy the bad, to attempt the control of circumstances towards that reasoned aim, is a process requiring an altogether more powerful mentality. As Bertrand Russell has so admirably put it, 'none of the higher mental processes are required for conservatism. The advocate of change, on the contrary, must have a certain degree of imagination in order to be able to conceive of anything different from what exists'.[2] Mob rule and uncontrolled violence are dangerous, active ignorance, if it may be so expressed; in the long run there is equal danger in ignorance at a standstill, the static futility of attempting to remain

---

[1] *A New World in the Making*, p. 18, Jean Piaget (Switzerland), published by the New Education Fellowship.
[2] *Education and the Social Order*, by Bertrand Russell, Chap. 1.

at the head of a waterfall, mental and spiritual inertia. This conservative attitude is latent in the public-school tradition, which will brook no change in any detail. In Arnold Whitridge's life of Dr. Arnold of Rugby, he says: 'He (Arnold) also knew, what many statesmen have ignored, that stability is achieved in a nation or a school by making it to the interest of as many people as possible that the *status-quo* should be maintained.' This is, of course, 'the greatest happiness of the greatest number' in another guise; but the interesting thing is the static conception of prosperity. Arnold had a great deal to do with founding the public-school tradition, yet even he in his day was looked on as a dangerous reformer. This conservatism is found not only in the schools. 'No child in the Western capitalist world can possibly escape from propaganda in favour of things as they are; it stares at him in the newspapers, it blares at him through the loud-speaker, it pursues him every day whenever he makes any contact with the outside world. All that progressive schools can hope to do is in some measure to redress the balance.'[1] The writer is here maintaining what is incontrovertible, that pressure to preserve the *status quo* is very strong and that it is the business of education to try to cultivate such mental alertness as will withstand that pressure, and sift the good from the bad by intelligent criticism.

The curricula of the schools of England have been evolved in the traditions of a governing class; and that the extension of education to the working class has been carried through without much consideration of their particular needs may be seen from the fact that the curricula of their schools are predominantly academic. The great public schools and the universities

[1] *Progressive Schools*, by L. B. Pekin, p. 97.

have set the tradition which it has been the aim of girls' schools and state elementary and secondary schools to imitate. There are many variations of this atmosphere but it has been in general the main source of the chief types of education peculiar to this country. One of the main concepts of the English tradition of education is the importance of character as opposed to mere knowledge, and no subject can really pass by the theorists unless it can, by some contortion of reasoning, be made to appear to provide some moral training as well. Matthew Arnold, an apologist for humanist education, had little following in his day, and the traditional curricula were justified on other grounds. His plea for sweetness and light can be found, by reference to his more detailed arguments, to demand among other things consideration of all great literatures and an appreciation of beauty in all parts of life. His support of the classical tradition in teaching was due to a firm belief that all that was good in European civilization derived from Greece and Rome, and that the way to combat the gross commercialism of the Philistines was to bring up their sons in the broad sunshine of classical learning. The absurd curricula of the nineteenth-century public schools, derived from mediaeval tradition when the classics were practically useful, were, however, justified frequently on other grounds; Matthew Arnold was himself brought up under the influence of his father, Arnold of Rugby, who was considered an outrageous revolutionary through attempting to introduce a little of the humanist conception of broad culture into his school. The doubtful theories of transference and formal training, which suggested that the mental training acquired in any one subject could be transferred to the study of any other, accounted, with the force of tradition, for a far less imaginative treatment of the classics than Matthew Arnold had envisaged, as the stand-by of public-school curricula. The classics became a discipline for growing mental powers; the glory that was Greece and the grandeur that was Rome have not yet rid themselves of the misery of grind and incomprehension that wrapped them round in the earlier nineteenth century. *Tom Brown's Schooldays* shows how even under Arnold the greater part of the school work was concerned with hammering some sense from the classics and laboriously manufacturing Latin and Greek verses. Kinglake, whose imagination was fired by the early teaching of his mother, tells in *Eothen* how dismal was the contrast between the classics at home and at school; at home 'you form strange and mystic friendships with the mere names of mountains, and seas, and continents and mighty rivers; you learn the ways of the planets and transcend their narrow limits, and ask for the end of space'; at school, 'instead of sweet knowledge, vile, monkish doggerel, grammars, and graduses, dictionaries and Lexicons, and horrible odds and ends of dead languages are given you for your portion . . . cold rations of *Poetae Graeci* cut up by commentators and served up by school-masters'.

The controversy over the educational value of such curricula is well-nigh dead, and our modern schools show a strange mixture of the remnants of this tradition and the commercialization of education that demands a vast number of subjects taught frequently with little connection between them. That commercialization can be dealt with later, but it is from this traditionalism in curriculum and in general school life that arises the tendency in English education to guard jealously what is old and to resist change. The classical languages form the most pointed example in curriculum. Their practical utility is now confined to the few professions where they are still in use for documents, notably the law. Otherwise their utility is solely that of a gateway to the ancient literatures and civilizations, and depends on the acquisition of considerable fluency in these languages. Yet they are still considered slightly superior to other 'sides'; the 'moderns' in a public school are felt to have taken the easier course; in girls' schools, which should be freer from clogging tradition, Latin is frequently begun at eleven; when in reality it is much sounder to defer its study until later. The older universities demand Latin for their qualifying examinations and many children are taught it solely because they may have the opportunity to go to Oxford or Cambridge. The mentality that insists on the study of dead languages by children far too young to get past the barriers of grammar to the imaginative fields beyond, is typical of the attitude that has made English education to-day; the education of the ruling class, culminating in access to the store-houses of academic learning at Oxford and Cambridge, is that which the benevolent wish to 'extend' to the working class. It is still considered somewhat socially inferior to demand an education that has an immediate relation to one's economic conditions. The invasion of the public schools by the middle class, who are naturally utilitarian in their demands, has not altogether ousted the more aristocratic preparation of a 'man of parts'.

Subjects other than the classics in the curricula are less obviously connected with the traditional education of the *élite*. Although the science and modern sides of advanced work are given their full place, if not full prestige, the struggle for the recognition of the crafts, demanding manual skill as well as intellectual qualities, is by no means over. In kindergarten departments, the study of psychology has made it the recognized procedure to let the child develop through handling material, and it is probable that the elementary schools are better off in this respect than the 'prep' schools which are far more closely connected with the public-school tradition. To choose the right amount of training in crafts and technical skill to coincide most exactly with the child's development from perceptual to conceptual levels of thought, is a theoretical question for the psychologist and educationalist; but the problem is complicated by the fact that there has undoubtedly been a class prejudice, possibly unconscious, against the use of methods that can in any way be likened to manual labour; that prejudice is illustrated by the far better technical equipment for craft-teaching in state secondary schools than in public schools generally. There are, of course, exceptions, as notably that of Oundle under Sanderson, who was a pioneer in a recognition of the importance of manual constructive work, but on the whole the public-school tradition has been reluctant to accept technical subjects. The county schools for girls are usually better equipped for teaching the feminine crafts of housewifery than the public girls' schools, whose aim, too often still modified by the suffragette outlook, is to prove equality of boys and girls in the intellectual traditional subjects; in such schools domestic work is left for the 'rabbits', an attitude which does not encourage good teaching in these subjects. The same is apt to apply to drawing and music, because in a crowded curriculum such subjects have to appear as 'extras' to the real meat of mathematics, languages, and arts subjects. It is also considered that a person of general public-school education can acquire an interest in and appreciation of these arts outside his usual school training, a supposition which is frequently made correct by the fact that such a person often comes from a home where the arts are held in high repute. But for children whose homes are without such cultural acquisitions as good books and pictures, the school must provide the impetus to interest in the arts. The advance in schools of practical training and expression in various arts has been retarded, on the one hand, by the attitude of the unimaginative official who cannot visualize the cultural poverty of the working-class home, and on the other by the commercialized mentality of capitalism which cannot see what use they are anyway.

The really thorny aspect of class-bias in school subjects comes of course in the teaching of history and literature; and here the dogs delight to bark and bite and to shout accusations of propaganda at one another. When the London Labour Party in 1934 announced its intention of inspecting the text-books used in the schools that come under the authority of the L.C.C., there was a howl of righteous indignation in the capitalist Press which declared that the children of London were about to be made vessels for perverted socialist propaganda. The L.C.C., however, was acting on a sound educational policy, that a history text-book should provide not merely true facts but truly proportionate facts, that is, should be a book which as far as possible will leave the child to decide for himself. A text-book of recent history which, though it may not be guilty of a single lie, gives several chapters to the Great War and a few lines to Lenin and the Bolshevik Revolution, is, nevertheless, perverting the truth, by Stalky's methods of *suppressio veri* and *suggestio falsi*. Take, for example, a modern text-book very fair in its positive statements, Book Four of *The Kingsway Histories*, by E. Wynn Williams (1935). It speaks of the Unemployment Insurance Act of 1934 without mention of the Means Test (p. 72); it gives a fair account of the antagonism of the English and the Boers in South Africa, but gives no comment on the status of the native population (pp. 104-5); it details improvements in Japan due to industrialization, but does not refer to the present appalling conditions of the Japanese workers (p. 136). While admitting much social improvement in Soviet Russia, it specifically mentions the horrors of the civil war and the anti-kulak drive: 'Many of the old landowners and professional classes were driven into exile or put to death, as were also many who opposed the new government' (p. 176). The fascist revolutions in Italy and Germany are described without any reference to cruelty and bloodshed. There is no mention of the foreign intervention in Russia in 1919, which did so much to aggravate the horrors of the revolution; on the other hand, there is no mention of the Jew-baiting or persecution of socialists and communists in Germany who was allowed to have her revolution unhindered (pp. 176-9). The inference by comparison is that the communists use force and encourage bloodshed, and the fascists do not.

The whole possibility of extensive capitalist propaganda in schools has been due to a vicious educational doctrine, that education can be conducted without reference to its environment, that a teacher can be both unbiassed and interesting; it is impossible for one human being to present an unbiassed case; all that happens is that the present situation becomes surrounded with a false aura of sanctity, well above argument. The doctrine is involved with the really sound point of view that no child should be presented with one argument without its counterpart, that he should be given the facts of the case and allowed to decide for himself, and that no kind of personal, moral, or social pressure should be put upon him to accept any doctrine or theory. But this is quite another thing from attempting to deliver education in a vacuum. Socialists are often accused of bandying names about, in their more hysterical moments, without really considering whether these abstract entities exist. 'Let those who can define them,' say the critics, 'shout "Liberté, Egalité, Fraternité".' Educationalists are perhaps of all people most prone to this sin of argument without reference to immediate environment. In reality nothing in a school from the character of the headmaster down to the stationery can be judged without reference to surrounding environment. The demand that education should exist a thing apart, sacred to its own self, although it has, for instance, stirred up teachers of all political opinions against government economies, and is responsible for some of the good in the professional spirit of teachers, has also led to a great number of misconceptions on this question of bias and propaganda. It is impossible for an institution, unless it is economically self-sufficient, to be uninfluenced by the structure of the society in which it exists; a school, which is a community cutting across the lives of many people and never totally absorbing the interests of any individual, must therefore reflect the society in which they spend the rest of their lives.

Education cannot exist without being socialist, capitalist, or fascist, or without bearing some other mark of political form; it goes without saying that England being a capitalist country, English education is capitalist education; it has sprung out of and exists because of a capitalist society, and no amount of high-minded principles on the integrity of educational theory can wriggle out of that position. Similarly, unless a person is in a state of intellectual apathy, which, of course, is unfortunately most often the case, he must either be in agreement with the surrounding order of society, or in revolt. Even the apathetic must, by the very selection of facts they make, put some personal interpretation on those facts. A teacher presumably has spent some time studying the subject he is teaching, and, if he has come through that study without making a personal judgment of his subject-matter, he must be an extraordinarily dull person. Personal enthusiasm for the subject taught seems to me as great a necessity for a teacher as a liking for children; he will not evoke interest from them unless he is interested himself. I am not suggesting that the teacher will necessarily flagrantly push his own point of view and demand from his pupils passive acceptance of his argument; if he is an educationalist, he will know better. But if he attempts to teach his subject without any reference to social problems, to present it as a mass of unrelated facts, he will not only have returned to the dark ages of psychology, but he will be performing a nice experiment in humbug. We pride ourselves on knowing better than Dr. Arnold, who remarked of young boys: 'It is a great mistake to think that they should understand all they learn; for God has ordered that in youth the memory should act vigorously, independent of the understanding —whereas a man cannot usually recollect a thing unless he understands it.'[1] We believe children must understand to remember. Understanding facts means putting

[1] Stanley's *Life of Dr. Arnold*, Chap. 3, p. 123.

them into a relation; relationship between facts presupposes a judgment on them; and a judgment means bias; and a very good thing too, one feels inclined to add. How it is possible for education to retain its integrity and accept this inevitable bias, I shall try to show when dealing with socialist education and propaganda. I merely state here that it is inevitable, and that England being capitalist the general tendency is to capitalist bias; that is, the majority of individuals accept present society, and the air of impartiality that breathes from our schools consequently surrounds the *status quo* with a cloak of axiomatic infallibility. Some personal orientation is present in all teachers and all text-books, and not even a text of geometry is a totally impersonal thing. The teaching of history, scripture, and English becomes barren and dull unless related to the living forces of political theory, social change and a general philosophy. William the Conqueror, 1066, has become a standing joke, but the theories of Marx are not yet sufficiently antiquated to be entombed in history teaching. The Old Testament may be taught as a guiding rule to life in the twentieth century, but it may not be whispered that some have called Christ the first socialist. Milton is sufficiently far away to be a glorious defender of our liberties, but it is safer to read the odes of Shelley without trespassing into his inflammable doctrines of atheism, polygamy, and republicanism.

Inevitably one must take history teaching to illustrate this problem for the simple reason that its subject-matter brings it nearer to the most controversial of modern problems, the political and economic. There are no bitterer battles except possibly in religion and that also is subject-matter which is closely connected with class-bias. For religious teaching, according to the present dogmas, tends to be static and not to encourage the dynamic interpretation of life. It rightly wishes to cultivate the spirit of reverence for things holy; but, as I have tried to show, through mental laziness reverence becomes attached to mere antiquity and not necessarily to worth, whereas creative imagination, which envisages change, must go hand in hand with real reverence. Not even the most reactionary of Tories will deny that the problems of modern civilization are primarily economic, and that our first necessity is to discover a cure for poverty in the midst of plenty. The majority of the various doctors who proffer their pet remedies for this disease, appeal to Clio for divine support. The capitalist says: 'This is what we have done in the past; let us preserve it.' The socialist says: 'By the study of history was the Marxist theory evolved; if you want to realize the predestined rôle of the working class, read history.' No wonder there has been wrangling as to the guidance of children in this controversial field; no wonder the harassed schoolmaster has sometimes wished that a history text-book could be an impersonal thing.

It is impossible without actually taking the reader into class-rooms and letting him listen to many history lessons, to prove personal bias; we must perforce return to the question of text-books, though it must be remembered that a blatant text-book can be toned down by a judicious teacher and a relatively good one be mangled by bad teaching. Arrangement of a history syllabus may reveal where a teacher fears to tread. A great many children leave school from the upper fifth forms having taken the Schools Certificate Examination, and many schools do not deal with nineteenth-century

BIAS IN CAPITALIST EDUCATION

history until the sixth-form stage. How can a child understand the difficulties of the present world situation, how can he come to use a vote intelligently, if he has never heard in school of the Industrial Revolution, of colonial expansion, of trade unions and factory legislation, of the European political revolutions of 1830 and 1848? But even when nineteenth-century history is taught it is infrequent to find that the social and economic factors are given the same prominence as the political and military, whereas the modern text-books of mediaeval history show that the authors have learnt that the economic and social aspects of history, the tale of how common people lived, ate, worked, and died, is the most interesting to children. It is seldom now that a text-book of mediaeval history wades through the tales of war and kingship that still clog nineteenth-century history;[1] yet hardly any school of economists or historians will deny that the Industrial Revolution, with its social consequences in producing an urban working class and the whole imperialist trading machinery of capitalism, is the key to the interpretation of the facts of nineteenth-century history. Yet how many children have heard of Peterloo as well as Waterloo, how many are as closely acquainted with the Chartist movement as with the jubilees of Queen Victoria, which of them knows the significance of the French Commune?

It is necessary to give some actual examples of bias in history text-books. This is how Sir Charles Oman in *A Junior History of England* sums up the effects of the Industrial Revolution on the working-class standard of life. 'The condition of the working classes, both in town

[1] Compare, for instance, *History, Junior Course*, Book Three, by E. Nunn, and Book Four, by Catherine Firth (1931), with *Highroads of History*, Book Three, produced by Nelson (1913).

and countryside, in the years after 1815 was one of great distress and the discontent of the ignorant multitude was at the bottom of the political troubles of the time. The wilder spirits among them talked of a general insurrection and of an assault, not only on the government but on all forms of property and established institutions' (p. 637). This is the only comment on the theories of Marx; it would indeed have been a magnificent revolution. In describing the Indian Mutiny the same writer talks of an Indian prince as a 'revengeful and treacherous villain', which possibly he was, but an Englishman who, it is stated, shot some Indian leaders without trial, is merely 'a daring cavalry officer' (p. 747). On the subject of trade unions Sir Charles allows himself such a biassed statement as this: 'they had not yet assumed the inquisitorial and dictatorial tone which they have adopted in our own day and were still defensive rather than offensive in their character.' This book is, however, admittedly an extreme instance of bias, though this Victorian product is still sometimes used in schools. The newer text-books seldom produce such prizes for the heresy-hunter, except in a reference to post-war history. The *New Statesman and Nation* for January 19, 1935, has an article quoting some fantastic statements, as, for instance, that Lenin was a German spy, from school-books as much used as Brendon's *Britain and Her Neighbours* and Miller's *Beginner's History of England*. The earlier chapters of history are now, more naturally, presented with little bias, their controversies being dead; the social and economic side of mediaeval history usually receives its right share of attention. The last chapters of a history text-book covering post-war history are usually the worst. The following quotation is from *Britain and Her Neighbours* and reveals an unconscious attitude of superiority. 'The most notable event in recent years has been the passing of an Act by the Imperial Parliament granting to the people of India a greater share in the government of their own country. This measure will, it is hoped, put an end to the unrest, some of it seditious, that has sprung up in India as in all eastern lands' (Book 6, p. 185). The hysteria engendered by the war still colours descriptions of it in text-books. The following re-hash of atrocity stories comes from *A History of England; The Nineteenth Century and After*, by Cyril Robinson. 'In one respect, indeed, they (the Germans) could boast an advantage which we need not envy them. They had little or no regard for the etiquette or chivalry of war; and ugly tales were told of the misuse of the white flag, of traps which traded on our men's humanity, and of Germans who deliberately surrendered and then struck down their captors from behind' (p. 274). The same book has the following account of the British intervention in Russia at the end of the war. 'So in 1918 a British expedition was sent out by way of the White Sea, and a tentative offensive was begun from Archangel. It was an utter failure. The Russian people, *oddly enough*, showed no signs of wanting it, and our men had to be brought back' (p. 328, italics mine). Both these quotations are lacking in the imagination which can regard the foreigner as a human being, and the width of vision that can take into consideration the psychological origin of evidence.

Here is a further selection of comments on various controversial questions of to-day. The passions of the Great War are still evoked in some text-books; a chapter on the war called 'The Threat to our Empire and How We Met It', begins thus: 'The shame of having deliberately caused the greatest and most terrible war in history—over five millions of human beings lost their lives in the struggle—must for ever rest with Germany' ('*New Guide*' *Histories*, Intermediate, p. 207, *c.* 1921, by A. Yoxall). The same book gives the following opinion of the Germans 'as courageous fighters; but they did not fight fair. It was they who began the use of poison gas, they who first planned aeroplane attacks on civilians; it was they who tortured prisoners, murdered old men and boys, women and children, and laid waste with needless and deliberate destruction the fair cities of Belgium and France' (p. 212). The senior book of the same series declares that at the end of the war it was recognized that 'God had done great things for us' (p. 240). Soviet Russia also provides much dubious statement; in its section on religion, *History, Senior Course*, Book Three, by Catherine Firth, suggests that in the Greek Orthodox Church the Russians have lost something of great value which was dear to them. The following statement is of dubious accuracy: 'The Russian government does not allow Christmas or Easter to be public holidays. It arranges for festivals in memory of Lenin and the Revolution' (p. 11). It is perfectly legitimate to consider these as state ceremonies, such as our own Empire days and coronation festivals. Book Four of the same series, in its account of Russia in the nineteenth century, represents the Tsars as primarily concerned with the welfare of the people and Lenin as a man who led the workers like sheep and even dictated to them in taste. The chronic economic condition of the peasants and soldiers is hardly emphasized and the foreign intervention in aid of the Whites is not referred to. The statement that Lenin taught the people that 'they should . . . imprison the Czar, his ministers, and the nobles', is a complete misrepresentation of the communist doctrine, which does not encourage acts of violence, particularly against isolated individuals. An illustration of a monument planned by a communist is possibly genuine, but must have been included to ridicule the communists, whereas a great deal of tasteful opinion has praised very highly some of the post-revolutionary buildings as artistic creations. In *The World To-Day*, by E. N. Fawcett and M. Le S. Kitchin, vol. eight, the failure of the socialist experiment of Louis Blanc is fairly accurately described, but that the failure was inevitable seems to be the opinion of the authors; an account of the doctrines of Marx is followed by this statement, hardly flattering to this thinker's intelligence: 'He took it for granted that the State could do these things (i.e. take over industry and agriculture) successfully' (p. 183). The Soviet experiments in planning are given fair treatment, but it is not made clear that those experiments belong to the despised doctrine of Marx.

The fault of the less violent text-book writer is not so much in commission as in omission. More subtle perversions of truth are thus perpetrated than by obvious incorrect statement and over-colourful description. Mark Starr, who in *Lies and Hate in Education* (1929), has made a valuable collection of examples of such perversions, says: 'What is more deadly is the lie by inference. A disproportionate attention is given to the home country and silence maintained upon the doings of other nations. There is a glorification of the particular empire and the glossing over of its methods of acquirement with incorrect or incomplete descriptions of its present state' (p. 13). Even an eminently fair book, such as *A Text Book of Modern English History*, by

G. W. Southgate (latest revised edition, 1932), which confines itself to simple statements of fact concerning the Russian Revolution and the General Strike, and which ends with the serious contemplation of the disappearance of competition in favour of co-operation, even such a book can include a chapter on the South African colonies, without any real appreciation of the fact that the negro has any claim to be considered along with the Boer and the Englishman. There are very few mentions of the shifty conduct of the British in connection with the Danish fleet in the Napoleonic wars, of the British intervention in Russia in 1919, or the allied blockade of Germany after she had surrendered. Not the least serious fault of even the fairly impartial text-book is the air of complacency which the last chapters effuse. The tale of past difficulties in the nineteenth century may be told accurately, but it is rare for the difficulties of the present time to be seriously considered after the complacent contemplation of past achievements. The writer of this book can hardly endorse this rosy picture of modern education: 'All young people can now get a good education, and the best are able to carry on their education right through to the university' (*The Headway Histories*; Junior Series, Book Four, by F. W. Tickner, 1932, p. 113). Complacency in the following quotation is explicitly linked with the latest developments of the capitalist society: 'Thus there are signs that our post-war difficulties are beginning to pass away. The leaders of industry in the new trades are showing courage and enterprise. In the older industries—in cotton, coal, and iron and steel—great amalgamations are taking place. Soon we may expect each of these industries to be made up of a small number of very large, powerful, and well-equipped firms, well able to hold their own in the world's markets' (*The World To-Day*, p. 307).¹

Yet the capitalist talks of socialist propaganda! Perhaps socialists would not be able to write a more unbiassed history text-book than many now current, but it seems only fair that they should have their turn after so many generations when the enemy has had the field to himself. These text-books have had a great ally in the natural conservatism of the child's mind and if for no other reason, I should prefer socialist to capitalist bias in the present society, because it is more likely to disturb the easy acceptance of things as they are, the natural assumption by the child that because things exist they must persist; because it breeds the beginnings of the critical frame of mind that will accept no institution, no idea, no tradition which has not been tested and found satisfactory by its own powers of reason.

Direct political pressure on the children of the school is not common, except where there are evidences of uncommon and precocious interest in politics, such as was shown by the authors of *Out of Bounds*, Giles and Esmond Romilly, who caused not a little disturbance in that respectable military academy, Wellington, by carrying on a campaign of active communist propaganda; incidentally by their relationship to Winston Churchill they provided the newspapers with grand copy, a choice illustration of the irrelevant circumstances that will throw an individual into the headlines. Their journal, also called *Out of Bounds*, was, of course, banned at most large public schools, a restriction which shows the limitation of the impartiality of these schools. It is

---

[1] All the text-books quoted or referred to in this section of the book are to my personal knowledge among the stock of some school.

permissible to discuss in debating societies most controversial subjects, but it is not permissible to read a paper which professes to prove the socialist theories by an appeal to facts concerning the economic conditions of the present world; facts will win over the adolescent mind where no amount of hysteria and 'gas' has any effect. However, the usual child in his teens does not wish to take an active part in politics; the method of direct pressure is used far more forcibly when it concerns the staff of a school. Writing in connection with the lack of liberty in Russian schools to inculcate any other than communist doctrines, the Webbs point out similar restrictions on English teachers. 'In no part of the country could a teacher in a public elementary school keep his (or her) job, however sincere and fervent his belief, if he was known to inculcate atheism, communism, the abolition of parliament, republicanism or the dissolution of the British Empire' (p. 1029). The theory that education in a vacuum is possible and that a teacher must forget his individuality and his personal judgments, has been responsible for allowing class-bias to restrict the political activities of teachers. It usually passes unnoticed that the active socialist is penalized far more often than the conservative, mainly because active membership of the Conservative Party does not always mean more than being polite to middle-aged ladies at a garden-party, while the socialist frequently feels called upon to stand on soap-boxes at street corners and shout. There is as usual a vast amount of sanctimonious humbug concerning this question, and the justification of political pressure by appeal to high educational ideals. Sir John Adams, in his new book *The Teacher's Many Parts* (1930), in a chapter on the teacher as citizen, after a very sane recognition of the fact that virile teaching must go along with personal opinions, concludes by saying: 'With regard to the out-of-school activities of the teacher as a citizen, I feel that it is not my business nor anybody else's to deal, beyond making the simple demand that his outside activities shall not be such as shall in any way interfere with his usefulness in his profession. Outside of school the only obligation laid upon the teacher as citizen is to be a good one', and he leaves it to the individual teacher to decide for himself what is a good citizen. Such refreshing sanity and generosity of mind does not, however, distinguish many of the school authorities in England. The left-wing group of university educationalists at Oxford has felt called upon to express their disapproval of the pressure put upon the teacher to refrain from all political activity.

The only argument that has any validity against the politically active teacher is that his is a full-time job and that any other interest will mean that he is not giving his best to his work. Personally I consider that when a teacher has got his hand in, and that should not take him more than a few months, he will teach far better if he indulges in some activity outside the school, than if he spends his whole time sedulously preparing every word of his lessons, and spattering masses of red ink over exercise books, in remarks which no one will trouble to read. One notices that this type of argument is not applied to such teachers as spend their time out of school playing games, collecting butterflies or writing novels. There are cases of definite political persecution cited in Mark Starr's book *Lies and Hate in Education*, including the dismissal of a left-wing schoolmistress and her temporary replacement by a member of the local fascist executive. The authorities may wink the eye at party work as long as it is not too public, but few will allow a teacher in their employment to stand for the county council or for parliament. We hear so much talk about training children in civics, yet, when a teacher, who is supposed to be a shining example of all virtues, has the public spirit to take on the thankless and unprofitable work of a town councillor, he is politely required to remove himself. Nor is it always necessary to stipulate political activity as the reason for dismissal. Any opportunity, including the frequently advertised national economy, may be taken, and in these days of unemployment the teacher has little redress. Rarely can he afford to walk haughtily out of his post; the weapon of unemployment is as crippling to the teachers as to any other body of workers; there is a constant stream of unemployed teachers ready to fill the gaps and to toe the line obediently. The National Union of Teachers has as yet no feeling against blacklegs, and to toy with socialism in this trade as in others often is to juggle with your bread and butter. Teachers are some of the best informed and keenest thinking people in England, but so strong is the sentiment that they are public figures, who must not come down from pedestal into the arena, that they deserve Sir John Adams' unconscious stigma: 'The teachers are always found to be on the whole more conservative than the bulk of their fellow-citizens. It seems to be a characteristic of the profession that its members are lovers of law and order, and less inclined than the average towards change . . . they are pre-eminently respectable, and unwilling to strike out into new lines for themselves' (op. cit.). It is only seldom, therefore, that we have a case of open conflict between a teacher and his education authority on this subject, such as that revealed by a correspondent, a schoolmaster at Clifton, to the *New Statesman and Nation* in 1934. It is tacitly agreed that while it is respectable to make public profession of a religion by attending a church regularly, while it is supposed that a public appearance on behalf of maltreated animals or in the interests of culture will have no undesirable effect on a teacher's pupils, nor bias them towards any one opinion, it is yet highly dangerous for the child's susceptible mind for him to see his teacher addressing an audience or even attending a meeting on a political question.

When we have discussed the unequal machinery of modern English education, and admitted the inevitable bias in text-books and class teaching, we have not covered all the types of capitalist influence in schools, nor perhaps its most subtle and irradicable form. War has raged over the teaching of history, but while an honest attempt at impartiality may be made in such teaching, the more insidious influence of the general school life may be inducing a bias of which the teachers are unaware. In the hands of an imaginative headmaster or mistress morning prayers, an almost universal practice in schools, may be made an occasion for the awakening of a vast number of useful and interesting ideas. On the other hand, and more frequently, they are both boring and unintelligent. Where is the boasted impartiality of schools where a daily ceremony is conducted in terms of a religious creed which is publicly acknowledged by a minority of the population?[1] Let

---

[1] Accepted religious dogma will be harder to disconnect from traditional conventional respectability than any other body of ideas. Witness a book on civic and international problems, produced for children by the S.C.M., *World Problems of To-Day*, by Hebe Spaull, 1935. Its comments are remarkably fair and show recognition of unpleasant facts, even those that detract from

us teach comparative religions, and attempt to induce sound moral judgments, but why act also as though after all the Christian religion according to the Church of England is the final established truth, accepted by society? How is the spirit of critical intelligence to be bred by such inconsistency? The chapel in public schools has had an enormous influence since the days when Thomas Arnold strove to drag back the souls of his pupils, which he considered to be trembling on the brink of hell. The place in society of religious worship and its connection with dogma, the possibility of its survival into the socialist state, raise questions too big for this book, but there is no doubt that religious ceremony in schools now stands with the *status quo*. I have heard Blake's revolutionary outburst, *Jerusalem*, sung on occasions of patriotic zeal; I have heard read passages of the Bible, which have been dear to me for their expression of pacifism and comradeship, in such a

---

British prestige. It has, for instance, a full description of the workings of the colour bar in South Africa, a fact unmentioned by the usual school history text-books. It recognizes the comparative failure of the League of Nations and attempts to explain the economic causes of the problems of poverty and unemployment. But it begs the religious question and cannot apply the same attitude of impartiality to the tenets of Christianity. The book opens by asking: 'What kind of a world are we living in to-day? How many of the people living in it are happy and contented—are, in fact, living the kind of lives God means them to live?' (p. 9). Every chapter ends with a text and what Jesus says is taken as being the final authority on the present world problems, an authority beyond all question. For instance, this is the comment on the Marxist theory of the inevitability of revolution, which follows an historical appreciation of the anti-religious propaganda in Russia, with reference to the degeneration of the Greek Orthodox Church under Tsardom: 'When one hears arguments of this kind used to defend *wrong* methods to bring about something *good*, one is reminded of the searching question asked by Jesus: "Can Satan cast out Satan?"' (p. 63).

BIAS IN CAPITALIST EDUCATION

context of militant hymn-singing and prayers that their meaning was diverted. I have heard the story of Lazarus read as an illustration of the Marxist gulf between class and class, and I have heard it read as an eloquent and complacent thanksgiving that our beggars are not so treated now. There is no safety but in the statement of more than one opinion and only one is given at school prayers. Do not most schools on Armistice Day praise God for the death of thousands who are supposed to have saved the world by their sacrifice? How long are we to go on pretending that anything came out of that war worth the sacrifice of a single life? The only thing that can be said for school prayers is that they produce their own reaction, as can be judged by the emptiness of college chapels where attendance is not compulsory. Wordsworth long ago poured scorn on such forced piety:

'Was ever known
The witless shepherd who persists to drive
A flock that thirsts not, to a pool disliked?'

Day-school children are saved some of the more oppressive boredoms of religion, but Sunday at some boarding-schools is still a horror of Victorian gloom, of stiff uncomfortable clothes, of enforced attendance at two or three religious ceremonies, of ban on free and interesting pursuits. The pity is that the reaction is not always intelligent, and that the adult too frequently, looking back, likes to think the system did him good, and to subject his children to the same treatment. What was, must be.

Along with school prayers go the various special days that are celebrated in schools. Prize-givings and founders' days belong, of course, chiefly to the public-school tradition, and are not of the same importance in elementary schools. These ceremonies, where some dignitary, or some famous product of the old school, declaims on the joys of childhood and the superiority of this particular school to all others, warm the hearts of the listeners and entrench them in their determination that the good old school and the good old England shall remain as they were in the beginning. It is rare to hear any criticism of the school at a prize-giving; the atmosphere is one of complacent self-congratulation. The other days that are ceremoniously observed in nearly all schools are Empire Day and Armistice Day. The latter has merely special prayers along with the two minutes' silence, and poppies are sold in the school; the service is not usually so military as the town one where the local regiments take part, although it is sometimes the practice for schools to be taken to a local church for the ceremony. Empire Day varies according to the school where it is celebrated, in the intensity of its nationalism. Sometimes it entails merely a flag flying and a particular emphasis in the morning prayers. Nowadays it frequently includes a wireless talk to schools on the Empire, given by some government or military official, who usually has little or no idea how to talk to children. There is no criticism of the part England played in the war, no suggestion that it could have been avoided, and no positive proposals for stopping the next. Once near Empire Day, without any previous comment, I gave as an alternative essay subject 'The British Empire', to a class of twenty-five girls aged about fifteen; two only mentioned any criticism of the empire, and they finally determined in its favour quite easily. The class seemed mildly surprised when I praised those two essays for showing the beginnings of logical argument. As with the influence of the text-books, the harm done by these special days lies not so much in what is said or done, but in the wrong emphasis given by what is omitted. More virulent propaganda appears sometimes in the elementary schools, and Mark Starr gives instances of schoolchildren taking part in the town celebrations of Empire Day. He also quotes from some empire plays provided by the *Teachers' World*, and at one time, anyway, certainly used widely. Their literary and intellectual standard may be judged by their frequent quotation and imitation of such poems as Henley's *England, My England*, and Newbolt's *Drake's Drum*.[1] But there are, however, no celebrations of Labour Day in schools; no day when the emphasis is on international affairs to counterbalance the nationalism of Empire Day. Every May 24th we suggest to children that our empire is a wonderful and divinely-appointed institution, what manifest benefits it confers on our subject peoples, while in the next breath we are sanctimoniously disapproving of Italy for disregarding the authority of the League of Nations where her imperial ambitions are concerned. By such lack of proportion we are creating the type of mind that cannot see the inconsistencies of such a position. The schools also took a great part in the ceremonies connected with the jubilee and funeral of George V, both of which provided plenty of emotional appeal, but no impetus to the intellectual appreciation of the monarchy as an institution.

As the wireless and the cinema have become a most powerful weapon for propaganda in everyday life, so they have a similar significance in schools. Private cinematographs are not yet common, as they are too expensive for the normal school, and the films that are

[1] Cf. *Lies and Hate in Education*, Mark Starr, p. 71.

available are mainly scientific, showing more clearly than can be done in the laboratory the life of some creature, for example, or a chemical experiment. These films are obviously of great educational value, and are yet so new that they have not become imbued with the traditional propaganda, if it may be so called, though they form a medium that will have to be watched closely in the future, as it is well known that normally no impression is so lasting as the visual. The wireless, as used in schools, has also been freer from bias than the general work of the B.B.C. The talks of Commander Stephen King-Hall may be sincerely admired by the socialist for remaining interesting while at the same time achieving a remarkable degree of impartiality. Wireless talks and lessons in all subjects are arranged, but it is doubtful whether they are much used, as most schools have already over-crowded time-tables, and extra periods are not easily inserted. The most frequent use of the wireless in schools is probably connected with special days and state occasions, notably the jubilee and royal funeral celebrations. Then the importance of the occasion is felt to be sufficient to cut across all timetables and the school assembles to hear the voice of His Majesty declaiming to his loyal Lords and Commons. The occasion is impressive and the speeches dignified, inspiring just that emotional sincerity of reverence for tradition that can be so dangerous when unaccompanied by thoughtful criticism.

More frequent breaks are made in the ordinary curriculum by visiting lecturers. Many of these people seem to think it their right to deliver their sentiments to any school they choose, and the head has no guarantee of their intelligence or fair-mindedness except the name of the organization they represent. They talk on a variety of subjects, careers, hobbies, and travel; those who concern us here are those who come from charitable organizations or from the League of Nations Union, the only organization who sends a speaker to deal with definitely political subjects. Fortunately many of these orators have little idea how to talk to a school or often, to judge from their voice-production, how to talk to a large audience at all; a great part of what they say is frequently inaudible. Most schools have the custom of charitable effort and often adopt some special charity for which they raise money by bazaars, concerts, and all the rest of the paraphernalia of social patronage. A great many schools, particularly those for girls, subscribe to Dr. Barnardo's Homes. Visiting lecturers describe the excellent work of their particular institution in helping the blind, giving country holidays to slum children, or harbouring the homeless, usually delivering a final peroration on the need for money. The socialist attitude to charity generally, is well known; it is obvious that a socialist cannot ultimately approve of an institution which, while it may do good to a number of individuals, does it by methods that are bad for the giver; though such activity may awaken some social consciousness, it fixes also an unconscious feeling of social superiority; to say the least, it is apt to insinuate that the 'poor' are always with us and always will be. Children in day-schools do not often meet the objects of their charitable endeavour, unless they are in London, where schools entertain their protégés with a certain charm of good manners. A girl in a high school may show a curious mixture of good manners and snobbery, showing a graceful politeness to a slum woman who is the guest of the school, and at the same time indulging in some subtle form of persecution of the 'scholarship' girl working with her; such a mixture seems typical of Lady Bountiful. It is very difficult and probably unnecessary to criticize such a phenomenon as the Duke of York's camp, obviously run on lines designed to avoid any air of patronage or superiority. It is one of the problems of the socialist thesis, to reconcile the economic theory of class-war with the common decency latent in most individuals of all classes; it is probably true to say that capitalism gives fewer natural opportunities for its display than socialism.

The League of Nations Union had the wit to see that a hold on the schools would provide one of its most powerful channels of influence. The Union has junior branches in many schools and sends a constant stream of visitors, who attempt to explain the covenant and the idea of international law. No one could possibly object to any activity that works for international sanity, and we may be thankful that so much is allowed and we are saved the extremes of vicious nationalism demanded in the German schools to-day. My quarrel with these lecturers again concerns not what they do but what they leave undone. One cannot help being struck, when listening to them, with the air of delicate unreality, almost of dilettantism, that is diffused from their arguments. Their speeches are often excellent examples of how not to present historical material to the young. I have never heard one of these lecturers face the fact that the League is in danger of subsiding into a clique of imperialist powers, using it for their own national ambitions; they deal far too much with the abstract notion of internationalism and with the laws laid down in the covenant; they fence gracefully with the major issues and refer only lightly to the crucial points of the League's history. I have heard them admit failure in the case of Japan, but never the true significance of that failure. I have heard one of them indicate that the loss of Japan was compensated by the entry of Cuba; that, in fact, as long as the League keeps its numbers up its prestige is unimpaired. The futility of such a point of view, its patent wish-fulfilment, rocks the listeners into a false and dangerous sense of security, and does nothing to develop that individual vigilance into public affairs that alone can make for the strength of international law.

Athletics might possibly have come under the heading of curricula, as now they usually have their set times in school hours; but as there can be no direct propaganda in their teaching, they must be considered as one of the less obvious influences towards bias of the school atmosphere. The English have been considerably praised by themselves and others for the evolution of organized games in their schools. Lyrical have been the praises of the team-spirit and the Englishman's loyalty to his comrade, engendered by athletics. Their influence may not be so wholly good as we like to imagine; individual children have swelled heads over their performances at games more frequently than over anything else. Is there any school where the captain of the eleven does not tower above the leader of the school orchestra in importance? That physical training is an absolute necessity in a good education goes without saying, but games obtain their most fulsome praises not for their effect on the body but on the character. Far be it from a socialist to sneer at the team-spirit of co-operation, but is it not possible that capitalism itself is not so individualistic, even economically, as it would like its critics to suppose, and that in some aspects of society it stresses co-ordinated effort as much as the schools do in their athletic work? Is it not an iron discipline, a superb team-spirit, that holds together an army, that induces millions of men to obey their superior officer and let themselves be killed or wounded in doing it? I believe that the spirit of English athleticism is dangerously near the military spirit. Of course in a team-game, as in war, quick wits are needed from some individuals, but the general atmosphere of war and of most organized games is obedience to rules, self-obliteration, and subordination to the captain. A great deal of that discipline can be harnessed onto any enterprise, and would that socialists would learn some of it. But the schools at the moment are harnessing that discipline onto the honour of the school and the good of the nation; and for the nation that means superiority, prestige, prosperity, in short, colonies, to be ruled and shaped with the same type of discipline that rules a game of rugger or hockey. Not for nothing does *Stalky and Co.* end with a chapter on India, with the public-schoolboy chasing Afghans; and you will find the same parallel in those unspeakable verses of Henry Newbolt's *Vitae Lampada*, with the ringing refrain, 'Play up and play the game', verses—I cannot call them a poem—which are popular with many children to-day; I will not quote them.

Finally the O.T.C., whose influence is practically confined to boys' public schools, a fact in itself significant. There is a vast amount of hypocritical writing on this subject, the kind that always appears when an institution is being championed for the sole reason that it exists and it is too complicated a business to destroy it. The plain facts are that boys are given military training by the O.T.C. and that in a nation supposed to be working for peace that is inconsistency bordering on the malevolent. Dr. Cyril Norwood[1] says that until disarmament is a reality it is a good thing that boys should learn voluntarily to defend their land. Other apologists excuse the O.T.C. on the grounds that the tactics and weapons used are out of date and cannot therefore have any bearing on modern warfare. It seems hard that if and when war comes, we shall have to depend mainly for our defence on officers with obsolete weapons. There are no privates' training corps in the elementary schools. The O.T.C., therefore, is guilty of class bias as well as military propaganda.[2] It has even been suggested that the O.T.C. is a self-denying institution, for, says Dr. Norwood: 'Boys do not acquire a spirit of militarism thereby, or a desire to go to war; in fact, there are few deterrents more strong than a knowledge of what rifles, machine-guns, and bombs can do. The men who train the boys have no militarism in them as a whole, for they are largely men who have fought in the war.'[3] I, for one, am not convinced that it constitutes an extremely subtle form of pacifist propaganda. In any case, it makes war seem more likely, if not desirable. But the pacifist attack has obscured what is really a more formidable aspect of this organization, its class-bias. It trains boys to understand the discipline of the military spirit, so that they hold together as a class and impose their will on the undisciplined workers, or on the subject peoples of the colonies. The O.T.C. provides an interesting example of an idea put forward by Delisle Burns, that 'the traditional education is largely a training in "waiting

[1] *The English Tradition in Education*, p. 295.
[2] The bias, of course, consists not so much in denying the working class the doubtful advantage of military training, as in training the public-school boy to regard them as inferior.
[3] *The English Tradition in Education*, p. 295.

for orders" or swallowing what is provided. The education of "the upper classes" has been largely of that kind, partly indeed because it is to the advantage of those who enjoy privileges in any social system to maintain even in themselves those virtues which tend to conserve rather than to change the system'.[1] One of those virtues is obedience to the superior officer. The discipline of the O.T.C. and of team-games develops the typical public-school virtues, and there is a recognized connection between the product of the public schools and the empire; the apologists for the public-school type often bring up this point as a matter for congratulation; public-school boys 'are, in short, to use a convenient if tiresome expression, "builders of empire", some on a large and some on a small scale and they do it on the whole well'.[2] By such disciplinary methods have the ruling class always held their authority, and it is for that reason that the O.T.C. has its strongholds in the great public schools, the bearers of the ruling-class tradition. As the crowning absurdity of this controversy we have the elaborate pretence that this military training is voluntary. It is true that in no school rules can we find any compulsion to join the O.T.C., but there is hardly a public-school boy who will not admit that it was 'the thing' to join, or as the more intelligent would say, the social pressure in favour of the corps was too strong to resist. There are some interesting revelations on this point in *Out of Bounds*, by Giles and Esmond Romilly; Giles, who was more or less automatically drafted into the corps, says: 'Every week was spoilt by dread of the next Corps parade. I detested Field Day which was supposed to be the

[1] *Leisure in the Modern World*, p. 195.
[2] *The English Public School*, by Bernard Darwin, p. 30.

great consolation which everyone looked forward to.' When he determined to get out of the corps, he found it very difficult. 'Night after night I was sent for, and every night my tutor and I spent at least two hours in earnest conversation.' It was only after resisting such continuous pressure that he finally emerged. Pressure may even go so far as a warning to parents that their sons cannot become prefects unless they are members of the O.T.C.[1]

It would be as well here to sum up some of the points concerning the public-school tradition, for though the public schools educate only a few of the children of England, those few belong to the ruling class; besides which the tradition of these schools spreads far beyond their own territory and is responsible for much in the forms and spirit of English education generally. Educational democracy in England has not yet been achieved. The following figures are quoted from *Public Schools* (1932), by L. B. Pekin, an admirable diagnosis of this educational system. 'Between 1851 and 1929 no less than 60 per cent of the British Foreign Office and Diplomatic Service had been educated in the eleven most exclusive public schools; over 70 per cent of the legal profession during the last fifty years have been drawn from the upper and middle classes, for which such schools cater; while it is not surprising to learn that 69 per cent of bishops and deans are drawn from

---

[1] The following figures from L. B. Pekin's book, *Public Schools*, might interest the economy-mongers.

'The cost to the parents of this organization (O.T.C.) is something under £50,000 a year; the cost to the tax-payer is about £160,000 a year. Our country contributes to the expenses of the League of Nations to prepare for peace £120,000 a year; on the training of public schoolboys to prepare for war it spends £200,000 or not far short of twice that sum.'

these same ranks of public schoolmen; 71 per cent of Indian civil servants and governors of Dominions, 72 per cent of high officials in public departments at home, and 75 per cent of directors of banks and railways have been educated in the same exclusive fashion.' These are the men who rule us; it is as well to see how they are prepared for the task. The English public-schoolman is admittedly a Philistine, usually uninterested in art or music; these schools themselves boast that they prefer to emphasize character, whatever that may mean, rather than intelligence or scholarship or creative ability. The curriculum is therefore not of such importance as the general school atmosphere. The uncriticized military discipline of the O.T.C. is reproduced in the school itself, so that loyalty to the school means, not its improvement through intelligent change, but the recognition of the sacred inviolability of all its institutions and customs, good or bad. 'They glory in the absurd curricula which often leave unexplored whole tracts of human knowledge with which every modern citizen should have some acquaintance; they glory in dirt and bad management; they glory in the inefficiency of many of the masters.'[1] The discipline of these schools rests ultimately on force, on corporal punishment in particular; it is extremely doubtful, to say the least, that such a weapon in the hands of adolescents forms a good preparation for men who in adult life are to have power over their fellows; indeed, it has been proved over and over again to be psychologically harmful. The prefects, who, with the masters, administer this punishment, are not such democratic figures as are frequently supposed. They hold absolute authority if their personalities are strong; no minor person would dare to criticize their

[1] *Public Schools*, L. B. Pekin, Chap. 1.

methods of government, that is, of course, to their faces. Their rule is that of an oligarchy, with a delegated authority from the superior oligarchy of the staff. The ordinary schoolboy in the lower and middle school has no say in the choice of prefects and cannot criticize their actions in any way. The system of fagging only makes their servility more complete. L. B. Pekin says of the institutions of prefects and fagging: 'At their best they are a source of much waste and casual annoyance; at their worst and all too common they amount to absolute slavery.'[1] The inevitable reaction to a youth of fagging is a tendency to bullying, laziness, and uncontrolled domineering when finally the victim comes into the privileges of the prefect himself; nothing in his education encourages the prefect to have the imagination to put himself in the place of his fag, or if he does so, it is merely to gloat. Our colonial officials, our directors of factories and banks, our civil servants, have in large proportion been brought up to demand absolute obedience, without regard to the rights of the underling. Mr. Chaning Pearce, a not entirely unfriendly critic of the public schools, nevertheless maintains that the system produces a rigidity of mentality. 'Form implies limitation; if his defects were modified his qualities would lose their hard and keen spear-head. An open-minded, unconventional, cosmopolitan public-school man is a contradiction in terms.'[2] There is good teaching in some of these schools, enlightened disciplinary methods, and a respect for knowledge, but individual exceptions will not dispel the general condemnation of them as inefficient, brutalizing, and

---

[1] Op. cit., Chap. 4.
[2] *Chiron, The Education of a Citizen of the World,* 1931. To-day and To-morrow Series, p. 21.

narrow. The education they provide is often hardly worthy of the name, but its worst aspect is its preparation of a few children as rulers, expecting to find a subordinate mass below them; while our rulers are educated in this wise, democracy in this country will remain what it is now, a very thin disguise to the power of the capitalist class.

CHAPTER FOUR

THE FAILURE OF CAPITALIST EDUCATION

WE have discussed capitalist influence on the organization, teaching, and tradition of contemporary schools; that in itself is not necessarily bad, as a bias in favour of existing society is inevitable in schools. It remains to be shown whether that influence works towards a satisfactory education, judged from the educationalist's standpoint. It is necessary to prove the comparative failure of capitalist education, before going on to discuss the general socialist attitude to educational ideals and the possible methods of remedying incidental inefficiencies. We need not labour the point that for the great majority of children in this country, capitalism does not provide enough education, and that the elementary schools, through which pass the greater number of English children, are inadequately equipped and staffed. The whole organization of education is worked out on a class basis, a differentiation according to wealth and not to capability, one which is not bridged successfully by the scholarship ladder. It has long ago been recognized by psychologists that a child from any class of society has the same possibilities of development if given the benefit of prolonged satisfactory education. Yet in England we allow thousands of children to receive inadequate training for adult life. Such short-sightedness in educational policy is due mainly to a fanatic devotion to 'economy' finance; it is one of the necessities of the modern fascist or semi-fascist state to find large amounts for expenditure on armaments, and one source of revenue is afforded by cutting down the money available for social services. It is an absurd perversion of values that allows the capitalist state to spend far more on the preparation of murder than of life.[1] In this sphere England is particularly retrograde, and when we sneer at the supposed shallowness of American culture, and the fictitious poverty of her scholarship, it is as well to remember that in some states she provides free education for her citizens up to the age of eighteen. Social-democrat countries have also realized the importance of education and the Scandinavian and pre-fascist German systems are more progressive than ours.

The existence in England of a large number of private schools, which carry with them the traditions of English education, and which are the guiding light to most educationalists, is the main reason for the lag in progressive state organization. As so frequently in the history of English institutions, we find that individual enterprise has been allowed by state negligence to monopolize the tradition. Individuals in the first place did what the state refused to do, and their institutions have grown to be jealous of their independence. Consequently we have the anomaly that to many people English education does not mean the state schools through which the majority of the children pass, but the so called public schools which touch only a few. Whereas in America or France private schools are very few and

---

[1] For the year 1935–36 the total cost of education in Great Britain was £44,556,787, as compared with £400,000,000 on past wars and preparation for the next. For every £2 spent on education £18 is spent on war. The maintenance cost of an elementary school child is £15 per annum; each cadet at the Royal Military Academy, Woolwich, costs £292 per annum, and at the Royal Naval Academy, Keyham, £385.—Cf. *The Ploughshare*, June–July 1936.

considered to pander to an exaggerated social snobbery, in England the man who declaims against spending public money on state education thinks it no absurdity to pay the ludicrously high fees of a school whose principal advantage in his eyes is its social standing. Incidentally the capitalist argument that the individual spends his own money more economically than that of the state is shown to be somewhat ridiculous when the finances of the state secondary and the public school are compared. The position is little different from that which induced Tawney in 1924 to say: 'The refusal of full educational opportunities to the children of the workers is a perpetual assertion of social privilege in its grossest and most insulting form.'[1] The English, who are proud of their political democracy, are guilty of the most blatant class-bias in the forms of their education. It is one of the unfortunate results of the educational tradition in this country that it has been an influence against the spread of state control, and though the rich will always find schools when they have money to buy them, no one other than the state, except possibly a few religious zealots, will provide the poor with any education at all.

The great force of conservative tradition in education, a tradition which capitalism has allowed to go practically unchallenged, has had a retarding effect on many aspects of education that do not seem connected primarily with politics. Thus, for instance, women have had to fight for their right to education just as for their political vote. The equality of the sexes in education, an idea that is taken for granted by the normally civilized person, is still not completely achieved. It causes the American visitor justifiable amusement when he hears

[1] *Education. The Socialist Policy.*

of the lecturer at Oxford or Cambridge who will not throw his pearls of wisdom before women. A woman's grant at a university is often smaller than a man's, her salary as a teacher less; when she marries, in many parts of England, she automatically loses her employment. These latter facts are, of course, an isolated example of the tendency of unemployment in general to bind a woman to domestic work which she may not like or do well, while depriving her of work for which she is qualified. It is one of the particular meannesses of capitalism that it puts such a large measure of the discomfort, if not always the more serious consequences, of unemployment on the shoulders of women by these indirect methods. It has its peculiar effect on education also and accounts for the continuous difficulty in girls' schools of relationship between staff and children, a difficulty that affords endless material to the satiric or adolescent novelist and to the jester. Psychology has enabled us to face the fact that the great majority of adolescent girls have homosexual tendencies, and often go through periods of maladjustment and consequent depression in their last years at school. It is the business of education not merely to provide knowledge, but to help children through such periods of mental adjustment. Who is more likely to help girls to sublimate their instincts into appreciation of the arts and cultural development, into the pursuit of some favourite study, and to bring out of a G.P. a satisfactory personal relationship, the married woman or the unmarried? Which of them is more likely to be flattered and attracted by her admirers? However much a teacher may be aware of the homosexual atmosphere in her class, and deliberately avoid exploiting it for disciplinary or personal reasons, the problem is always present needing a restraint imposed by the will; while from her own point of view at least, it is solved if she is satisfied in marriage. One would like to complain to certain conservative local education authorities who refuse to employ married women, that such a ban encourages homosexuality in schools and what they would call immorality outside them. Girls may count themselves lucky that the comparatively late development of their schools has allowed much good education to be provided for them outside the conservative tradition of the public boarding-school, though there are few schools that can escape its influence entirely. But capitalism, which, in its use of the Victorian notion that the home is the woman's place and her prison, for the alleviation of its unemployment problems, has provided, along with the whole system of segregated schools, special disadvantages for girls' education, until they have become a byword for morbid adolescent excitement.

If education is to be preparation for life by living, if it is to be as little artificially differentiated from society as possible, the child's environment must be as like that of his adult years as possible. This is the argument, educationally sound, for allowing both married and unmarried to teach; it also forms the best argument for co-education. The conservative force of the English tradition has been set against this departure; there are a few state co-educational secondary schools, but, generally speaking, English education stands for the segregation of the sexes, and so strongly, that we have examples of such absurdities as two schools built side by side, one for boys and one for girls, coming out at different times in order that boys and girls shall not go home together. Such an arrangement produces the unnatural curiosity that it was designed to avoid, as any psychologist would know. Neither employment of married women nor co-education, of course, are incompatible with capitalist society;[1] the American schools are co-educational, and though the old-fashioned English may be caustic on the subject of lip-stick and bridge-parties at school, no one can fail to be impressed by the assurance and ease with which the young American meets his fellow men; good manners are more likely to grow out of such easy bearing than out of the bluster which so often covers over the nervousness of the Englishman. In England, the land of traditions, the conservative forces of capitalism have themselves been nourished by the educational system, and in return have resolutely set themselves against any educational change. Education in this country has been far less influenced by liberalism than many continental systems. This is yet another reason why it is unnecessary for the present government to be admittedly fascist and to make such an open attack on educational integrity as Hitler or Mussolini has done. It is sufficient for their purpose to allow the steady conservative force of middle-class education to continue and with this background they feel even sufficiently secure to contemplate the restoration of some of the expenditure on working-class education.

Generally speaking, it may be said that English education has been very little and very slowly influenced

[1] Economy may drive the conservative into curious reforms. Thus in two adjacent state schools of my acquaintance, one for boys and one for girls, co-education has been introduced into the sixth form, on the grounds that it is a waste of money to have a few children taught in separate parallel classes, when, by combining them, time can be saved and consequently the numbers of staff can be reduced. Psychologically it is difficult to imagine a worse age than fifteen to sixteen for the commencement of co-education after previous segregation.

by new educational theories; experimentalists have frequently found it necessary to found schools of their own, finding the atmosphere of traditional education incompatible with the practice of their theories. Such educational masters as A. S. Neill and Bertrand Russell have to go into the wilderness. Either from fear of spending money or simply from conservatism, the progress of nursery schools, of handicrafts, of free discipline, of small classes, and of many another development which most serious educationalists consider necessary, has been retarded. In our schools, we accept crammed and potted knowledge, arid academicism, and feudal discipline. This may be admitted but its relation to capitalist society denied. I maintain that, though the immediate connection may not be strong, this backwardness is ultimately due to the conservative forces latent in capitalism. The greater progress of education in other capitalist countries, in Scandinavia, in America, and in pre-Nazi Germany, was not due to the benevolence of the capitalists, but to the fact that education is a social service that the social-democrat and the humanitarian are anxious to wring out of the state in times of prosperity. In England public opinion has never been strong enough to insist on the Hadow reforms, which would make English education comparable to some of the better continental systems. The slow progress of experiment in state schools is due, partly to the tyranny of public examinations, but largely also to the great force of the public-school tradition that influences the spirit of most state schools. That tradition stands against the equality of class in education, as is admitted by F. S. Marvin, not an unfriendly critic of the public schools: 'The well-established system of boarding-schools with its great merits and cherished traditions, acts and will continue to act as an effective barrier to the complete mixture of class in schools.'[1] Dr. Cyril Norwood, the apologist for the public-school system, puts forward as one of its merits, the fact that it stands against freedom of discipline; strangely enough, he uses a Prussian metaphor to describe the disciplinary attitude of a public-school headmaster: 'He should let it be known that under the soft glove there is a steel gauntlet. For boys need to be protected from themselves.'[2] His definition of real freedom, which he claims is to be found in these schools, is comparable to that of every dictator, in the home, the school, or the country generally: 'At its best it is a system of training in which the boy is taught to choose what he ought to choose, and that is the real freedom; not the pseudo-freedom of many-headed uneducated democracy in which there is at the worst the negative freedom by which each one chooses what he individually desires, and the common life is denied.' So finally it is not the socialist but the capitalist state that demands the sacrifice of individual choice; it is the capitalist state that will dictate what we ought to choose, and a common life which encourages the individual to develop in the way he desires is impossible under present society. Experiments in education, freedom in study and discipline, mean real democracy and liberty, and the public schools, the educational vehicle of the ruling class, are set against such experiments and their political consequences.[3]

Finally there is to be found in contemporary schools

[1] *The Nation at School*, 1988, Chap. 18.
[2] *The English Tradition in Education*, 1929.
[3] In the last chapter, I have given my reasons for believing these progressive educational developments to be compatible with socialism.

that reliance on the motive of competition that is also the psychological basis of capitalism, and the commercialization of that which should not be bought or sold, due to the appeal of education to the profit-seeking desires of the individual, an appeal that characterizes capitalist society. The study of psychology has undoubtedly added force to the arguments for competitive methods of discipline, as the competitive spirit has an attraction for our more primitive nature. In the early days of educational theory, from the growth of the public-school tradition in the beginning of the nineteenth century, the main appeal was to fear: 'If you don't do this, something unpleasant will happen to you,' an appeal still extant in much school discipline to-day. There followed the discovery that it was often more effective to say to a child: 'If you work very hard you will do better than Tom, Dick, and Harry, and everyone will think you very clever; if you work harder than anyone else, we will even give you a reward.' So Marmaduke worked very hard and glowed with conscious pride when he reached the top of the form. Now there is a good deal to be said for this as far as Marmaduke is concerned; the apologists for the complete reliance on competitive motives, however, say far too little about Tom, Dick, and Harry at the bottom of the list. What are their feelings, and what has competition got to offer them? Even if two of them are lazy, the third probably owes his place to some factor not within his control—mental slowness, physical deficiency, or psychological maladjustment. Competition in schools frequently does for the dull and the slow just what it does for the poor in economic society, deprives them of all interest in their work and produces the kind of mentality that does as little as possible, not as much. For the rich and the boy at the top of the form, there is much good in competition; it has possibly stimulated them to efforts that have developed their talents that might otherwise have lain dormant. But poverty is not ennobling and the mental poverty that is consequent on being always bottom of a class is enervating and demoralizing.

Ruskin in *Fors Clavigera* went so far as to say: 'Of schools in all places, for all ages, the healthy working will depend on the total exclusion of the stimulus of competition in any form or disguise. Every child should be measured by its own standard, trained to its own duty, and rewarded by its just praise. It is the effort that deserves the praise not the success; nor is it a question for any student whether he is cleverer than others or duller, but whether he has done the best he could with the gifts he has.' This is an extreme statement and it is probable that competition even when it ceases to be the main or sole motive evoked, will, nevertheless, remain among others. The existence of socialist competition in Soviet Russia shows that it is possible to combine competitive and co-operative motives so as to obtain the value of both.[1] But as far as the individual is concerned the last part of Ruskin's statement is absolutely true, and the competition that pits one child against another, regardless of their native capacity, is one which induces a false set of values in both the successful and the unsuccessful. The latest educational theories have, however, gone beyond this complete reliance on competitive motives and maintain that interest in the

---

[1] 'In education no less than industry, socialist competition is a powerful factor in "the struggle for quality". Not only individual students and professors take part in socialist competition, not only separate teams and groups of students within the one school, but also entire schools as such.'—*Science and Education in U.S.S.R.*, Pinkevitch, p. 87.

subject-matter for its own sake is the only lasting appeal, the only one that will ensure that work is done well, with intelligence and interest, not memorized without understanding. Interest in the subject will set a higher standard for the clever child than the examination results of an average form; it will not discourage the dull and the plodding; it is the only weapon against which laziness has no defence. Sir Percy Nunn, in his well-known book *Education; Its Data and First Principles*, condemns 'the excessive use of competition, in which the school reflects one of the greatest evils that affect the modern world, for competition, like alcohol, though it may begin by stimulating tends to bring men in the end, to one dull, if not brutish level' (Chap. 15). I can remember well the one lesson I had from this fine educationalist, during which, by means of walking up and down a tennis court, algebra became so fascinating for forty minutes that I entirely forgot that I had had 100 per cent in the last examination, a thought which in algebra lessons was seldom otherwise far from me.

Despite the fact that the deadening effect of competition, when the motive is overstressed, is recognized by most educationalists who take any interest in their trade, the majority of English schools to-day are hampered in their work by a plate-armour of marks, lists, and examinations. The system of grading has lessened some of the worst effects of competitive marking; yet some schools still tot up marks every month or even every week. Seldom now are marks taken in in class, thus avoiding the public announcement of individual good or bad results. But the very fact that homework or classwork is set, for which a grade will automatically be given, makes the child much more interested in the grade

I

than in the work. Any teacher knows that comments on work had better be given before the grade is revealed as there is a distinct slackening of interest afterwards. Comparisons of work are nearly always odious in school and grades invite such comparisons. The terminal examinations merely form a culmination to this process, and the mark fever becomes rabid. The staff perform extraordinary feats of arithmetic in order that a child may have the satisfaction of knowing that he has on the sum-total two or three marks more than his neighbour. Then come the holidays, during which most of the knowledge 'mugged up' for examinations is speedily forgotten. Much of the school work that is most educative, individual reading to choice, dramatic work, handcrafts, debating, and all appreciative sides of artistic work, are not adapted to grading, which is part of the reason why mathematics and Latin loom so large in the minds of schoolchildren; they can be ticked off and marked very easily. Marks tend also to make the teaching of English and history crass and inhuman, as it is obviously easier to mark exercises on notes than a child's sensitiveness to the beauty of poetry; where artistic subjects are taught well without much reference to grades, many children are led to suppose that they are a soft option, not to be compared with the sterling stuff of science or languages.

The competitive urge in schools finds its completest expression in the external examinations, institutions that also account for much of the commercialization of education. These examinations form the rungs of the scholarship ladder; the scholars to a secondary school from an elementary school are selected by examination; so also are those from the secondary schools to the universities. Besides these tests, the General Schools

Certificate forms the pivot of the system; nearly all secondary schools send in the majority of their pupils, usually at the age of sixteen. The universities recognize this examination in certain subjects as the equivalent of their preliminary test, apart from the scholarship competitive examinations. Most employers for all kinds of clerical or non-manual work demand it. F. S. Marvin says: 'Its system of Credits is cunningly devised to appeal either to the universities or higher scholarship authorities, or to the employers dispensing the jobs, or to the guardians of various professions. Hence, as every boy or girl in these hard times wants either a scholarship or a job, the School Certificate Examination catches them all.'[1] The majority of children who stay at school until they are eighteen take the Higher Schools Certificate from the sixth form, an examination recognized by some universities as a first part to a degree course. These examinations, particularly the Schools Certificate, have been expanded in late years to include many subjects such as housewifery, music, and woodwork, so that the academic mind shall not have the advantage. All skill of hand, all artistic creation and appreciation, have been made grist for this mill as well as mere knowledge. The examination questions are set and corrected, of course, by people who have no personal knowledge of the examinees; the teacher has a syllabus to work on, and as this is usually too long to work through intelligently and with the detailed study demanded, it is often sheer luck whether the questions cover the field of the child's knowledge or not.

Such an examination, with its serious consequences for the future of most children, naturally colours the methods and scope of teaching in any school. Answers

[1] *The Nation at School*, 1933, Chap. 11.

to probable questions can be dictated in a few minutes, then learnt by heart and reproduced in a written test with very little trouble. But as a teaching method this is contemptible; to make a child think out problems himself, search for facts by himself, and make his own judgment on them, is a much longer process. A syllabus that can be covered by unintelligent cramming is frequently too long and too detailed to allow of more desirable psychological approaches. The influence of the examination is not confined to the year during which it is taken, but its effects spread further; it is a temptation to let some of the syllabus spread downwards to lower forms, so as to prepare the way beforehand. Thus in one school of my acquaintance a certain period of English history is taught the year before the examination; it is taught again for the examination; if any members of the form stay on at school they cover the same period for the Higher Schools examination, so that any scheme for covering a wide stretch of history during the school course is impossible. Such a deplorable disregard for the aims of education may have led Professor A. N. Whitehead to remark: 'I suggest that no system of external tests which aims primarily at examining individual scholars can result in anything but educational waste.'[1] Edueationalists have agreed long ago that examinations conducted on the present lines are deadening, and tend to retard the use of new educational methods. No teacher can work from any syllabus as well as from one he has devised himself; no one can fairly test a child who does not know him personally, with all his circumstances and individual talents and difficulties; no one can produce the best that is in him, writing to set time on material he has had to learn

[1] *The Aims of Education*, 1929, p. 21.

THE FAILURE OF CAPITALIST EDUCATION 117

unintelligently. Examinations are particularly bad for the teaching of literary subjects; how can a child's appreciation of poetry be tested fairly in a written examination on a particular day? Mr. Raymont, in *Modern Educational Aims and Methods*, says that 'external examinations are a tremendously conservative force. They form the dead hand that tradition places upon all attempts to get out of the rut of established educational custom.' Dr. A. W. Pickard Cambridge said, in the presidential address of 1935 to the Educational Section of the British Association, that 'examinations as they are treated in most schools are among the worst enemies to education in freedom of thought and independence of judgment. . . . Under these conditions the teacher dare not encourage his pupils to think and is afraid of the statistics by which the local education authority judges his fitness for promotion.'[1] It has been proved over and over again that the Schools Certificate examination in particular, and most external examinations along with it, are very inadequate tests of intellectual ability and even of real knowledge. Most teachers would agree with Professor Whitehead that 'no educational system is possible unless every question directly asked of a pupil at any examination is either framed or modified by the actual teacher of that pupil in that subject'.[2] Such a system worked very well in the German schools where the first examination was taken at seventeen or eighteen years, and the questions set were sent to each school to receive comment and revision by the teachers.

There is this considerable body of opinion among reputable educational thinkers and the teachers

[1] Quoted in the *Daily Telegraph*, September 7, 1935.
[2] *The Aims of Education*, p. 7.

generally, against the system of external examinations as we have them to day, an opinion by no means confined to socialists or actuated by a dislike of competition in any and every form, but one bred by the realization of the evil results of this system on the practice of the profession. Yet nothing is so firmly entrenched in our educational system as the external examination; which goes to show how impossible it is to consider education apart from society generally, something to be moulded and given its own particular ideals and methods by those who deal in it. The external examination is imposed on the school from outside, by the pressure of society demanding a visible return for its money. The teacher who cares at all for his art cannot afford to be indifferent to the influences in society that are responsible for such inroads into his province. One of the main excuses for external examinations is that they form an essential part of the scholarship ladder which is supposed to obviate the worst class-divisions in education. By means of examination the worker's child can get from the elementary school to the university; we might feel more comfortable about this if we were sure that examinations were fair tests and always gave the opportunities of further education to the most deserving. How often have we heard the lament from secondary-school teachers that the brightest and best of the elementary scholars fall off sadly in the next years! In any case, capitalism is guilty of inequality in education and that it tries to remedy it in some measure by the method of examination does not make that method a good one. It seems probable that a far better idea of a child's suitability for further education could be obtained from a report from all the teachers who had been in contact with him in his previous career. While children who can pay fees are admitted on a different test from that for scholarship children it remains true, as F. S. Marvin claims, that 'the system of examinations now in vogue cannot act as a general solvent of class divisions in education, and is by no means completely effective in drawing out the real powers of those to whom it is applied'.[1] When it is remembered that the fees paid for a child in a secondary school do not by any means cover the cost of giving that child secondary education, and that that child is probably obtaining a larger subsidy from the state than the child in receipt of free education in an elementary school, where the expenses of staffing and equipment are not nearly so high, then the examination ladder seems an extremely poor mitigation of that inequality.

The Schools Certificate examination is a very minor part of the scholarship ladder and yet it dominates the whole of secondary-school teaching. The reasons for its predominance are those given by Mr. Marvin, that it is accepted by universities as exemption from their preliminary test and is very widely demanded by employers who offer the jobs likely to be wanted by the school-leavers of sixteen plus. This demand reveals the fact that the capitalist employer has learnt to put a commercial value on education, and it is this commercialization that prevents the teacher from successfully attacking the external examination; he cannot run the risk of prejudicing the child's future. There is, of course, every reason why a child should have some specialized training for the work he is going to do when he leaves school, but the attitude of most employers towards vocational training shows a false set of values and the Schools Certificate examination does not stand for a

[1] *The Nation at School.*

specialized training for any particular employment. Technical or vocational education has become a synonym for training in some particular craft or manual labour, and in a capitalist world such training has been despised by the academic tradition at all stages of education, right up to the universities; Oxford has, for instance, been extremely reluctant to afford parity with more traditional studies to the practical sciences such as engineering. Vocational training in a wide sense has an important place in socialist education, as I hope to show later; here it is enough to say that capitalism has produced a false division between humane and practical education, breeding an unnecessary contempt for the latter as belonging to a lower social order. The Schools Certificate examination, therefore, while showing signs of commercialized values, in its forms and curricula still largely reflects the tradition of a ruling-class education that has seeped down to the middle-class schools. When the employer, wanting a clerk, an office boy or a cashier for his shop desk, demands a child who has passed this examination, he is not asking for specialized skill, but for a guarantee of general intelligence and a gentlemanly education. This attitude is due partly to the idea that he wishes to get some return for the money spent in taxes and used in state schools, and partly to a desire to keep the black-coated trades on a higher social level than manual labour. The employer in a small office or, in particular, the shopkeeper, desires to have an air of refinement about his establishment. That the employer does not get what he wants and that the Schools Certificate is no indication to education in the best sense and frequently not to intelligence, does not make this system any better.

Skill or even knowledge may, under capitalism, be

bought and sold, but education cannot. The development of personality, the ability to acquire knowledge, to use it and to pass judgment on it, the capacity for abstract thought, the tolerant, broad, reasonable state of mind, all the high-sounding aims that have been claimed time and time again for education, these cannot be put into the money market, for these there can be no bargaining by any values of our modern commercialized world. It is perhaps the supreme indictment of capitalist education that it allows its economic system, with its pressure of unemployment, to attempt a valuation of what should be the cream of a nation's civilization, its culture and learning, in terms of money. The state has been driven to invest so much money in the nation's children; it demands its return in crude terms, a certificate, a label, which means little but potted knowledge. For that certificate society will pay; did not the state once pay a teacher with a second-class degree more than one with a third? We come round here to the first point of this book, the poverty of capitalist cultural influence in the daily life of its citizens. A man or woman wanting to take up an artistic career must have private means, or be commercially successful, or starve. Education, say some critics of this state of affairs, will cure this, will make the mass of the people demand what is good. But that education itself is commercialized; it appears as a commodity; so much more education, so much better a job. The majority of children who write on the desirability of remaining at school as long as possible, give as their main argument the fact that further training will procure them better employment. This is a vicious circle, and the poverty of much that passes in modern life as of artistic value is a sign of something badly wrong in education itself. An education that is parcelled out on a class basis, whose traditions stand against freedom of thought, of discipline, of experiment, which offers its wares for sale, is as much the enemy of civilized culture as, though in a subtler way, the blatant nationalism of fascism, which wrecked the fine artistic life, both Jewish and home-grown, of modern Germany. There is much fine teaching, many great ideals, sensible psychological attitudes, courageous individual experiments in English schools to-day, but all of these can make little headway against the economic structure of society which presses on them the structure of capitalism that surrounds them with its class divisions, its competitive psychology, its concentration on money values and profit-making. No amount of tinkering with the administration will alter these false values; in America, where there is free secondary education for all, there is a commercialized culture in ways more depraved than our own; Robert and Sylvia Lynd found Middletown in America, and how often have the English laughed at the American millionaire hunting trophies in Europe with a fat pocket-book? We, who make a fat profit out of American visitors to Stratford-on-Avon, might think twice before we laugh. Real lovers of literature would like to reveal Shakespeare to children for what he can be, a perpetual source of wonder and delight, a treasure-trove, a fairyland, and they find him set in an examination, as a task and a labour; he has to be taught with notes, every reference explained, every famous passage paraphrased; and the examination must be taken, or the children will be out of work, for a job requires a label, an examination passed: in short, a Schools Certificate. Is it too far-fetched to say that many children leave school with a positive dislike for English poetry, because they live in a competitive, capitalist society, which debases our literary heritage into a counter in the great job-hunting game?[1] The facts are not totally unconnected. Nor is it to be wondered at that such children when they leave school will at once spend money on second-rate films and novels, thus making it still more difficult for the first-rate artist to earn his living without debasing his art. The labour and socialist movement can and must stress the inequalities of the capitalist educational system, but it should also emphasize the fact that capitalist society cannot to-day produce an education that has a generally high level of culture and civilized aesthetic values. When we succeed in breaking capitalist society, and setting up one founded on more equable and enlightened principles, then teachers may perhaps be able to realize their cherished ideal and turn out from their schools that paragon of nobility that is always lurking at the back of their minds, a human-being sensitive, self-reliant, responsible, reasonable, appreciative, well-informed, and tolerant; or if there are few of such perfect beings even then, we shall at least have better opportunities of letting a child develop the best that is in him, for his own satisfaction, and the well-being of the community.

[1] We should be surprised to find in many working-class homes good taste in decoration or any real love or knowledge of our literary heritage. The cultural tradition of our civilization is in the hands of the very few. It comes as a shock to find, as I have done, a Russian factory worker, not so long ago an ignorant peasant, spending a half-hour break in his work reading *King Lear*. How many workers in an English factory have even heard the names of our literary masterpieces, much less those of Russia or any other foreign country?

PART TWO
SOCIALIST EDUCATION

CHAPTER FIVE

IMMEDIATE AMELIORATIVE MEASURES[1]

IN the first part of this book, I have tried to prove the existence of capitalist influence on modern English education, and to make plain the connection between capitalist society and the more deadening aspects of our educational tradition. Socialist propaganda cannot afford to ignore this most subtle force of capitalism, a power by which it manufactures something, as ultimately deadly as any of its less gracious products, munitions and poison-gas—that is, the capitalist mentality itself. The Labour Party has always been fully aware of the importance of education for the success of their plans for a socialist state, and their educational spokesman, R. H. Tawney, is one of the most penetrating writers on the subject. In stressing the need for an educational revaluation in the first part, I have wanted to make it clear that the problem is not merely one of administration, and that the question of education has very close connections with the cultural life of a nation and, indeed, with all aspects of its civilization. Consequently in this part of the book I shall not confine myself to dealing with the educational measures put forward as the policy of the Labour Party, though these, of course, have great importance, but I shall also discuss how in my opinion the socialist state should deal with special educational institutions, such places as, for instance, the great public schools not under state control at the

[1] I am indebted in this chapter to material made available to me by the New Fabian Research Bureau.

moment. Finally we must take stock of the ultimate aims of education, and face the question whether those aims are reconcilable with socialist society; whether educational ideals have more or less chance of realization under socialism than under capitalism. I am purposely not attempting here to give any opinions on the method of transition from capitalism to socialism, which is a political question outside the scope of this book. I can only state, for the sake of clarity, that I make certain suppositions, and if a reader considers them quite impossible, the administrative changes that I propose or support will also probably appear to him absurd, or at least impracticable; that, however, is not a point that can be argued fully here. I take for granted, first of all, that the transition will not have been so violent as to destroy the main outlines of the educational system at present extant; that the principal institutions, as I have described them in the first part, will remain essentially the same. I also suppose for the sake of convenience that in re-organizing this educational system the socialist party will do so through Act of Parliament; if the reader chooses to replace parliament in his imagination by some new legislative and executive machinery, it makes little difference to the forms of the necessary educational alterations. Finally, I accept the idea that it is a real socialist state that has been set on foot, whether by the Labour Party or by some other body; that it is not a mere patching of capitalism that is proposed, but the destruction of that form of society and its replacement by one run on principles of state-ownership and co-operation.

Though in the long run the re-organization of education is probably the most important reform for the continued existence of a socialist state, since ultimately a state of society depends for its life on the mentality of its citizens, yet it will not, of course, be the first thing to be tackled; nationalization of the banks, of land, of the key industries must come first. Even then it will be impossible to start with more than ambulance measures for the immediate reforms, for education is a long business, and though it is possible to re-organize institutions fairly quickly, a change of mentality is of necessity a much longer process. We may therefore begin with a consideration of the immediate reforms necessary to improve education, remembering that many such reforms are also compatible with capitalist society and do not make education socialist, in themselves. The first measure that could be carried through even under capitalism, to the profit of society, is the raising of the school-leaving age, and the National Government has now put forward a bill which proposes to raise the school-leaving age to fifteen in September 1939. The specifically socialist argument for this measure is that it is a move in the direction of dissolving the class inequality of age-limit, and such class distinctions in society it is the business of the socialist state to destroy. The proposal is stated as follows in *Labour and Education*; 'Legislation should (a) fix a date in the immediate future after which all children must remain at school till the end of the term in which they become fifteen, and a further date, the earliest possible, after which they must remain at school till sixteen.

'(b) Empower the raising of the age to sixteen in particular areas, before the date fixed in the bill, either (a) by Order made by the Board of Education, or (b) by by-laws made by local education authorities.' This is obviously an ambulance measure, as, of course, compulsory education to sixteen will not destroy inequality, or we should not have a capitalist government putting forward a similar measure.

These proposals, which go far beyond the present government bill, are, however, probably all that could be done immediately, as it is no good making education compulsory until there are sufficient schools to receive the children; one has to be realist though not necessarily gradualist; banks may be nationalized by a stroke of the pen, but schools cannot, unfortunately, be built overnight. The raising of the school-leaving age to fifteen at once and to sixteen very shortly, is, however, quite practical politics owing to the fluctuations of the population. We are at the moment just at the bulge in the numbers of the school-leavers made by the exceptionally high birth-rate after the war. In the next few years the school population in the higher forms will be decreasing and there is now the space and equipment ready for the fifteen-year-olds that could be kept at school. Thus in 1933 the number of young people between fourteen and seventeen available for employment was 1,872,000. That number rose to over two million in 1935, and if the school-leaving age remains at fourteen the estimate for 1937 is 2,357,000. *Labour and Education* calculates that should the school-leaving age be raised to fifteen now,[1] the increase of children on the school-roll would in 1937 be only 60,000 or 1 per cent; in certain areas there would be an actual decrease, all of which suggests that 1939 is an absurdly late date to fix for the enforcement of the government measure.

Financially speaking, there can be no objection to this measure even under capitalism; the refusal of the National Government to carry it through until 1939, when they have had every opportunity of doing so since

[1] This was written late in 1935.

1931, can only be due to class-prejudice. Owing to the desperate state of unemployment, even among young people, it would probably be possible to save money by this measure. Juvenile unemployment was set at 150,000 in January 1934, and Tawney, in *The School-Leaving Age and Juvenile Unemployment*, has estimated an increase in that number of another 100,000 to 150,000 by 1937, if the school-leaving age is not raised. This great increase is, of course, due to the same fact, the larger birth-rate after the war. The Tory argument against this measure has always been economy. Lord Hugh Cecil has said that 'to raise the school-leaving age, to pension off old workmen, and to shorten hours of work is a policy of national impoverishment'.[1] If these young people are not accommodated in the schools where there is room and useful work for them, the state will have to pay them, though very inadequately it is true, for the privilege of roaming about the streets with nothing to do. There are also, of course, a great many unemployed teachers who would be available to meet any increase in the school population.

The raising of the school-leaving age must not, of course, be made the excuse for enlarging classes, and doing without full equipment. In fact, this measure should be made to go along with the Hadow reforms, and the beginnings of a unified secondary education. With four or five years of post-primary work to cover, it will be necessary to develop the senior school into a real secondary institution, and it will no longer be possible for children in the higher grades of the elementary schools to get through the post-primary stage with the minimum of fresh material. A really satisfactory senior course seems only worth while when it can be continued

[1] Quoted in *The Socialist*, November 1935.

for some years. But with the proposed exemptions in force, continually whittling away the senior pupils and giving no security of tenure, such reorganization is impossible. The Hadow report states that 'the extending from three to four years of the period available for post-primary education would not only make it easier for such education to be planned as a coherent and progressive course with a character and quality of its own, but would also (and this is of much more importance) ensure that it continued sufficiently long to act as a permanent influence for good on the lives of those who passed through it'. Psychologically such a change is all to the good; it is very undesirable that the adolescent child should be drawn into the business of wage-earning, and should be forced to feel a premature responsibility towards his social welfare. He should be free to explore many channels before he comes under any necessity for supporting himself, much less anyone else. As the Hadow report says, great good and great harm can be done in these years; they are only less vital to future development than those of very early childhood.

The general problem of unemployment must be considered in this connection, a problem which in this country will undoubtedly persist during the transition to a real socialist state. Not only juvenile unemployment will be affected; the socialist government will take every means in its power to lessen unemployment and raising the school-leaving age to sixteen as soon as possible will be one of them. The presence of a large number of boys and girls who can be employed at a cheap rate, of necessity puts out of work many older people who would expect to be paid more.[1] Employers

---

[1] Juvenile employment still shows some disgraceful episodes, that are not too unlike the worst excesses of the Industrial Revo-

find it cheap to take on a boy when he leaves school, for a few years, then turn him off when his wages are increasing too rapidly and find another. This practice would be impossible but for a large juvenile population wanting work; remove this source of cheap labour, and many more adults will find their proper places in the social system. It should also be made illegal to take children in part-time employment while they are still at school. Maintenance grants will relieve the financial pressure on the family that leads it to snatch every penny, even at the cost of the effectiveness of the child's education.

lution to allow us to be comfortable on the subject. *The Socialist*, November 1935, gives the following figures:

There are 100,000 juvenile workers whose legal limit of hours is seventy-four a week; in the Argentine the maximum is thirty-six. [This maximum has been considerably reduced by the government's Factory Act (1937), but not to the lowest extent possible.]

At an aerated waters factory in Merthyr boys of fourteen work fourteen hours a day, starting in summer at 7.0 and finishing at 10.30 at night, for 5s. a day.

In Bristol there are many boys and girls working sixty hours a week in factories for wages of 1d. an hour or less.

And there are many more such cases.

The proposed new Factory Act and the report of the Chief Inspector of Factories have brought to the light some further interesting facts. The time-limits for work in factories have hardly changed since the beginning of the last century, and though many employers find it compatible with private profit to employ young persons only forty hours per week and to insist on attendance at day-continuation schools, the general tendency during the latest boomlet, according to the Chief Inspector, is to work young persons and women up to the legal maximum, even when the men, organized in trade unions, are working much shorter hours. There is a consequent increasing accident risk among children in factories; in 1928 it was 3 per cent above the adult rate; in 1935 it was 22 per cent higher than the adult rate (cf. *The New Statesman and Nation*, November 7, 1936). These facts make the government's concern for the fitness of the nation somewhat ludicrous. The physical exercise after hours, such as they propose, can be of no benefit to any child who has already worked ten hours and is very possibly also under-nourished.

It should, of course, be impossible to contemplate this reform, unless the government is prepared to couple it with adequate maintenance grants. In the present standard of living, it is not sufficient to give free education; most families consider that a child of fourteen is a potential wage-earner, and their finances are planned with an eye to his earnings.[1] To keep him at school means not only a sacrifice of those earnings, but also of the money that will have to be spent on his food, clothes, and other necessities. It is for this reason that so many working-class people are opposed to the raising of the school-leaving age, although it is a reform ultimately much to their advantage; on the short-sighted view—and poverty makes people short-sighted—with no maintenance grants, it involves a financial sacrifice. Education will never appear for what it is worth, in the eyes of the workers, until it is separated from the idea of money value altogether; their present general indifference to the true value of education is

[1] It is this aspect of the question that makes the National Government's educational proposals absurd, for they are introducing the system of exemptions for beneficial employment or home duties. To a struggling family, existing on the dole, all employment is beneficial, and many a mother can earn a few pence charing, if she can leave an elder child at home to mind the baby. With such exemptions in force the absence of maintenance grants will more or less nullify the ostensible object of the bill.

Sir Walter Citrine in the *Daily Herald*, February 7, 1936, says of the National Government proposals: 'In its own memorandum, published with the Bill, it estimates that children will be retained at school, not for an extra year, but only for an average of an extra six months. . . .

'In nine out of ten of the areas in which the age has been raised in this way the proportion of exempted children exceeds 70 per cent. In six of those areas the proportion is 90 per cent or more.

'In the remaining area exemptions were kept down to 37 per cent. In that case maintenance grants were paid in necessitous cases by the Local Education Authority.'

only one example of the false commercialized point of view induced by poverty. These maintenance advances should be available for children staying at school till fifteen, and also should be offered to parents who voluntarily keep their children at school another year before the sixteen year limit becomes actual law. The allowance could be fixed at a national minimum, say 5s. a week, with discretion given to local authorities to increase the amount in particular cases, if necessary; an income limit could be imposed as long as it was a generous one, and included all insured people and those coming under the income scale of the National Insurance Acts. There need be no stigma attached to the payment of this grant, such as are frequently found to-day when a child is receiving free meals at school, or is helped to buy school uniform or equipment. The fact is usually kept hidden and the grant regarded as a charity, a deadly secret. A maintenance grant should be more in the nature of a wage, like the salaries paid to Russian university students, as payment for work done which will ultimately be of value to the state. In the future socialist state, the question of maintenance is connected with the whole problem of the school as a form of society, and its relation to the family, a problem to be discussed later when we are considering matters beyond the immediate reforms and ambulance measures. If the family is still held responsible for the financial burden of children, and if necessitous families still exist, then maintenance grants will also be necessary.

Building is the next most important item on the list of reforms, as obviously the reconstruction of education into a unified system of primary and secondary schools requires a background of adequate equipment. The first National Government abolished the special building grant established by the last Labour Government, and by official coolness with regard to local expenditure at the central board and by 'economy' pressure on the part of its inspectors, put a stop to a large percentage of the capital expenditure on education by local authority.[1] *Labour and Education* suggests as well as the re-establishment of the special building grant, 'the restoration of the system under which the Board paid in grants not less than 50 per cent of the expenditure of local education authorities'. Such a restoration is being made under the second National Government, but then Circular 1444 states that 'the grant will be for a limited period, the end of which will be determined when the proposed Bill for raising the school age has become law, and the operative date is known'. The Labour proposals, with no such limitation, would provide a general basis of financial assistance, as an indication of the progressive tendencies of the Board and their good faith in urging the local authorities to go on with the work of re-organization. The initial policy of the National Government is not merely responsible for crippling financial economies with regard to education, but also a general discouragement of all educational progress and reform. Interest and initiative have been killed in many localities and it will take more than the lukewarm reforms of Circular 1444 to revive them. Thus, while the cut in teachers' salaries has been restored, the grant paid to local authorities in respect of teachers' salaries remains reduced, with the result that they have less to spend on equipment and building, a state of affairs

---

[1] The Board of Education report for 1934 (published in August 1935) shows seventy-two black-listed schools abolished out of 1,244 (Labour abolished 500 in two years), and one nursery school built.

that induces parsimony and obstruction rather than interest and development. The full building grant is necessary to encourage activity in various directions; adequate equipment must be provided if the senior elementary schools are to become anything comparable to the secondary schools; special rooms for scientific subjects and handicrafts, libraries, studios, maps, pictures, and models are all required if even the Hadow scheme of reform is to be put into operation. Much reconditioning is necessary for primary schools, especially in rural areas; the socialist state should recognize no difference in claims for building and equipment between primary and secondary schools. Many schools that are not actually on the black-list are in a most deplorable condition; those on the black-list, even if they are not under direct state control, should be closed right away, and private schools have their fair share on the list. Many schools in the country have leaking roofs, damp walls, old clumsy furniture, outdoor sanitation; every school should have adequate indoor lavatory accommodation, means of drying wet clothes, good heating apparatus, and modern pleasing furniture. Finally building grants are needed for many new nursery schools and departments. It is unnecessary to dwell on the poverty of our nursery-school accommodation; but a campaign to obtain sufficient nursery schools in the country demands, as a necessary preliminary, generous building grants.[1]

[1] I have not dealt here with the special schools for mental defectives and children with tuberculosis and epilepsy. But it is obvious that a progressive and just educational policy aims at giving every child the fullest opportunity to develop to its best capacity, and that particular care should be taken with children thus handicapped by physical or mental defects. It goes without saying that the provision of such special schools should be encouraged.

The retention of a large number of children at school beyond the age of fourteen must not be made an excuse for conniving at, and possibly worsening, the present unsatisfactory conditions in schools, any more than it should be allowed to bring financial hardship on any family. For this reason building grants are very necessary, and for this reason also great care must be taken that classes are not increased in size. As already stated in dealing with the inequalities of capitalist education, there are far too many classes in elementary schools with over fifty children in them and even more with over forty. The limit in secondary schools is thirty-five, but all experienced teachers would agree that, where a subject is being taught in forty-minute periods, it is impossible to give the individual attention needed with much more than twenty-five in a class. The limit of forty might be set at once, though the Board of Education would have power to exempt particular schools where present building conditions made it impossible. But such exemption should only be granted on the condition that schemes for enlargement were immediately set on foot. Such a limitation now and the statement that a further limitation to thirty in a class was proposed at a future date, as soon as possible, would give a convenient fillip to the energies and initiative of the local authorities in receipt of the building grant. The limitation to forty at least in the primary schools might be set at once, as even with the school-leaving age at fifteen, the fall in the school population will make the question of accommodation much simpler. The limitation of classes to forty in many localities, particularly in slum areas where clearance has done something to decrease the number of schoolchildren, is a possibility now; further limitation should be a progressive process, continuing with the growth of new buildings and the removal of senior pupils over eleven to new senior and secondary schools. It is important that the limitation should not be confined to new and secondary schools, but should also be applied to primary schools, when they are relieved of the pressure caused by having the senior pupils in the same block of buildings. For it is just possible to work a class of over thirty adolescents, by using methods of individual work at the child's own pace, and by effective grouping, but limitation is absolutely essential for smaller children who need continuous individual attention.

The problem of staffing these schools with smaller classes and increased populations should in its first stages present no difficulties, owing to the large number of teachers out of work at the moment. No school which, through these changes, requires more staff, should be allowed to take the opportunity to employ uncertificated teachers at less than the standard Burnham scale of salary. No grants should be made unless the staff of a school met the Board's requirements as to qualifications. Part-time uncertificated teachers should be dismissed, and if they are serious in requiring full-time employment, they should be given the opportunity to acquire qualifications by means of scholarships to training colleges; as most of these are married women, their places could be taken, if a shortage occurred, by qualified married teachers who have been obliged unwillingly to leave their employment. Full-time uncertificated teachers, if elderly, could be pensioned off early, and the younger ones impressed with the advisability of improving their qualifications at summer-schools and refresher courses. It may be doubted whether, as the school-leaving age is progressively raised and the number of children in a class lowered, there will be found a sufficient number of people able and willing to qualify as teachers. The doubt is increased by the indisputable fact that many people now train to teach only because the Board of Education grant, available to them on the condition that they train for the profession, makes it possible for them to afford a university education. How many people, especially women, have declared their intention of taking up teaching for a few years only and going on to some other work! Once they have discovered the extreme difficulty of getting out into some other work, teaching becomes for them a prison, from the narrow windows of which they stare at the great world outside. Add to this that for many people there remains a faint aroma of priggishness about the trade that would to-day make them avoid it if possible; men fear to be regarded, as Lamb and Samuel Johnson looked on schoolmasters, as men who have grown used to being petty gods, who cannot be natural in their behaviour or inspire natural feelings in others; and women have an unholy dread of the spectre school-marm with her loud voice, authoritative manner, and fearsome clothes. One suspects that a vast number of teachers would rush out of their profession to-morrow, if some more congenial and well-paid employment were offered them.

Yet for all that I do not think that in future years there will be a shortage of teachers. In the first place, a socialist state if given a fair chance to live, should enable its citizens to develop far more balanced views and saner judgments; it is inevitable that as a country becomes more civilized, it will realize more and more strongly the importance of education, its position as the keystone to its cultural life and even to the continuation of that state of society itself. Many people, including many teachers themselves, already have this point of view towards education, if not towards its individual practitioners. It will be a sign of a healthy state if there are sufficient people willing to enter a trade that is of vital importance to the continuance of that form of society. A saner, freer school discipline, a pleasanter, friendlier atmosphere in the class-room will mitigate the popular conception of the teacher as a walking encyclopaedia, a disciplinarian concealing the iron gauntlet under the glove. It is also the business of the state under socialism to see that, in the first stages of its educational administration, no effort is spared to make the working conditions of the teacher as pleasant as possible. Most people consider the teacher to be exceptionally well off in this respect, and I, in maintaining that there is much room for improvement, will inevitably be suspected of teachers' grouse. I do not deny that compared with many workers to-day the teacher, especially in secondary schools, works short hours and is well paid; between three and four months' holiday looks on paper very generous. Secondary-school teachers must expect the first reforms to benefit the elementary-school teachers and bring them up to equality of advantages, just as in general school reform the elementary children have first claim. Certain changes are, however, essential before the profession of teaching can be attractive. Before general equality of income is established in the socialist state, the teacher must feel secure against such inroads on his income as that made by the first National Government. He will also be encouraged to take a keen interest in his work, if he feels that the state is also interested. Adequate equipment and pleasant buildings are not merely desirable because they are necessary to the elements of teaching and good health, but also because they induce a state of mind in both teacher and taught in which they may realize that their work is important, interesting, and decidedly worth doing well. Similarly, small classes enable the teacher to feel unhampered by disciplinary problems, by the necessity of teaching his class as a regiment not as individuals; with the right number in his class he has time to be interested in his pupils and to give expression to his own appreciation of his subject. A teacher should not for reasons of economy be asked to teach a number of subjects that are of little interest to him; there is no reason for absolute specialization unless individual teachers desire it, but they should never have to teach anything that has no attractions for them. It is also unfair and unnecessary to expect a teacher to do the mass of clerical work that usually falls to his lot to-day. Most schools are miserably under-staffed on the secretarial side, whereas it should not be teachers' work to keep registers, make lists, and percentage marks, take off copies of examination papers, collect and file evidence on each child's circumstances. In Russia they have realized the importance of leaving the teacher free to do his own work, and to our one secretary for the head of the school, they have a staff to do the clerical work.[1] The gradual disappearance of

[1] On the other hand, the recent drive for extra efficiency in Soviet education, and the number of out-of-school activities in which he is expected to take part, at present make the Russian teacher far more busy than his English fellow. Beatrice King considers the Soviet teacher to be overworked, but sets against that fact his economic security and his certainty that the government is interested in his work; he has no sense of frustration and is assured that conditions will improve as rapidly as possible. 'The teachers have to help to initiate libraries, reading-rooms, and Red Corners for the adult population. Once a month the

the system of competitive marking will lessen the burden of out-of-school work, whereby the teacher will avoid the more monotonous labour of correcting exercises and examinations.

As far as actual hours of work are concerned, there is much to be said for very short hours. Indeed, this has been realized in some countries already and in a school in Copenhagen that I visited in 1935, the English mistress who showed me round taught from eight in the morning to 12.30, except for two days in the week when she worked till one o'clock. Out-of-school corrections would of course increase these hours to a certain extent, but to many who look on the eight-hour day as a goal to be achieved, this will seem an absurdly short working-day. I can only make the age-old plea that every teacher can understand, some harassed mothers and nurses, but otherwise few outsiders, that eight hours of the company of children is not at all the same thing as eight hours of adding columns of figures, of hewing stone or tending machines; in fact, that human nature is the most exhausting material that anyone can have to work on. A great deal of the traditional manner of the school-marm, her domineering nervousness, is due to the fact that she has to be in contact with children too long at a stretch with resultant irritation and boredom. It is in the nature of children to be fidgety and noisy; they are only quiet and silent under artificial restraint; adults either have to impose the restraint or stand the racket. Again, teaching in my opinion should be the sharing of a mutual interest;

class teacher is expected to visit the homes of the younger pupils. . . . The Soviet teacher has to spend much more time writing up notes of lessons than his British colleague. Very detailed records of the pupils' progress, psychological and social as well as intellectual, have to be kept.'—*Changing Man*, Beatrice King, pp. 219–20.

consequently a successful lesson is as exhausting as an unsuccessful one; the extension of enthusiasm and interest is a type of creation and has its consequent reaction. The material of the teacher, human nature, that which he has to handle in his art, is not, or should not be, as clay to his touch, as words to his pen; it must be worked on, yet allowed to grow, stimulated but observed, given interest, sympathy, initiative, and criticism. The reason for so much bad mechanical teaching, so much routine boredom in schools, is frequently that the teacher's store of nervous energy is used up, and with it his sympathy and interest in the children. Bertrand Russell's statement that no adult should have to be in the company of children for more than four hours is no exaggeration, but the sober truth. It is also desirable from the educational standpoint that the teacher should have sufficient spare time to engage in pursuits and hobbies outside his profession, for the more versatile a man, the more broad-minded, the better teacher he will be. A teacher should not only be free, he should be encouraged to spend his spare time in any pursuit he desires, artistic, political, or administrative. Education will gain if the state sees to it that he has sufficient spare time and entire liberty to express himself outside his profession, howsoever he chooses.

One further ambulance measure will be essential in the early stages of socialist education, one which grows out of capitalist evils, and which the socialist state in itself, if it succeeds in abolishing poverty, should do much to make unnecessary; it concerns school feeding and medical supervision. It is, of course, impossible to ignore the state of children's health in education, and particularly in a society that keeps so many of its citizens in a state of poverty, it is a question that the educationalist must think of primarily. Medical inspection will form a regular part of socialist education; it will be part of the medical attention that will be available for the child from conception onwards. It should be an axiom in socialist education that, as a basis to all socially necessary activities, physical and intellectual, every effort should be made to secure for all children in the country a sound state of health. There should be doctors and nurses attached to each school, and regular medical supervision. It will probably be found advisable to give all schoolchildren free meals, in order that the school shall be a real community; even if, in the more distant future, the family subsists, it is desirable that the idea of community in schools should be removed from the vague abstractions of present schoolboy honour, to the more solid actualities of social life. The school should be a place where the child expects to meet with all the communal phases of daily life, and school meals have a function to perform here. They provide also a means of ensuring that a child is eating the right things.

If the family continues as a real unit in the future state, the system of health-visitors will have to be extended considerably. A new point of view must be encouraged towards health, one that is already prevalent in Russia; a doctor should be thought of as a man who not merely cures an illness when it comes, but prevents it coming if possible. The ridiculous notion that a mother knows more about her child's health by instinct than a trained nurse, is one that must be combated. A procedure for health visitors might be worked out, by which a trained medical adviser would be a constant visitor to a child's home right through his school career. Far too little is known about the home conditions of children in the later stages of their education, and a teacher meeting poor work and inattention obviously arising from tiredness and strain, too frequently can only guess at the reasons for that condition, whereas he should have the knowledge and services of a health-visitor at his disposal. I should also like to see a parallel system devised for the psychological side of health. Far too many people dabble in this new science and teachers even with a certain amount of training are not competent to deal with the extremes of psychological maladjustment. It would be as well if we could realize that a psychologist and psychiatrist are as necessary as a doctor to the community for the prevention as well as the cure of malady. Maladjustment in certain individuals is bound to occur even in the best regulated communities, and much depression and unhappiness might be saved children, especially in adolescence, by intelligent observation and scientific treatment.

These developments, however, belong to the more distant future, and require a different mentality from that so prevalent to-day, which makes a mother declare jealously that no one can understand her child, physically or mentally, as well as herself. There are fortunately more immediate things that the socialists can do when in office, to counterbalance the worst effects on health of an unequal capitalist society. At the moment the elementary schoolchildren must be inspected medically between the ages of eight and nine, and again between twelve and thirteen. Medical inspection in non-state schools is just beginning and there is great variety of competency here; but as children from these schools usually come from homes where they are well-fed and clothed, and where building conditions do not induce disease, they do not suffer much from lack of

IMMEDIATE AMELIORATIVE MEASURES

school medical attention; parents supply that deficiency in the holidays. It is the elementary schoolchild, whose home is poor and uncomfortable, who stands in particular need of school supervision. Local authorities are given a wide liberty in the matter of the provision of medical care, some confining themselves to the regular inspections, others providing school clinics and making arrangements with local doctors and hospitals for treatment of the children. One of the main reasons why nursery schools are so much to be desired, perhaps the chief reason, is that they would provide opportunity for early and continuous medical inspection. A child to-day may be taken to a clinic for its first two years, if there is one locally; even then attendance is not obligatory. It is very rare for a mother to take a child to a clinic from the ages of three to five, so that for three years a child is without medical supervision. Thus, while the amount of disease in schools, that is from the ages of five to fourteen, has been greatly reduced in late years, mainly owing to school medical supervision, the health of children just entering school, that is at five years, has hardly improved at all.

School medical inspection has already shown its value, but the conditions under which it is practiced leave a lot to be desired. Mr. C. E. McNally, in his book *Public Ill Health*, gives some examples of extra investigation bringing to light far more cases of malnutrition than the routine examinations had revealed. In Chester, for example, such an extra investigation was made, and consequently the number of children treated for malnutrition rose from three in 1932 to seventeen in 1933, and those requiring to be kept under observation from twenty-five to fifty-eight. 'These figures would suggest that the routine inspection in which the Ministry of

Health takes so much pride is completely inadequate as a method of finding out if children are suffering from malnutrition.'[1] The three routine examinations during school life seem hardly sufficient, and four as in London should be the minimum. A doctor usually has an average of six minutes to inspect a child, talk to its parents, arrange treatment if necessary, and make a detailed report, which may involve filling in a form of over thirty columns. Then, again, when treatment is ordered by the school doctor, it is not by any means certain that the child will ever receive it. It is claimed that not more than 60 per cent of dental cases ever get attention. This is, of course, partly due to the fact that parents do not often realize the importance of treatment in cases of slight decay; medical education has itself far to go; but this fact is also partly due to inadequate provision for treatment.[2] Private practitioners do not welcome cases of defect in ear, nose, or throat, which have to be attended for a very small fee; outpatient departments have not the provision for the numbers of children requiring attention. A school clinic is a necessary and logical addition to medical inspection. It is well known that a child that has left school at fourteen is under no medical supervision until he is sixteen, when he is entitled to go to his panel doctor. The raising of the school-leaving age would get over that difficulty, but until sixteen is the limit, schools should be requested to invite former pupils to the school medical inspection during those two years. The report on the

[1] *Public Ill Health*, C. E. McNally, 1935, p. 75.
[2] 'Durham S.M.O. states: "The subject of dental treatment has been dealt with at length for several years. There has been no addition to the service during the year. The numerical inadequacy of the staff and clinics requires no reiteration." '—*Public Ill Health*, C. E. McNally, p. 112.

child's health that is kept from five to fourteen years, should be handed to the school-leaver to give to his panel doctor. To-day clinics do not hand on their records to the schools nor the schools to the panel doctors, whereas the whole value of such records is in continuity. Socialist legislation should therefore make it incumbent on local authorities to provide for adequate medical supervision right through childhood, and under conditions that ensure that the inspection will be efficient. As soon as the growth of equipment and buildings will allow, attendance at an ante-natal clinic should be obligatory, unless a woman can prove regular attendance to a doctor. Children should also be obliged to attend the infant clinics until they are five years, unless nursery schools are taking the place of the clinic. All such treatment should of course be free. At the moment the local authorities are forced to recover the whole or part of the cost of treatment from the parents, if they consider they can afford it. This merely deters many parents from giving their children the treatment ordered by the doctor, particularly in the case of slight dental decay or minor ailments; there is, for instance, a close connection between the charges made and the number of dental cases treated. The total sum collected from parents is only £30,000 a year, and considering that lack of treatment in early years usually means illness in adult life, which has to be paid for by the state, the collection of such a sum hardly seems economical.

Medical inspection in schools in the present state of society will not, however, solve the problem of ill-health among schoolchildren. Detection and cure of disease are very necessary, but prevention depends on healthy living. Trained advisers in matters of diet, sleep, fresh air, and dress can now do much to improve the health of babies under the care of ignorant mothers. But no amount of advice and good intentions can repair the effects of poverty on health. Good soap and hot water cost money and are necessary to cleanliness; food, which not merely satisfies hunger but gives a balance of food values, is needed for full healthy growth;[1] slum-dwellers do not prefer the putrid air of their alleys, but cannot afford a home in fresh and agreeable surroundings. That this is so makes it imperative that light, pleasing buildings should be erected for schools as soon as possible, in order that the squalor of the home environment in slum areas should be counteracted by good school surroundings. For, in fact, capitalism, that keeps so many people in such conditions, virtually makes a greater claim on education to meet the deficiency than a state of society that can maintain its citizens in health and decency; it automatically makes the demand for an environment healthy enough to prevent the physical and mental maladies bred by slum-dwelling poverty. It is impossible for a socialist state to abolish poverty at once; poverty is a disease in the body of a nation, not a growth that can be cut out by the surgeon's knife, but one that must be lived out of the blood, by means of wholesome food and fresh air. Consequently, whatever may be said for and against free meals in the future socialist school, now they are an immediate necessity. The Provision of Meals Act (1906) makes it permissive for local authorities to give free meals in

[1] That the working-class housewife should be expected to have a knowledge of dietetics that is unnecessary for her richer prototype to possess is hardly just. Again and again we hear the blame for malnutrition laid at the door of the ignorance of the housewife; the wealthier woman is usually just as ignorant, but natural taste and desire for variety in food, unrestricted by considerations of cost, will usually arrive at satisfactorily balanced meals.

schools where there are judged to be individual necessitous cases; cost must be recovered from the parents if they are deemed to be able to afford it. The scales of unemployment relief, the dietary charts drawn up by the British Medical Association, have brought the question of malnutrition into the news; controversy still rages on this point and the conclusion of Sir George Newman, in his report on public health, that unemployment has no ill-effects on the health of those individuals receiving benefit, has been vigorously challenged, particularly by Mr. C. E. McNally in his book *Public Ill Health*, in which he quotes extensively from local Medical Officers of Health to refute such an idea. In the first place, he challenges the notion of a possible minimum standard of health, such as that on which the British Medical Association's food scales are based. An optimal standard is all that will ensure really good health. Various experiments have been carried out by competent investigators to show the difference in physique resulting from an addition to a normal diet, such as that of cod-liver oil or varying quantities of milk (pp. 21–5). The now familiar comparison of the heights and weights of Monmouthshire schoolchildren in elementary and secondary schools shows quite clearly that, though the elementary schoolchild may be properly nourished, a still greater degree of physical development can be achieved in better social surroundings.[1] Another

[1] HEIGHT IN INCHES

Age	Boys		Girls	
	Elementary	Secondary	Elementary	Secondary
11	53·6	56·2	54·6	55·3
12	54 7	57 4	56·9	58·9
13	55·8	60·6	57·8	60·4
14	58·3	61·3	58·9	61·6

[*Footnote continued on page* 152

interesting comparative experiment was carried out by Dr. Spence in Newcastle-on-Tyne, among pre-school-children of different social circumstances. He found 36 per cent of the poorer group to be unhealthy or physically unfit; in height and weight measurement, in the comparative prevalence of rickets, anaemia, and deficiency diseases, and in liability to infection, the poorer group was found considerably inferior. This inferiority Dr. Spence believes on the average to be due to '(a) The housing conditions, which permit infections of young children at susceptible ages.

'(b) Improper and inadequate diet, which prevent satisfactory recovery from their illnesses.'[1] Mr. McNally gives the following interesting figures which prove fairly conclusively that poverty and the inadequacy of the unemployment assistance in particular must lead to the limitation below the danger level of the food supply of some children.[2]

Age of Child	U.A.B. Scale	B.M.A. Food, plus 1s. 2½d. for Clothing, Cleaning and Light	Deficit
	s. d.	s. d.	s. d.
2	3 0	4 3½	1 3½
4	3 0	4 7½	1 7½
6	3 6	4 9½	1 3½
8	4 0	5 4½	1 4½
10	4 0	5 11½	1 11½
11	4 6	6 6½	2 0½

Footnote continued from page 151]

WEIGHT IN POUNDS

	Boys		Girls	
Age	Elementary	Secondary	Elementary	Secondary
11	68·5	77·6	68·5	77·9
12	72·6	78·6	74·6	79·9
13	80·8	89·5	82·4	88·9
14	87·1	93·5	87·2	91·2

Cf. *Public Ill Health*, p. 25.
[1] *Public Ill Health*, p. 95.   [2] Ibid., p. 210.

IMMEDIATE AMELIORATIVE MEASURES

Sir John Orr has gone so far as to suggest that 20 per cent of the population are living on an inadequate diet.[1] Immediate efforts must be made to see that the growing generation does not suffer.

The results of malnutrition are not always obvious to the eye even of the medical practitioner, and, in fact, the deadliness of this condition is that its effects are far-reaching and often delayed. 'Malnutrition does not show definite signs, even to the expert, until it has been exerting its influence for some time. It is most undesirable that children should remain untreated until they show signs of malnutrition, for by that time serious damage may have been done.'[2] There is something grimly humorous in the fact that in 1935 47 per cent of the volunteers for the army were rejected as unfit; and yet the National Government has set its face against the improvement of this state of affairs

---

[1] These are more facts concerning malnutrition published in *The Socialist*, November 1935.

'In Lancashire malnutrition among school children has risen each year since 1931. In 1934 it reached the figure of 2 19 per cent, the highest point reached since 1924. In Aberdare the percentage of malnourished children increased during 1934 from 7·1 per cent to 8·6 per cent. In Swindon eighty-three cases were recorded, as against thirty-three in the previous year.

'In Monmouthshire 14·4 per cent of 1,614 children examined from thirty-six rural areas were found to be under-nourished.

' "Most of our children are suffering not so much from tuberculosis but from starvation ... 75 per cent of the cases admitted to the society's sanatorium are definitely due to starvation", declared Dr. J. O'Hara, M.O. of the sanatorium of the Durham County Society for the Prevention and Cure of Consumption.'

Even in Ipswich, a comparatively very prosperous small town, with a small proportion of unemployment, the School Medical Officer's report for 1935 gives the figure of 21·9 per cent of the schoolchildren examined as slightly malnourished, and 0·4 per cent as bad.

[2] Cambridge S.M.O. Report for 1933, quoted in *Public Ill Health*, p. 71.

and put pressure on local authorities to cut down expenditure, so that one education committee to my own knowledge has passed a resolution against providing free meals unless a child shows definite signs of malnutrition, by which time, of course, irretrievable harm has been done. The Board of Education now demands that the Medical Officer of Health, in his examinations of schoolchildren, shall divide them into groups, classified as excellent, normal, slightly sub-normal, and bad. The division is insidious as the larger number of the malnourished children go, of course, into the slightly sub-normal group, where the 'slightly' invites complacency. The argument that technically malnutrition is not always due to lack of food holds no water except in individual cases; in this country the bulk of malnutrition is admittedly due to poverty. Meat, fish, eggs, milk, fresh fruit, and vegetables are expensive, and it is frequent to find a working-class diet containing less nutritious but cheaper foods, such starchy meals as consist mainly of bread, porridge, rice, and potatoes. Thus actual malnutrition is frequent where there is no shortage of food; and many people are without the means of buying nutritious foods, for which the British Medical Association reckons 22s. 6½d. a week is necessary for a family of two parents and three children.[1] It is the business of socialists when in power to ensure that no children in school are suffering from malnutrition; it is far better to feed some whose parents do not need assistance, than to risk missing a single child who is in need of free meals. A national minimum income

---

[1] The report of the Ipswich S.M.O. for 1935 is interesting in that it gives the incomes, rents paid, and residues for food, etc., of fifty representative poor families, with the inference that poverty, in those cases at least, is the main cause of malnutrition.

scale could be decided upon if necessary, but it must be a generous one and those in receipt of public assistance must be allowed to apply for free meals in addition. The school canteen must be open to children of all ages, for in adolescence as in infancy right feeding is essential to good health. Milk has been declared to be ideal food for children of all ages by a great body of medical opinion; the National Government, as a form of advertisement for the Milk Marketing Board, has supplied cheaper milk to schoolchildren, but the Labour Party, quite rightly, in view of the surplus of milk in this country, proposes to give half-a-pint of milk a day to all children attending a state-aided school, free of charge. They also propose, to avoid any taint of charity or class discrimination, that they should aim at giving all schoolchildren free meals.

The question of the financial provision for these educational developments will be the first concern of the capitalist critic, though his argument cannot be met without a consideration of the whole socialist scheme of financial rearrangement, which is, of course, outside the scope of this book; that type of criticism leaves untouched the position that such developments are necessary. It is the business of the state to provide what its citizens have a right to demand; it is one of the most important arguments for the socialist régime that it will be able to increase the proportion of the state's wealth spent on social services, whereas the dependence of capitalist finance on private enterprise obliges it to sacrifice the needs of the poorest, in spite of the good intentions of many of its individual supporters, who would never willingly impose hardship on anyone. It might be well to make one point here for the benefit of the economy maniac. We are sufficiently civilized to believe that the state has some obligations to its citizens in the matter of health. The ill-health of the adult population sends in a heavy bill to the nation. A conservative estimate of our total bill on ill-health, its prevention and cure, is £300,000,000 per annum, which, of course, is in addition to the loss of productive power. Of this sum £4,500,000 only goes on school health services. The expenditure of a little more at the earlier stages, making a really efficient school and infant health service, would almost certainly result in a great reduction in the total cost of ill-health. We allow 7,000,000 insured persons a year to go to the doctors under various national schemes, a number that might be considerably reduced if the health of schoolchildren were adequately cared for from the start.

CHAPTER SIX

THE MACHINERY OF SOCIALIST EDUCATION

THESE are the mere tinkerings that will, it is hoped, counteract some of the worst defects of the present educational system. Even with these ambulance measures in force, the system will be far from being a suitable vehicle for socialist education at its best. They may, however, if energetically applied, be a stepping-stone to the formation of a fully socialist educational machine. The form of that machinery I propose to discuss in this section, attempting in the next section a synthesis between it and such existing institutions as are worth preserving.

The stated aim of the socialist movement with regard to such machinery is that it should provide free secondary education for all. The principles of universalism and equality must form the basis of socialist education. It is these principles in action that make the machinery of Russian education so impressive. The Webbs emphasize this aspect of Russian education in suitably forceful language: 'The most important feature to-day is the extraordinary "universalism" of the system. In the whole of the U.S.S.R., education, in the full sense of training for life, has now to be provided, as a matter of course, gratuitously and with attendance made compulsory, in every town and village, for every child, irrespective of sex or race or colour or creed or nationality even among the numerous backward races of the U.S.S.R. There is no fragment of the earth's surface, at all comparable in extent, in which anything like this conception of an educational service prevails.'[1] And they add to this a note: 'Compare the position of the service of education in India which has had the advantage of British rule for more than a century; or in the manifold colonial empire of six European powers over nearly the whole continent of Africa; or even in the United States, which still has 5 per cent adult illiteracy and in 1935 literally tens of thousands of schools closed because of lack of funds.' It would be a comparatively simple matter to abolish fee-paying in grant-aided secondary schools, a change that would bring English education in sight of 'universalism'; no legislation is required, but only an amendment to the regulations of the Board of Education.[2] The entrance examination to secondary schools, with its different standards for fee-payers and scholars, and the dead-weight it brings to bear on elementary education, will automatically disappear. The transformation under socialism of our present unequal system of education into one providing universal free secondary education, consequently depends mainly on the building of new schools, and of additions to the present ones that can be converted. All children should be able to receive free education to the age of eighteen, if desirable, as soon as building has progressed sufficiently.[3] This will also mean the avoidance of that

[1] *Soviet Communism*, Sidney and Beatrice Webb, p. 891.
[2] Cf. *Labour and Education*, p. 13.
[3] Sixteen must be the legal limit to a general secondary education, in the preliminary stages. Under socialism, I believe experiment alone can decide whether that age should be compulsorily raised. Free education to the age of eighteen must be provided optionally; but it is possible that when the pressure of economic insecurity is lifted from society, the combination of part-time education in school with light employment may be found to be most educationally sound for a number of children between the ages of sixteen and eighteen.

great change in educational environment which comes for the public schoolboy at the age of thirteen or fourteen and for the elementary schoolchild at ten or eleven. If there is to be a break at all the latter age is probably preferable psychologically, but there is little to be said for such a violent change in a child's school life at either stage. The new schools of the socialist state will consequently be a series of correlated departments, much like the departments of infant, primary, and senior teaching already found in some elementary schools. These departments will have separate buildings, each planned according to its separate needs, but the school will also be conceived of and built as a whole, so that the children may have the double advantage of surroundings suitable to their age, and of life in the same community right through their school years. Thus they can proceed from one department to another, with the valuable sense of starting a new phase of their lives, but without the great dislocation consequent on a complete change to a new community with new faces, new rules, new clothes, and new traditions. The departments would be normally three—kindergarten, primary, and secondary—but it might well be found an advantage to make the voluntary nursery school a fourth department of the community. The advantages of this system of correlation from the organizational point of view would be very great; just as the medical inspection services suffer at the moment from discontinuity, so also does the teaching, especially in secondary schools, from ignorance of the previous records and attainments of the children. Within a planned community which correlates all stages of development, it will be possible for kindergarten teachers to hand on valuable experience to primary teachers and primary to secondary. There would also probably be a certain overlapping of teachers, so that a child on entering a new department need not necessarily come in contact with a totally new staff, for continuity in teaching is sometimes as important as variety. This system will also enable the teacher to have some choice in the ages he teaches, ranging over a variety or specializing on that which suits him best if he prefer. The school will be under the central authority of one head or organizer, with departmental heads working under him, so that the maximum of variety of method can be encouraged without dislocating the central plan.

Free secondary education for all and the provision of nursery schools where needed, mean therefore a great increase in the number of state day-schools; so that, whereas now secondary education acquires its pupils by means of skimming the cream off a number of elementary schools, with rather inadequate tools, in the future we must expect to find communities providing all types of education, for all types of intellectual attainment, where now we have a single elementary school. Our present elementary schools, altered and expanded beyond recognition, will probably form the basis of most of the new secondary schools. The old secondary schools will have to be expanded downwards, unless they already have kindergarten departments, to produce a uniformity of type in educational institutions. One school for a large village or small town may be all that is necessary, but obviously more will be needed for larger communities, and correlation and planning will be possible between the several schools resulting. It is a matter for experiment to decide whether all schools should attempt to provide all types of education or whether a group of schools should each try some form of specialization in the secondary stage, one, for instance, showing a technical, engineering bias, one a musical and another a scientific. The question is complicated because it is connected with the whole problem of vocational training, which must be discussed later; a few points concerning such organization, however, may be noticed here. First the argument that it is cheaper to have specialized schools, since extensive equipment for all sides of teaching is not necessary for all of them, should not be given undue weight. It is to be hoped that the saving of money will not be considered an end in itself by socialist educational officials. The most considerable argument for such specialization is that it facilitates the adoption of various schools by parallel productive, cultural or scientific organizations, and factories. It is a desirable educational principle, as I hope to emphasize later, that there should be a friendly and practical relation between the schools and other organizations of a town. Thus it is obviously simpler to achieve a working relation between a factory for machine-goods or a musical society and a school, if that school has a definite leaning to music or engineering. The main argument against such specialization is that it may put undue pressure on a child to adopt a specialized course that is not really suited to him, as, even if he can change schools at the secondary stage, the fatigue and expense of a journey, possibly across a large town, will discourage initiative in choice. Even though choice of change is made such fatigue is bad in itself, a practically useless waste of energy.

These are the schools of the future, day-schools giving free education to all the children of the district, planned within themselves to meet the needs of the children at all ages, with due regard to the psychological aspect of change from one stage to another; planned also in groups and districts according to the needs of the population and its occupations. The machinery of government of this great body of schools I will deal with in considering whether the present governing organizations can be brought over to control these new institutions. Two points only want emphasis here in this very generalized picture of the socialist schools. First, they must be really free; even if all children automatically receive secondary education, and the entrance test for the secondary stage becomes obsolete, it is still dangerous to allow anyone to pay fees. The socialist state presupposes equality, and if equality of income is not reached by the time these schools are in being, the inequality must be levelled by taxation not by fee-paying, in order that no suspicion of class-difference shall be in the minds of children growing up in a state based on the brotherhood of man. The division between the free and fee-paying child may cast opprobrium on the subsidized scholar, as now in England, or on the fee-payer, an opprobrium similar to that under which the bourgeois lived at first in Soviet Russia. In either case the division breeds nothing but evil, and no retributive hate, no idea 'of making the rich pay' must be allowed to obscure the principle of equality in schools.[1]

The other debatable point in my description of the socialist schools is that they are day-schools. There are many who envisage the schools of the future as com-

---

[1] To quote the Webbs on the Russian educational system again; 'There is, alike in practice and formal regulation, none of the segregation of pupils according to parental rank or profession, wealth or income, which in other countries has so much influence alike on the schools themselves and on the pupils.'—*Soviet Communism*, p. 893.

munities covering the whole of living from day to day, who believe that real commonalty of feeling is impossible until children sleep, eat, and play together, as well as learn, and that therefore these schools must be boarding-schools. The problem and its solution is entirely a matter of speculation, and opinions are frequently put forward with reference to very different stages of the future, with consequent varying degrees of imagination employed. I have said day-schools because I have envisaged this change to a socialist state in the not too distant future, when our social institutions, apart from the machinery of the state and of economic production and distribution, will not be much changed. If the family, as we know it, persists under this new government—and entrenched as it is in the English character I see little possibility of its dissolving for a very long time—then day-schools we shall have to have, so that the child may continue to move in the two circles of home and school; the appeal of the day-school is made stronger by the fact that now the boarding-school is usually a place for the privileged few, the sons and daughters of the rich, and as such will be better abolished. Even so, I personally believe that the community life of these schools will be greatly strengthened if at least one meal is taken in them; this might be free and compulsory, thus allowing the state to have some control over the nourishment of all children. Leisure activities, clubs and societies, and so on, are already rightly regarded by educationalists as valuable additions to day-school life. I should also like to see large holiday-camp schools run in connection with the day-schools, providing a possible use for some of our older boarding-schools when they have become obsolete; camps where the children would live entirely together and apart from their parents for some part of the summer. Finally, my personal provision does not contemplate the perpetual persistance of the family as an economic group of such rigid bonds as now exist. I look forward to the family relation being fairly close in the earlier years of childhood, though even that does not preclude the school's having the major part of the child's time under its care at the nursery-school stage. After the early years, the family, it seems to me, must stand or fall with its success in creating a friendship to supersede the earlier more physical affection, and I would wish to see that friendship tested for its reality by allowing the child from the age of twelve, or earlier if he desires, to live in a different community with a totally different way of life from his parents. That, after all, is only what the 'sons and daughters of gentlemen' are doing to-day, and the system of new school communities need not destroy all contact with the family, any more than do the contemporary boarding-schools. Holidays, or change as I hope they will come to be known, will exist then as now. Consequently the school of the more distant future, if my supposition be correct, will have to be something rather different from the normal contemporary day-school, so far referred to. It will have to be a community, covering the daily life of the children in all aspects, and one where it will be possible to learn much not by mere study, but by the process of making the community function by the simple means of just living. Meanwhile I do not wish to increase the fears of those who regard the socialist state as intent on the destruction of all sacred social institutions from marriage to Christian burial, and though I wish to see a different attitude to the family arise, I am convinced that should we initiate the socialist state in the near future, then Englishmen will continue to live in their self-contained dwellings, cabbage patch attached, with their wives and families around them; and in that case the socialist state must provide day-schools for the education of their children.

As far as university education is concerned, it is not necessary to provide that for all, for all do not need it; it is only necessary to provide it free for all who do. The big cities of this country already have their universities which work in close collaboration with the schools; the same process must continue to provide university institutions for the smaller towns and rural districts; Oxford and Cambridge are obvious special cases marked out for other treatment. The number of universities required will have to be determined by experience and the prevailing educational thought. At present academic education is a possible means of escape from manual labour and its accompanying social inferiority; there should be a new attitude to the desirability of university work when the idea of the value of labour has been reorientated. It may not be found necessary to provide academic training for as many as would now accept it if the opportunity were forthcoming. When the application of socialism has relieved the producer of the necessity of looking for cheap labour, the system of apprenticeship may again take on a valuable educational function, and part-time work in factories, shops, theatres, and in trade will be a possibility even before the leaving age of eighteen.[1] In this

[1] Most educationalists now recognize the cultural value of practical and manual labour. 'There is evidence to show that the average human mind does not educate itself generally before proceeding to special subjects, but the teacher can often bring to bear more readily general educative influences from a specialized interest, because it is only then that the child's will and attention are fully aroused. For this reason and on educational grounds

way the university may grow into an organization for placing apprentices and watching over their careers, and this practical side of its work may be as important as, if not more so than, the academic. I visualize the future university working in close collaboration with, if not actually approximating to, the local educational planning department, dealing with a vast variety of educational efforts, apprenticeship, technical and academic training, adult education, evening lectures and classes, musical, theatrical, and literary societies, in fact, becoming the hub round which turns every cultural movement and function of the town outside the regular schools. The local education board should also attempt to connect closely the work of the universities with that of the public libraries and museums, and, when the state comes to control them, the films and theatres of the town. It will probably be found advisable to pay maintenance grants to all students of whatever calibre. This will give them complete independence from their families, and freedom from financial worry when they are studying. Again, there must be no suggestion of pauperism in these payments, but they must be given as wages to workers, who will make an ultimate if not immediate return to the state in the increased value of their labour. The argument that such a system would invite a large number of spongers to waste public money is one which will trouble only the capitalist mentality, like the argument that the dole should be withdrawn because a few people will try to swindle the government of a paltry sum. I have hopes

alone, the more practical type of course would seem to be that best adapted to the needs of at least a large proportion of children.'
Technical Education, Barbara Drake and Tobias Weaver, N.F.R.B., pp. 17–18.

that society will induce the belief that work may be a possible pleasure and certainly not a very onerous duty, so that the desire to 'slack' will not be a very serious problem; and a government which trusts its citizens to make good use of public money will have to educate them to receive trust, using methods very different from those in force to-day, which threaten, coax, plead, demand work from a child, but all too seldom allow him to work because he likes it.

The labours of the Board of Education and its subsidiary bodies will have to be immensely expanded to deal with this mass of state enterprise. The activities of the Board do not, however, cover the whole field of education to-day; certain special institutions I will deal with in the next section, but there will be obviously a hang-over into the socialist state of many private and semi-private schools now providing education in various degrees of efficiency. It is absolutely necessary for the state to be in complete control of education; it is the ideal method of correlation if the central control is not abused in the interests of official rigidity and red tape; if the backbone of capitalist mentality is to be broken once and for all, it is essential that the socialist state assume immediate potential control of all schools. The extension of state powers may remain merely potential for some time in the stages of transition, much as the nationalization of the land is a measure designed as a safeguard and does not mean the immediate expropriation of all landowners. In practice such control means the planned working and unification of all education, and extension of control will, of course, be more marked in secondary schools where private enterprise now has a large interest. This extended control means more efficient planning, so that no institutions will retain the rights of privilege, and all advantages existing may be fairly and equally distributed. Thus, as it is unwise to allow any parents to pay fees in state schools, so also it will be impossible to destroy inequality in education if special schools for fee-payers are allowed to persist, schools to which parents with money may send their children if they do not wish them to use state schools. The atmosphere of privilege and snobbery would condense round such schools even more so than it does round the public schools to-day, as they would come to be regarded as the last ditch of decency and breeding grounds of all the virtues of the *ancien régime*. The mentality of capitalism must be destroyed along with the economic capitalist system, and no educational organization that allows leakages away from the principle of equality will ever achieve this. Inspection will have to be efficient and sympathetic; all schools will be compulsorily inspected not only sanatorially but educationally, the mental environment of children being as capable of defect as the drains. A new attitude to inspection is necessary, and the announced visit of the inspector should not be the signal for a general clean-up and nervous strain. To-day the state is regarded as an intruder, even in state schools, to be watched with suspicious hostility until it removes its immediate attention from the school, an attitude not without justification towards a Board of Education that has evolved the present mixture of red tape and economy. The future inspector must be one who not merely sees that the school is up to standard, but also collects the requisite knowledge of the school and its problems and advantages, which is necessary for effective planning at the centre, a knowledge that he cannot attain if he never sees the school as it really is. The inspector should aim at being regarded as a means of correlation between various institutions, one from which the central board can profit, and also the officials of the school who wish to have at their disposal expert knowledge and the results of other people's experience as well as their own, for the benefit of the children.

I am well aware that most of the ideas in the foregoing paragraph will be anathema to a great many people, who regard state control as in itself bad, deadening to enterprise, and the personal element in education, reducing all that is spontaneous and vital in the profession to a mass of absurd secretarial detail, and finally fatal to all experiment, thus producing a monotony of method and organization. I am also well aware that there is much to be said for this attitude; it seems to me unnecessary and mistaken for the French to congratulate themselves that an official at headquarters can know exactly what any class in any state school in France is doing at any particular time, the exact place in the syllabus it has reached at any stage in the year. On the other hand, there are enormous advantages in planning and state control and many of the disadvantages could be avoided with intelligence: At the moment the laxity of our control allows a large number of very inefficient institutions to exist; for every valuable experimental school that thus comes into being, there are a host of second-rate preparatory schools, establishments kept in old houses by old ladies, cheap private academies: in short, all the riff-raff of private education, run on lines that appal the trained educationalist and with disastrous results for the children. If due provision is made, as it can and should be made, for experiment within the state system, further control will cut out a great mass of inefficiency and ignorance, which, where the lives of children are concerned, are as unforgivable as more positive harm.

It is scarcely to be wondered at that for many people, and especially for many teachers, state educational control has become synonymous with petty regulations and arid officialdom, and it is perfectly true that to-day the teacher and the school secretary waste a good deal of time in filling in forms in order to conform to the regulations of the Board of Education. I am arguing for a state control that goes far beyond the present one, and one that is embued with a different spirit, one that is not so much concerned with catching out offenders against its minutest order, but one that attempts to combine the maximum efficiency consequent on constructive planning with real educational ideals, a combination that I maintain can only be secured through such central control. The state can erect new institutions where a greater choice of educational avenues is desirable, where no private body would find it profitable to build. It can insist on the highest standard of building, and of qualification among its teachers; what is more, it can itself provide the means to that qualification, turning out roughly the right number of teachers for the various stages of education. Here, again, I do not mean that they will be turned out like sausages from a machine, strung to order, but that the knowledge of requirements that will be possible under state control will greatly regulate the supply. People will not willingly choose a profession that is full, whereas to-day many choose it hoping to do the other man down when it comes to the fight. But the day of saturation, after the full educational requirements of this country have been realized, is far off. The general advantage of planning in education is that which the socialist claims for all state enterprise.

It must be emphasized that such control will be socialist, not in the political sense of detailed scrutiny in which Hitler supervises the German school text-books, but in the sense that the commercial side to education as it exists to-day must disappear. There should be no need to set up some inefficient little dame-school to eke out a miserable income; no need to cut down expenses so that the fees may be lowered to snatch pupils from a wealthier rival; no need to wait to meet the requirements of a district until some private individual sets on foot the enterprise. Education will not have to pay; it will be able to concentrate on educating. Without private competition or commercialization it will be possible to provide the best or the worst. The socialist state will have failed unless it can produce the ideals that automatically provide the best. It may be a happy thought to those who view human nature without much charity, that under such a system the educationalist will get what he makes. If he can turn out citizens worthy to live in a state founded on justice, equality, and freedom, the educational system under which he works will be capable of providing him with excellent machinery and material; if he does not and ideals fall short of the best, then the machinery will be corrupted and take toll of his initiative, turning him into a mere machine-cog in a soulless workshop.

This, then, is the machinery, a central board controlling a network of local and district boards which are in immediate contact with all local educational and cultural ventures. Plans for improvement and regulation must be devised centrally and revised locally. To avoid stagnation and dry officialdom this machine must be worked by education officials and teachers together with inspectors forming links between the two. Teachers should be well represented on all local boards and thus could keep the details and revision of plans in contact with the realities of education as no other body of people can do. Local and national conferences of teachers and psychologists should be held regularly on general educational principles, and on every conceivable problem bearing on their subject. These conferences should be regarded by the central board as indications of what specialist opinion requires of them, not as the wailings of a collection of monomaniacs, and they should make it their business to provide for these requests in their plans. Besides this, of course, the teachers' trade union (will it grow out of the N.U.T.?) must be fully represented wherever wages and hours of work are being discussed. It would be an excellent thing if it were possible to co-opt the counsels of parents at conferences and deliberations, and why not that of the children themselves? No one knows more about education than the child enduring or enjoying it; nor can anyone make more pungent if unconscious criticisms of the present system, and where it is the aim of an educational system to keep sweet a rigidly controlled machine by constant contact with broad principle and unofficial opinion, no influence could be more refreshing than that of the children. One day possibly we shall not think it funny to suggest that the President of the Board of Education should meet the representatives of the children's educational union, and I can imagine no better way of infusing a sense of reality into the life of a school. A school committee would feel itself to be of importance if it were recognized by officials and administrators as being something more than a mere adults' device for keeping children quiet. But much false dignity will have to be shed ere that happens.

CHAPTER SEVEN

SOCIALIST TREATMENT OF SPECIAL EDUCATIONAL INSTITUTIONS

IT is sometimes necessary to destroy much in order to build afresh, and there is much in our present educational system, from bad buildings to worn-out psychology, that will have to go by the board, before a really socialist education is possible. Nevertheless, some of our present machinery is fitted for use in the new system, and can be converted for general educational purposes or to meet certain special circumstances. In this chapter I want to mention certain of these institutions that can be thus manipulated, before I come on to the real crux of the matter, the discussion of what kind of education is to be provided through this machinery, what, in fact, is to be poured into the mould.

In the present state of affairs a great deal of the initiative in educational expansion comes from the local authorities; in fact, it may be said that the majority of progressive tendencies in state schools in recent years have been due to the interest of local authorities in education, an interest not encouraged by the retrogressive and miserly policy of the National Government.[1] It would be an ill reward for much

[1] The central government still defers all detailed initiative to the local authorities, as can be seen from any government circular. Thus, as an instance, we find in Circular 1444: 'The extent to which they (the local authorities) will avail themselves of this discretion is a matter which those responsible will no doubt wish to consider without delay, and the Board would be glad to be informed in due course of the action which they may decide to take.'

patient effort, and a waste of much valuable knowledge and experience, to sweep away the jurisdiction of these authorities to make room for entirely new local boards; for local boards there will have to be. Just as in planning the whole economy of their nation, its industry, finance, and agriculture, the Russians have found it necessary to have a pyramid of boards and authorities, collecting material and advising the central Gosplan, so almost certainly we shall have to devise some such organization to achieve unification and at the same time to make full use of expert local knowledge. The local authorities seem destined to take on such a position and to merge into the future Local Planning Boards with the Education Committee as its educational section. I may repeat here, by the way, that I am contemplating the transition to socialism being sufficiently calm to preserve the governmental and social systems existing to-day; if they are destroyed in the process, then, of course, new machinery must be built. The local committee will thus be in touch with the local plan for the whole district, and also under the direct central control of headquarters. For it is obvious that a town's educational planning, to be efficient, must have some reference to sanitation, transport, and other correlated departments of local government; whereas now a local authority may put up a school far removed from drainage systems and transport, owing to lack of real understanding between the various committees of the council. The educational section of the local government will also be in direct contact with the centre, not merely through the county or town council, so that the general plan is not too much interrupted by considerations not immediately connected with education. I have already indicated that that local board must include teachers among its numbers. It must not be constituted as so frequently happens to-day, of a number of vaguely philanthropic persons, entirely ignorant of educational principle and practice, with a sprinkling of clergy to safeguard their own interests. It must be a body representing expert knowledge and varied interests, with some understanding of what education is, and how to provide it. Intermediate councils for larger districts may have to be set up, but the county councils of London and the great industrial cities are already coordinating a sufficiently wide field for a single unit.

It is possible that new machinery will have to be invented to deal with rural education, for the problem of planning over an area of scattered villages, in order to provide the country child with the chief advantages of town education, is a new one and will very probably be outside the ken of the normal rural council. A new departure must be made in rural education, for some of the contemporary village schools, where one teacher deals with a dozen or so children of different ages, are among the worst in our educational system. The advantages of good equipment, specialized teaching, and adequate buildings are dependent on numbers, and community life. This seems to be a very strong argument for the type of boarding-school in the country which I have suggested for the pattern for all schools in the more distant future. To continue the day-school as it is at the moment in rural areas, and to have compulsory education until eighteen years under such conditions is to reduce the idea of free secondary education to an absurdity; the young man or woman of eighteen would gain nothing from such schools unless the staff far outnumbered the pupils. A country school might become a pioneer in the idea of children's communities, by force of circumstances made to gather together all the children of a thinly-populated district and to organize their lives apart from that of their families. The form of education in these schools is bound up with the environment, and the future of the rural school depends on that of agriculture. Supposing that agriculture persists in England as a profitable concern, and is even much improved by the application of the results of scientific research, there will be an obvious need for the type of country school that will not tempt the whole of the countryside's children to the towns by a smattering of that type of academic learning that has always been connected with the black-coated professions; yet the principle of equality demands that the children in the country shall have the same educational advantages as those of the towns. The solution seems to lie in a certain type of progressive school, known as the farm school; the educationalists responsible for these schools have decided that proximity to country life and the more elemental conceptions of birth, and life, and time, blurred for most children by the sophistication of town life, are a valuable influence in themselves, besides providing opportunities for light manual labour which is considered a useful balance to academic study, alternative to the more usual round of competitive games. The country school could graft onto these educational ideas the practical utility of training farmers, and easily become a self-contained community, approximating more to a village or large farm, than to a town school. School life could also be arranged so that the summer holidays were long and the children could come into contact with farm work in their own homes at a time when light work could be given them. If children were collected into such a village school to form a com-

TREATMENT OF SPECIAL INSTITUTIONS

munity of some hundreds, the numbers would enable the provision of opportunity for a child with a particular bent outside his rural environment, to develop his abilities and be drafted for university study to urban institutions. Other children would not be more influenced towards rural work, than they are already conditioned to it by the fact of their birth-place; and such work would gain enormously in intellectual and emotional value by being treated as worthy of educational consideration. It seems to me that development on some such lines is the only way of ensuring the advantages of large-school life to the country child, without too violently uprooting him from his accustomed surroundings. Such a development would probably be beyond the imagination of the present rural councils and their education committees, though they might find a place in the organization under new district planning boards, with a special rural department at headquarters.

But in whatever way the present local education authorities are incorporated into the pyramid of new planning boards, the control of the centre must be constructive and not merely permissive, as so much of the central authority is to-day. Headquarters must provide the main initiative, for there is no sense in planning unless it is done over the largest possible area from an authority that controls the whole of it. Policy must be directed centrally as it is now, and presumably such policy under a socialist government will be constructive and progressive and will use its subordinate boards as experts on local matters to criticize the parts of the general plan, and to control its immediate administration, but will not expect them to be the first to put forward concrete proposals. To-day even when after four years of inactivity the central government determines on an expansive policy, the initiative for producing the plan is still left to the local authorities; the Board will be glad to hear of expansion schemes but never commands them.

Socialist educationalists as well as anyone else who has anything to do with the matter will sooner or later come up against the religious problem. This thorny question is the price the state has had to pay for refusing to take on its educational responsibilities earlier than it did, and allowing elementary education to grow directly out of the church's missionary zeal. The churches, and no one can blame them, are not willing to let go their hold. The only way to face this problem is with courage; if the socialist shows common sense and justice, some will scream that he is destroying religion and all things sacred, but most people will approve his action; if he dithers and attempts a compromise, his whole scheme for equality in education will be wrecked and no one will ultimately respect him. Even the churches cannot seriously desire to stand in the way of educational improvement, unless they wish to suffer the fate of the Russian Church, which is undergoing a lasting and possibly eternal penance for its unholy alliance with the reactionary forces of Tsardom and ignorance. As the relation of the church and state stands at the moment it works as though the church were an obstruction to educational progress, though that is far from the general clerical intention; in their effort to retain their power over their schools, the churches have made special bargains with the state, but as the latter has gradually made up for its first educational indifference by building new schools, it has become increasingly obvious that the church cannot compete with the state financially, so that its schools on an average show a low level of equipment and qualification. There is no way out of this position except by the secularization of all education, a measure that will incur bitter opposition, but one that must be attempted, if all children are to have the best that can be given them. The principle behind this measure is that in a free, democratic, socialist country, all men must automatically have religious freedom; such an axiom can stand against all fears that socialism is the enemy of religion. But the state has other duties besides ensuring religious freedom; one of its prime duties is to see that every child in the country has the best education that it can provide, and to carry out that duty it must have absolute control of all schools and can allow no society to build its own institutions however financially sound, as the children in those schools may one day have to pay the price of declining revenues, in ill-kept buildings, underpaid staffs and poor equipment. All honour to the church for its pioneer work in education, but it can serve its own cause better, as well as that of the children, by resigning its direct influence in the schools.

The state has got to have the positive courage to prevent anyone else carrying out its own duties. Parents must rely on the home influence and any out-of-school training they may desire, to inculcate their pet dogmas in their children. It would be approaching dictatorship at this stage of educational development, to deny them that right. It may be objected that the reason why the churches require the control of children's lives, is the fact that so much clerical training depends for its effectiveness more on isolation from other influences than the teaching of any particular philosophy. This seems to me a condemnation of such a dogma, which to be healthy and vigorous must be capable of standing intelligent criticism. Anybody, who really believes in the value of the Christian Church, cannot wish to see it preserved by hot-house methods, and it is only a matter of tradition that the state subsidizes one particular form of Christianity or, indeed, any particular religion. I also believe that the rights over persons that must exist in any community are being gradually deflected from the family to the state, that this has been the process for some time past and is unavoidable if progression is to be possible on familiar lines. In this connection we have to ask ourselves which is more important, the child's right or freedom to receive a good education, or the parents' right to use the child as their property. The state now decides that the child must receive education and must not be maltreated or starved; the parents have no freedom to decide on these issues. It is only a logical step in the same direction for the state to decide that the child must go to a secular school, leaving the parent free to bring to bear what other influences he thinks fit. Again, it seems a suitable test, to have such parental rights removed, for the fundamental personal bond of the family. From the child's point of view this is an advantage, for the state can decide its educational policy after examination of every known opinion and with expert advice; parents may know absolutely nothing of either the theory or practice of education. With those who do not approve of the scientific approach to all problems, and who consider the issue of eternal life and damnation to hang on the acceptance on earth of certain beliefs, there can be no argument about the matter; the majority will decide and they will disregard its decision as far as lies in their power.

The socialist government must take the same attitude to the teaching of religion in schools:[1] to my mind again complete secularization is the only solution. Comparative religions may be taught with profit, reviewing the teachings of the great religions of the world, but all state schools have now some form of Christianity in their ceremonies, and there is just as much justification for the agnostic's withdrawing his children from school prayers as for the Roman Catholic's doing so to-day. There can be no real freedom to choose, only the possibility of reacting against, the Christian religion while school prayers and school chapels are adjuncts of Christian teaching. Assemblies for public readings, songs, and ceremonies in suitable buildings, may be necessary as training for the emotions, and many progressive schools not professing Christianity have such practices. But the state cannot offer the nearest approach to freedom of thought that is possible until it has removed such a bias from its school communities. Nor need religion necessarily suffer a decline; a faith is healthiest and most vital when it receives acute criticism and has to hold its own against all comers, rather than when it is coddled in a false isolation, and fostered in children by infinite small suggestions and influences.

Besides a host of private schools for which nothing but extinction is desirable, and the semi-state church schools which must be secularized, the chief educational

[1] Mark Starr, in *Lies and Hate in Education*, emphasizes the still existing control of the church over the schools, especially in the country where the school is sometimes as much in the pocket of the church as the living used to be in that of the squire. 'In many local Church schools the teacher is expected to act as unpaid curate and organist and the vicar sways the rural managers' (p. 21).

institutions outside direct government control are the public schools with their university corollary, Oxford and Cambridge, and the group of schools known as progressive, best represented in the *Modern Schools Handbook*. All of these cannot be literally destroyed without serious loss, if not always of good education, then of material in endowments, buildings, and grounds. I have already harangued against the public schools, trying to show them as the chief breeding ground of capitalist mentality, but I shall reinforce that opinion here, before going on to outline a treatment that may seem harsh for our most honoured and cherished educational institutions. First, their influence goes far beyond their own pupils, setting its mark on the internal management and curriculum of many state schools. Mr. Harold Stovin, in an interesting review of modern youth movements called *Totem*, claims that these organizations, the Scouts, the Buchmanite groups, Toc H, and others, are attempting to give to the children who leave school at fourteen certain of the emotional characteristics that belong to the public schoolboy. After a quotation from the Chief Scout, Mr. Stovin remarks: 'This, of course, is curiously akin to the familiar bombast prevalent in the Public Schools. But its appeal is inspired by the cult of Fitness, and the Scout Movement and the N.A.B.C. are, from one aspect, the diffusion of the Public School ideal of the Empire Builder among the less wealthy sections of the population.'[1] Secondly, the ideas and prejudices thus diffused are those of an imperialist ruling class, uncritical and often unintelligent, and are characteristic of a type which, though certain individuals may be clever and charming, is anathema to a classless equable society, and one dangerously out

[1] *Totem*, by Harold Stovin, 1935, Chap. 4, p. 105.

of touch with modern life. As Mr. Chaning-Pearce says in his book *Chiron*: 'England to-day is full of men chiselled by the public schools into a governing type who have nothing to govern.'[1] The only excuse for educating a ruling class is that they should rule and rulers without subjects are extremely dangerous to a political democracy.

Any clear-thinking person who cherishes an affection for the public schools should read an uncritical apologist for this type of education, Mr. Bernard Darwin, in his book on *The English Public School* in the English Heritage series, introduced by Stanley Baldwin. In what purports to be a serious study of this type of school, he mentions neither sex nor the O.T.C., two subjects that are the central points of all debate on this question. Nevertheless, I know of no better revelation of the public-school mentality. 'When trying to think on this subject,' says Mr. Darwin with touching but necessary humility, 'I asked one whose opinion I valued, what he deemed the essential quality produced by these schools. He answered that it was a readiness to be an officer' (p. 22). He congratulates these schools on the stupidity they generate:[2] 'It seems to me that when we stick up for public schools in a good stolid conservative

---

[1] *Chiron. The Education of a Citizen of the World*, by Chaning-Pearce, 1931, p. 61.

[2] The lengths to which the complacency and insularity of the public-school mind can be carried are sometimes almost beyond belief. The following quotation won a richly deserved prize in the *This England* column of the *New Statesman and Nation*, November 28, 1936: 'In England they had learned long ago that they must work as a team and sink their personal interests for the good of the community. The first public school man had been born in Nazareth, and his name was Jesus Christ; the second was his disciple, St. Paul.'—The Bishop of Portsmouth reported in *The Isle of Wight Chronicle*.

way, we are not so much sticking up for a particular English institution, but rather for the genius and the stupidity of the whole English people' (p. 29). And here is a remarkable example of the type of psychological truth by which the public-school master is apparently guided. 'I remember a much-adored fellow of my college saying to me as an undergraduate, "When you are fifteen years older you ought to be a different sort of person than you are now." These words that have stuck in my memory a good deal longer than fifteen years, seem to convey something of what a good housemaster can do for and suggest to his boys' (p. 98). My own feeling is that if this blinding glimpse of the obvious is all that a public-school housemaster can suggest to his boys, the sooner he resigns his job the better. Schools that foster class-division are impregnated with military discipline, make little attempt to develop a scientific or self-critical state of mind, and, in fact, have little respect for intellectual attainment and practically no psychological knowledge, have no place in a socialist state. Mr. Chaning-Pearce is balanced and penetrating in his criticism of these schools and makes a point that will have even a greater truth under socialism. He praises the public-school man for being an exemplary citizen in some circumstances: 'He is far from being a fool or a failure' (p. 19, op. cit.). But with regard to the public-school system of education, which, with the poetic justice that will appeal to the socialist, he calls 'this triumph of British mechanization', he maintains, quite rightly, that 'the question is not whether the process as a process is good or bad, but whether there is a market for what it produces' (p. 28). Obviously under a social system that has no use for capitalism, there is no market for the empire-builder and the

TREATMENT OF SPECIAL INSTITUTIONS

officer, in Mr. Darwin's sense of the word. In fact, the persistence of socialism depends on the irradication of such capitalist mentality. What then is to be done with the buildings, the endowments, and the property of the public schools? What is the socialist state to say to the Headmasters' Conference? It is a situation with a certain humorous charm.

In the first place, these schools will come automatically under the control of the central board as soon as the state takes on its new responsibilities. Nevertheless, it seems absurd to allow these schools to come under the normal planning system, though the idea of the respective local authorities administrating Eton and Harrow has a certain appeal. These schools call for special treatment owing to their traditions and endowments, and cannot necessarily be absorbed into the administrative network of normal secondary education. Being boarding-schools they have no relation to the surrounding population. It will probably be advisable to set up a separate central department to carry through the liquidation of the public schools, for liquidated they must be as they function now; one class of society must not be allowed to segregate its sons from the normal type of education whatever it may be. The department will be solely responsible for all financial matters in connection with these schools and will also have control over the selection of staff and pupils. A number of headmasters will probably resign in disgust, an event all to the good as they can then be replaced by men outside the public-school tradition. These schools will then be free to begin anew, and the special central department can set up committees to select applicants for admission as staff or as pupils, with a judicious eye to removing class distinction. The existing teaching staff, if old, can be pensioned early unless they show strong desires to continue their services. The young can be reminded, with pecuniary arguments drawn from the Burnham scale, that the socialist state expects its teachers to be trained, and that the sooner they acquire some knowledge of psychology and modern educational methods the better. Exemption from such training might be granted in individual cases, where experience seemed to have provided an adequate substitute, but judging from the results in the normal public-school boy, most of these masters, in the practice of their profession, never acquire anything but contempt for psychology and new teaching methods. By the introduction of teachers from outside the public-school tradition, its isolation will be broken, which at the moment engenders so much false sentiment around the old school. Far too many public-school masters go back to teach at the school that knew them as pupils, after their university years; such inbreeding is responsible for much of the easy acceptance of, and even pride in, the worst aspects of these schools, which so astonishes the outsider without the same tribal instincts.

The whole-hearted hater of the public school, the man who shudders at the mention of Thomas Arnold, will enquire why the socialist state should bother to replace one tradition by another, and will have fears, not without foundation, that it will only scotch the snake. Why not shut the doors of Marlborough and Wellington, Eton and Harrow on all boys forthwith, and let them be turned into rest-homes for tired teachers or nerve-racked busmen, or anyone else you choose? To me it seems a pity that, where money has been used for centuries for specifically educational purposes, it should not continue to form a special fund for special educational

TREATMENT OF SPECIAL INSTITUTIONS

needs. Some public schools are near enough to towns and thickly populated areas to become absorbed in the general plan, after such changes in their administration as I have mentioned; their endowments will automatically be pooled in the educational budget for that area. With the remaining schools, the selection committees might do their work after some time with a special object in view; if, for instance, in the more distant future, we are going to replace day-schools by school-boarding communities, some of the old public schools would provide excellent opportunities for experiment in this direction. Such parents who from principle considered it more desirable for their children to go away to school, could explain their preference to the selection committee, who from these children could form the nucleus of the new type of community. It might also be advisable to allow about half a dozen of these schools to become altogether depopulated, so that they would provide pleasant and suitable accommodation for holiday camps, teachers' conferences, and parents' meeting-places. Then, of course, there are children whose parents are abroad, or who have no parents, all of whom could be most conveniently accommodated in these communities. Nor need much sympathy be expended on such children, as it is now on children who have no homes to escape into, from the grind and boredom of their school life; if these schools are properly run on self-governing lines, they should be able to replace the home. The state in due course will take over all charitable institutions for homeless children, for it is a disgrace that a child without parents should have to depend on charity for its pleasures and even for its existence. Surely the new type of school community would be preferable to the best-intentioned children's home as it exists now, just because the latter depends on the whims of its patrons. In fact, orphans will find themselves in the same position as many children who wish to live their lives independent of their parents and immediate home circles. If we find these new foundlings' homes established in buildings which once housed superior public schools, we need not consider it a great indignity but merely a pleasing symbol of social justice. But such developments belong to the more distant future; the immediate necessity is to break the public-school tradition, which can only be done by state control making deliberate and far-reaching changes in the staff and pupils of these schools. As these schools are already obsolete in spirit, belonging in outlook more to a feudal society than to a political democracy, it should not be found that the public-school tradition is very tenacious of life. A breath of common sense should be sufficient to blow away this flimsy structure, now kept standing by the protecting walls of isolation.

The parallel to the public schools in the university world is provided by Oxford and Cambridge. These universities are of course changing fairly quickly, at least, in the type of students that compose them; just as the public schools, though more slowly, have opened their doors to various new types. These universities have naturally far greater freedom in their rules and methods of study, and owing to this atmosphere, they provide opportunities for the expression of very various ideas, far more various than anything that emerges from the public schools. Oxford, for instance, can have its Labour Club, even though the October Club be suppressed, and the authorities sleep in safety. Nevertheless, these universities have the taint of class privilege and they obviously cannot remain as they are in a social system that purports to give equal opportunity in education to all its citizens. Besides, these universities have traditions that date back far beyond those of the public-school mentality, grafted on to them in the nineteenth century, traditions that may well be worth preserving. Nor is it possible for the state to provide copies of this type of educational institution elsewhere, for while the socialist state can provide many good things that are new, it cannot mass-produce mediaeval colleges, nor traditions dating from Alfred. The universities might be made free and entrance strictly competitive, with no exterior circumstances such as the father's former residence in college, to be considered; but that would probably make competition so intense that university tutors would rapidly degenerate into mere examination boards. It is as well to inquire what exactly is the function of a university and how best Oxford and Cambridge can fulfil that function, while at the same time shaking off those class privileges and conservative constitutions that now obscure their real worth.

A university, as understood by most educationalists, not only provides a post-school training in academic and even in practical subjects, but is also a home of learning; it is engaged, not merely in handing on to the young what is already known, but in increasing the general body of knowledge; it is a place where the solitary worker in his laboratory or library has as vital a part to play as the student. In short, research is as much part of the university's business as instruction. The rival claims of research and instruction in universities have been debated by educationalists quite apart from the political considerations involved. In the new universities in the towns, the problem will not be so acute, as they will have little tradition of learning to maintain. Their activities will be mainly concerned with providing all kinds of training for all kinds of careers; they will also, if successful, diffuse a general atmosphere of interest in artistic and intellectual achievement, correlating the many aesthetic and scientific ventures of the townsfolk. It is unnecessary for every university to be equipped with a large research department; such scholars' work can be centralized elsewhere. More immediate practical research work can be closely connected with factory and farm, and departments for such research should be on the premises of the correlated enterprise.[1]

There is a type of opinion that reacts against the present ascendancy of so-called research; it has, in fact, become something of a joke in America. Thus Mr. Alderton Pink in *Procrustes* says: 'The intellectual and moral malady of this present age has infected our seats

[1] The authors of the N.F.R.B. pamphlet on *Technical Education* disagree on this point, and in advocating the building and equipment of higher technical colleges say: 'It is probable that the processes of the future will be found in independent research and teaching institutions rather than in the research departments of private firms, or even of public undertakings, where commercial gain or immediate financial considerations, consciously or unconsciously, restrict the freedom of enquiry' (p. 33). They quite rightly condemn the present academic exclusiveness of the older universities and suggest that 'the result is that Denmark, Germany, Holland, Sweden, Switzerland, and the U.S.S.R. can all show higher technical colleges better than, or at least as good as, the best in this country. British industry to-day is, on the whole, behind American and German industry in contribution to discovery and invention and, in proportion to resources, is behind many other countries' (p. 32). The authors are, I believe, thinking in terms of a capitalist environment for industry, but under socialism, though there will be a place for higher technical colleges, I consider that departments for research in factories will ensure a close relation to the practical necessities of industry, without necessarily being cramped by false economy.

of learning so that they appear to be abandoning the ideal of a liberal education and to be substituting the narrow aim of the acquisition of specialized knowledge. The modern university must be a centre of research; the danger is that it will neglect to be also a centre of education.'[1] He speaks also with scorn of the type of scholarship all too common in the universities: 'Criticism and enjoyment of the great masters have to give place to the study of tendencies and influences, of historical minutiae and bibliographical irrelevancies' (p. 89). Anyone who has endured reading for an Arts degree at a university will see the truth of this criticism. This regrettable mixture of cram and academic aloofness appears to me to be the result of attempting to do too many things at once and of combining too closely the worlds of the scholar and the educationalist; and for once I would make a plea for separation, though not for isolation, as against the present ineffective attempt at merging, not merely correlating, two different things. I believe that the liberal education should be preserved, that training for the emotions and aesthetic senses should be provided, and consequently that the general direction of cultural life will be as important a function of the new university as the training of its students for particular careers. I also think it of value that these two things, vocational training and humane education, should remain mixed, for the vitality of one conduces to the health of the other. What has happened to our present universities is that the academic training has become endowed with a false glamour of class privilege, which has resulted in a cheapening of that academic training itself, so that from real scholarship

[1] *Procrustes. The Future of Education*, by Alderton Pink. To-day and To-morrow Series, p. 77.

it has become crammed and potted knowledge, easily acquired by the social climber and used as a symbol of superiority. This commercialized conception of academic learning as a short cut to a larger income and social status, with its necessary corollary of examination labels, has almost swamped real scholarship in the resultant scramble for jobs. Delisle Burns in *Democracy* makes much this same point: 'Universities are not institutions for training in all forms of service; the most dangerous effect of a false conception of democratic equality in education, is the "levelling down" which takes place when great numbers attempt to use instruments which they are incompetent to use with advantage' (p. 181). There are very few real scholars, though a great number of people who can profit from a university training and a liberal education; these a new university can supply, and no student need, if that university is satisfactory, consider he has missed the best to be had, if his degree does not come from Oxford or Cambridge.

It seems an excellent opportunity for the preservation of real scholarship to turn our more ancient universities into large research departments. Such a departure would solve many problems; there would be no need for the intensive and objectionable competition that would result from any honest attempt to send the pick of the normal students to these universities with special advantages. It would also allow the scholar to be a scholar without being at the same time a don, for it cannot be too clearly emphasized that these two things are not necessarily the same, and are in fact frequently different; the man who has the gift for scholarship is usually wasting his time in attempting personally to hand on his knowledge to the young, and in expounding year after year the same ideas. Too frequently the don has no general ideas to expound, and year after year plods over his own select patch of detail which he had once made his own by a new departure in research and which is now more readily available in print. Such a man has not necessarily anything to do with education, but he has something to give to the state, and to the socialist state. Socialism cannot ignore learning, and a healthy state always has its scholars, men and women who are willing to devote their lives to details of knowledge, like Browning's *Grammarian*, and though they may remain outside the whole social system of production, on their work ultimately depends what we call civilization. The socialist state must respect learning so that it may be realized that its aim is not mere material comfort, and it is bound on an adventure with more at stake than its bread and butter. Nazi Germany is rightly suspected of barbarism, not merely for its physical cruelties and economic chaos, but for its cultural poverty and intellectual barrenness. Let socialist England never be in the dangers that have sometimes seemed to threaten Soviet Russia, especially when we consider the phases of scorn for the intellectual, the dangers of developing a contempt for things spiritual, dangers which one glance at her films, her earlier architecture,[1] and her scientific research will show she has avoided. What better use is there for Oxford and Cambridge than to let them return to their earlier ideals of scholar-

---

[1] A visit to Russia in 1936 has, I fear, forced me to insert the word 'earlier'. The latest buildings show considerable degeneration in taste. Soviet citizens in this respect suffer from a hang-over of the capitalist mentality, a commercial attitude to things artistic; ornament on buildings is welcomed as a sign of prosperity. Here is proof of the fact that education is ultimately the key to a new society, and that mentality or ideology, as the Russians call it, is not a simple thing to change.

O

ship. In fact, I would decarbonize Oxford from its attempts at correlation with modern industry. Let them exist apart from the more practical aspects of daily life, though related on the level of ideas, for it is the right atmosphere for the scholar; others must apply his work and its results. In a socialist state, new and glistening, let the tradition of mediaeval learning continue a little removed from the sweep and pressure of our time, surveying wider abstractions in the artificial but glamorous atmosphere of antiquity. Some may say that it is unfair to deprive the young of a supremely romantic episode, but scholarship needs that form of romance more than the young, who, if anybody, can find inspiration in the new and unknown. The Bodleian libraries and the science laboratories of Cambridge, for instance, seem worth preserving, but not the barges on the Isis, the bump suppers, or the pub-crawls. The young may turn their attention to other forms of excitement, probably more valuable as they come closer to everyday life, and learning can flourish (or if your temperament prefers the phrase, the don can stew in his own juice) undisturbed by the drunken flippancies of the tribe of young asses.

This does not mean that I wish to debar the scholar from the new university; often he is an educationalist as well, and his presence will prevent these new universities from erring on the other side from their present delinquencies with regard to masses of unchewed detail, and from developing into factories for sentimental vagueness and fatuous generalizations. Exact knowledge and dynamic interest in concrete fact are necessary; Whitehead is probably right when he defines the function of a university as the preservation of the connection between knowledge and the zest for life. 'The university

imparts information, but it imparts it imaginatively....
A fact is no longer a bare fact: it is invested with all its possibilities. It is no longer a burden on the memory: it is energizing as the poet of our dreams, and as the architect of our purposes.'[1] In fact, it is just that zest in the romance of learning and culture that I wish a university to diffuse throughout the whole of its town; it will be the special function of the new university to add that romance to the experience of the mass, instead of allowing it to remain the privilege of the few. In setting apart Oxford and Cambridge which have advantages that cannot be universally applied, I am merely arguing for a haven for the scholar who is not an educationalist, but emphatically not for the divorce of scholarship and education. It will be argued by a certain type of socialist that, by subsidizing the scholar to research, we would be merely giving a dole to pottering fools who have nothing to give to the state in return; such an attitude seems to me crass. A scholar may produce nothing in a lifetime save the knowledge of another form in a Greek word; yet he may not be merely futile, for by his way of life he will have contributed something towards the general atmosphere of learning and discovery, out of which grow the most adventurous new departures in scientific knowledge and artistic appreciation. It might, however, be possible, in order to quiet the clamours of the scoffers, when the hours of manual labour have been very greatly reduced by the application of machinery and planned economy to production and distribution, to insist on the scholar's taking part in such labour to earn his bread; he might possibly keep these universities where he lives clean and in good repair. But in the earlier stages it seems

[1] *The Aims of Education*, A. N. Whitehead, 1929, p. 139.

wise to trust to the value of the scholar to the state, though the individual may produce no discovery of interest.

Besides the scholars, the older universities might be inhabited by a constant stream of visitors, not merely students from the new universities, but adults who wish to spend a holiday away from their usual job, in some form of study. Every opportunity must be given to the casual student, in his home environment and in the universities. At the moment the worker who wishes also to read in a library, finds it difficult to find one open after his working hours.[1] The general standard of learning is as much dependent on this casual study as on the more concentrated labours of the specialist student, and universities must see that libraries and museums are open at convenient hours for this. These students might profitably spend some weeks in Oxford or Cambridge, as there are some people who find their recreation in study. Oxford and Cambridge in their new state as scholars' retreats will be preserved from a segregation that is petrifying, by being thus used as meeting-places for conferences on all manner of subjects and practical problems, and by the constant stream of the semi-scholarly, fresh from contact with the immediate economic structure of society. The opposite process could also be arranged through the network of new universities, whereby the scholar could refresh his brain by visits to the outside world, and in particular to observe the application of his own research to everyday life in factory, theatre, or school.

The socialist state is more likely to be accused of cutting short valuable traditions than of blocking up the

[1] Cf. Letters in the *New Statesman and Nation*, December 28, 1935, and January 6, 1936.

avenues to new fields of experiment Nevertheless, the educationalist is on the whole an intense individualist and rarely realizes the synthesis possible between his individualism and socialism. Consequently there will be many who will object that this system of state-controlled educational institutions that I have outlined, will result in a stereotyped rigid plan for every detail of a school's life, with the inevitable suppression of individual initiative. If such a thing were to happen, any educationalist has every right to regard socialist education as a failure. The next chapter will deal with the theoretical side to this problem, the possibility of individual freedom within the centrally controlled system; here we must consider a last group of special institutions that have to be fitted into the new system, a group that owes everything to individual experiment, viz. the progressive schools. By this term is usually meant a group of schools, privately owned, attempting, in various degrees of moderation, to put into practice modern psychological and educational ideas; such schools as are represented in the *Modern Schools Handbook*. These schools, such as, for instance, Summerhill, St. Christopher's, Letchworth, and Dartington Hall, provide the most hopeful signs of intelligence and understanding in English education to-day, and they exist in reaction to the normal educational methods in vogue in the state and traditional schools. Their contribution to educational experience has a wider influence than over the children with whom they come into contact directly. How is the socialist state to meet the claims of such innovators? How is this valuable educational research, so far entirely due to individual initiative, to be preserved in the network of state-controlled schools?

There are two aspects to the problem; what will be the attitude of these particular experimenters to socialist education, and how can the experimenter be incorporated into state-controlled machinery? In the first place consistency to socialist principle demands that these schools, as well as a mass of bad private schools, should not be allowed to remain private money-making concerns; that is, they should cease to charge fees and the staff must be paid the usual salaries in force by the state. If any person can be allowed to run a school, independently of state finance, on any pretext whatever, snobbish or experimental, the idea of selection and privilege to be bought for money is reintroduced into the educational system, and the way is opened to a host of charlatans more interested in fees than in education, thus jeopardizing the welfare of the children they teach and the general acceptance of socialist mentality. Nor should the owners of the progressive schools object to this in itself, since where they are real educationalists, and the majority are, they are more interested in their experiments than any profit they may obtain thereby. Indeed, they are sometimes at a loss for funds to further some educational project, and often the staff are willing to accept a low standard of pay for the privilege of working under congenial circumstances and in accordance with principles of which they approve. The problem is to ensure that experiment has the same chance of flourishing under this financial control as it has now in these schools. The fears of the extreme individualist that state control means rigidity and immobility are much exaggerated. Socialism from one aspect means experiment within control; what is a plan but an experiment? And the advantage of socialist planning is that it enables the results of any experiment

TREATMENT OF SPECIAL INSTITUTIONS 199

that proves successful to be immediately applied to the maximum number of people. Control that is concerned solely with the preservation of what already exists is fascism, and the control that denies the possibility of change is self-destroying. Socialism, on pain of death, must allow experiment, and must aim not at static inactivity, but at the intelligent control of movement. Therefore the socialist state must find means to reconcile the experimenter to its existence and if possible harness his activities to the state machine. The ideal seems to be a rigid financial control, so that education cannot become commercialized, with the maximum amount of freedom for the individual educationalist in matters of method and curricula. Consequently, except for the fact that no fees would be paid and salaries would come direct from the state, the progressive schools might remain exactly as they are now. If a genuine educationalist feels that he cannot remain within the state system that it is not sufficiently elastic to permit of the expression of his new ideas, that is a condemnation of the system. The selection of children to go to these schools may present a difficulty, as most of them are boarding-schools, without reference to the educational needs of their localities. Application from parents must presumably travel through their local education authorities, though nothing need stand in the way of their choice except the necessary balance of numbers.

The same freedom that will thus be granted to the experimentalists is necessary in the regular state schools, so that the head of the school can exercise his or her own opinion on matters of discipline, curriculum, or organization. The government will probably best ensure the development of that type of education that it requires by allowing such liberty in school management, if it is combined with frequent national conferences, and an insistence on adequate training for the staff, including a familiarity with all the latest experiments and ideas.[1] There should also be more fluidity of staffing, so that a teacher can be encouraged to move from school to school, rather than, as now, be bound to the same institution by fear of losing his job. The vigorous intellectual atmosphere that should result from such fluidity will do more to develop a modern progressive education than a policy laid down by the central authority concerning every detail of school life, dress, management, and time-table. The central authority can keep in contact with the general level of efficiency in its schools by the system of inspection, which will attempt not so much to see that the school is conforming to a preconceived plan in every detail, but to acquire and circulate the results of a host of small individual experiments. The central authority might with profit run a special department interested in the theory of education, a department responsible for calling conferences, for issuing memoranda and a journal, which could be a vessel for the opinions of numerous inspectors, teachers, and officials, and which could be circulated free to all schools. If an individual teacher wished to put into

---

[1] The tendency in modern Russia for the teachers to accept too readily any suggestions forthcoming from the central authority, is not likely to occur in England where at present there is a much higher standard of training and experience in teachers. 'Teachers are warned not to adopt slavishly all the suggestions in the research material. They are only to be used as guides. In practice the warning is frequently disregarded, as may be imagined, and unthinking wholesale adoption of methods described by the Central Laboratory as excellent occurs very largely . . .' (p. 110). 'Experience and an encouragement to experiment individually will in time remove this grave defect' (p. 111).—*Changing Man*, Beatrice King.

practice a particular method of teaching or system of organization, and was not content with expounding it in the journal, and could not experiment fully in his present subordinate position, he could apply for a headship. The serious desire to experiment could be taken into account as a valuable qualification when the authorities came to choose the heads of schools.

The socialist state may promise this amount of liberty and may fulfil its promises, but will our progressive educationalists, men and women like A. S. Neill, Bertrand and Dora Russell, W. B. Curry, and the late Margaret McMillan, be content to work within this system? Will this amount of liberty be sufficient or will they continue to demand complete independence from the state? They are in revolt against the traditional methods of English education; I have tried to show that those methods are inextricably woven into the capitalist system and mentality, and it will be obvious to anyone who reads the next chapter that much of what I consider should be the methods of socialist education has been borrowed from the ideas of the progressive schools. Excessive individualism is a revolt against a too rigid social tradition; if our educational tradition can become fluid, the individual experimenter may be incorporated into the tradition and need not go into the wilderness, to the great benefit of the state system. If he finds the main tendency of that tradition to be on the same lines as his own ideas, his feelings of revolt will be still further mollified. Revolt against a tradition has produced great ideas, and rebels have a large proportion of great men among them, but there is even richer fruit to be obtained from acceptance of a social system by a progressive, intellectual, critical individual. What Oscar Wilde says of the individual may be applied to ideas within the social system: 'What I mean by the perfect man is one who develops in perfect conditions; one who is not wounded or worried, maimed, or in danger. Most personalities have been obliged to be rebels. Half their strength has been wasted in friction. The note of the perfect personality is not rebellion, but peace.'[1] It should be the aim of socialism in education, as in every sphere, to provide a social background of dynamic peace, if I may be allowed the term, not rebellious indignation, to its great men. I only wish to show here, by way of illustrating the possibility of the experimental educationalist taking more kindly to socialism than he has done to capitalism, the general similiarity between the ideals of progressive schools and those of socialism. A more detailed comparison can be surmised from the next chapter.

It cannot but impress the reader of *The Modern Schools Handbook* that there is a remarkable unanimous emphasis on the ideal of co-operation and its merits as a teaching method as opposed to competition. The new psychology has shown competition to be only one of many means of evoking enthusiasm, and one not nearly so strong as interest, which can frequently be best aroused by group work. Mr. W. B. Curry, headmaster of Dartington Hall, said at the 1932 World Conference of the New Education Fellowship: 'The individualism of the conventionally conducted school, which bases its academic work on individual competition, and treats all co-operation in the class-room as cheating, works in exactly the opposite direction to the ideal of collaboration which we set up for ourselves in the national and international field. Indeed, in such schools the only hours when co-operation and team-work are advocated

[1] *The Soul of Man under Socialism*, Oscar Wilde.

are those devoted to competitive athletics, in which one side is attempting to defeat the other. Too often the unanalysed team and school loyalties of which the conventional school is so proud are but a childish form of narrow nationalism. A legitimate pride in one's school should be a more rational and less competitive thing.'[1] Mr. Curry in his article on his school in *The Modern Schools Handbook* shows the more positive side to this criticism of the conventional school, explaining that, as it seems to be generally agreed that the economic system must evolve away from *laissez-faire* in the direction of greater co-operation, so 'the schools must endeavour to produce a type of human being who takes to co-operation more naturally than the products of our present schools',[2] and he joins in the chorus of progressive schoolmasters who condemn marks, competitive examinations, and too great a concentration on team games. At Beacon Hill, according to Dora Russell, a child may be 'interested in things and events for their own sake, but competitive education drives out this lovely quality and substitutes snobbish and financial values'.[3] St. Christopher's at Letchworth is called 'a co-operative community of education'.[4] At Bembridge, by means of common service in some joint enterprise, employing boys of all ages, 'the principle of service for all, by all for the common good was realized and respected by all'.[5] These quotations might be multiplied many times; there is hardly one of the schools represented in this book which is not being run with the major emphasis on co-operation and common service, while the headmasters and mistresses

[1] *A New World in the Making*, 1933, p. 291.
[2] *The Modern Schools Handbook*, 1934, p. 59.
[3] Ibid., p. 41.   [4] Ibid., p. 97.   [5] Ibid., p. 153.

are practically unanimous in their condemnation of marks, prizes, and competitive examinations as inducements to drag work out of children. Their essays show considerable variety of attitude to educational principles and the reader can guess at sharply divergent political opinions, but all these people proclaim the need for greater co-operation and presumably would welcome a state that was founded on co-operative ideals.

The other idea that emerges strongly from these essays is that of internationalism, an idea that is also naturally basic to *A New World in the Making*, a synthesis of the remarks of delegates from all over the world at a world conference of the New Education Fellowship. The idea is latent in the quotation from Mr. Curry at the conference, and it occurs again and again in the essays of the writers of *The Modern Schools Handbook*, especially when they are dealing with the teaching of history. Many of these schools encourage their pupils to travel abroad and Leighton Park gives scholarships to boys who travel alone, where they wish, as far as the money will take them. Mr. Harold Rugg, for instance, wishes to 'prevent the young nationals of our sixty-odd nations from growing up in the belief that the form of government peculiar to their own country is of proved superiority'.[1] Here, again, there is similiarity of idea between the progressive educationalist and the socialist who wishes to see economic and political nationalism superseded by a real international law. These ideas have been arrived at by different roads; the socialist economist, for instance, denounces competition and prefers co-operation from the utilitarian point of view as a more effective method of production and distribution; the progressive educationalist prefers co-opera-

[1] *A New World in the Making*, p. 79.

tion from an equally utilitarian standpoint, as a more effective psychological method in developing a child's mind and personality. This suggests two things; first, that there is probably something valuable in an idea which is both pleasing to the idealist and thought practically useful by persons in very different spheres. From that point of view the progressive educationalist is performing a very useful psychological experiment which can be more widely applied by the socialist. Secondly, this similiarity of idea suggests that these educationalists will experience little difficulty in finding their places in a socialist state system of education; and that incidently is the answer to Mr. Harold Stovin, who, with certain justice, accuses these schools of artificiality and superficiality. They are lifeless and vapid, according to this critic's wit: 'That infusion of life cannot be given by a "progressive school", whose roots spring from the stony soil of the intellect, whose rooms are light and modern and redolent of Cézanne, open-shirts, and a sex-barren camaraderie.'[1] That, and the rest of the essay, are well put, and have some justification, but Mr. Stovin passes far too lightly over the real point of interest in one sentence in mitigation of his criticism. 'It must be remembered firstly that they are blazing a new trail, secondly, that many of them are on a negative rebound from the public-school tradition, thirdly, that the approach of many of these people towards education is not one of intuitive response to the needs of children, but of intellectual interest in sociological experiment.'[2] There is certainly an air of artificiality in some of these educational experiments,

[1] *Education in the Wasteland*, by Harold Stovin. From *Growing Opinions*, edited by Alan Campbell Johnson, 1935, p. 14.
[2] Op. cit., p. 12.

which is a poor substitute for that richness of vitality and intuitive urgency that Mr. Stovin finds so important. But, as I have already pointed out, that is the price of an impoverished tradition and a worn-out system, which makes rebellion the only alternative to stagnation. Therefore the great educational necessity at the present moment is not so much the discovery of any new attitude to the problems, any unknown process for making a man, as for the creation of a social system into which all that is best in progressive education can fit; thus may acceptance replace reaction, without the sacrifice of the dynamic force that is in the rebel, and so also may educational method become more intuitive and less self-conscious; nor should love of the child, as the teacher's main motive, be in any danger of disappearing under a theoretical interest in psychological experiment. In short, we return to our text, that the social system must be changed first, before education can be revivified; capitalism allows it little choice between an obsolete tradition and too self-conscious and sophisticated a reaction.

CHAPTER EIGHT

THE AIMS AND METHODS OF SOCIALIST EDUCATION

OUR final problem is the most important; for so far I have pulled to pieces the tradition and administration of capitalist education, but have constructed nothing to stand in its place but an empty shell, a machine with no raw material to work on. We must, therefore, discuss the general aim of socialist education, and describe what it intends to produce by this fine array of machinery, what kind of men and women socialism is concerned to mould. We have been talking of dry bones hitherto; the question of how they are to be clothed with flesh is all important. Let it be said at once that socialists have no specific aims for education beyond the problem of education itself, although that problem must always be considered in relation to social environment. Each educationalist will have his own synthesis of the best that has been thought and said on the subject. The socialists are not primarily concerned with making socialists through their educational system; they believe that the state should be the servant of the individual in his youth as in his adult years, not that education is the mere slave of the state. Consequently their first object will be to provide the best education possible for every child in the country, whatever the best may be. The following account of the best type of education is, of course, coloured by my personal opinions and some socialists will be found to disagree with me in detail and even in principle. Nevertheless, I believe that the general trend of socialist thought on educational matters is comparable with the opinions here set down, and I shall attempt to give a socialist as well as an educational or psychological reason for those opinions wherever possible. I shall also try to make clear my reasons for believing that such education is more likely to emerge from a socialist than from a capitalist society. Incidentally, I hold no particular brief for Russian education, though naturally reference must be made to it, as the Soviet state provides our one example of socialism in action. In certain ways, such as by the reintroduction of school uniforms and competitive examinations, the Russians seem to me to be showing a retrogressive trend. The important point, however, is that we must judge the Russian experiment, even though we may regard it with particular interest, with the same critical attitude as we should employ towards any other educational system.[1]

The first necessity in education is fluidity; its golden rule is that the individual child is more important than any consistency in method or curriculum, than any ulterior motive of the teacher or the state, than any pet

[1] This change of attitude in Russia towards educational methods may be due to a feeling of inferiority in the matter of mere knowledge in comparison with the Western European countries; there is a consequent over-emphasis on the value of knowledge itself, and a characteristic determination that scientific technique should be home-grown. If this supposition is correct, it provides an example of the subordination of the good of the individual to that of society in times immediately following a revolution. In support of this view, Pinkevitch may be quoted: 'The Soviet Union has set itself the task of overtaking and outstripping the capitalist countries in the matter of technique and economics. It can fulfil this task only if it masters all the knowledge of science and technique to be found in the most advanced countries of Europe and America.'—*Science and Education in the U.S.S.R.*, p. 40.

project or enthusiasm on the part of anyone with whom he comes in contact. Prof. A. N. Whitehead gives spirited emphasis to this idea from the psychological point of view, showing that the individual is never a constant element, and that consequently the system, which is before all else concerned with that individual, must be in a constant though ordered state of flux to meet his changing needs: 'The mind is never passive; it is a perpetual activity, delicate, receptive, responsive to stimulus. You cannot postpone its life till you have sharpened it. Whatever interest attaches to your subject-matter must be evoked here and now; whatever powers you are strengthening in the pupil, must be exercised here and now; whatever possibilities of mental life your teaching should impart, must be exhibited here and now' (op. cit., p. 9). For that fluidity in method certain conditions are necessary. The old education, with out-worn psychological theories of formal training, laid far too much emphasis on the rigid observance of pattern and order, so that the mind might be formed by an external discipline of subject-matter, or of general school-life. Formal methods of approach to knowledge went along with a day divided by a bell into artificial sections. The realization of the psychological truth of Whitehead's statement has not yet ousted the elements of rigidity from our education. I have tried in my review of the machinery of socialist education, and of the place within it of the progressive schools, to show how fluidity of idea can be preserved within a state system; by the constant exchange of theories in conferences and journals, by the frequent shifting of staff, by the freedom of the head of the school to experiment seriously. As well as this interchange of idea, an educational system should provide

P

conditions of teaching that will allow for different treatment of different individuals; small classes will make such individual treatment possible, whereas now large numbers too often reduce education to military drill. Free secondary education in itself will prevent individual development being arrested too early. A larger quota of staff than that which now obtains will encourage elasticity of curriculum, so that each child can exercise some choice in what he will learn. For another psychological notion that will one day gain wide acceptance, is that a child will not learn satisfactorily unless he is fundamentally interested in what he is doing, if not for its own sake, then for the sake of a further activity for which the first is essential. In short, it is no good trying to teach a child Latin who does not like Latin and sees no logical reason why he should learn it; but if he becomes inspired with the aim of becoming a doctor, like the boy of Neill's whom he delights to quote,[1] then he will learn Latin with remarkable energy, and anything else he finds necessary for that purpose, however much he may dislike it.

The schools of the future, therefore, must be so constituted as to allow an individual approach to various subject-matters, so that while every child may as a matter of course range over the normal school subjects, he will be able to come to them from his own peculiar standpoint and activated by his own peculiar interests. The rigidity of the public schools I have explained as coming from an immobile and inelastic tradition in curriculum and method, connected closely with the specific training of a ruling class. The tradition of socialist education must never be allowed to harden in this way. Furthermore, the rigidity of the present

[1] Cf. *The Modern Schools Handbook*, p. 116.

state schools is due not only to lack of psychological perception, but also to lack of money, that is, to capitalist economics. To-day the staff of a school is not changed as much as it should be, because teachers are afraid, in view of the long unemployment list, of not finding a second job if they walk out of their first; when they have reached a certain stage in the income scale, no fresh school will employ them, as every school is concerned with reducing its salary bill to the lowest possible. In the same way, small classes, individual treatment, and an elastic curriculum and time-table demand a far smaller proportion of children to a teacher than is at present allowed; the government is more concerned with economy than education. The socialist state, according to its principles, should be far more likely to provide these opportunities for individualism, as it is prepared to find and spend the money necessary for such development. I would go so far as to say that only under a central planning system which can ensure real equality of opportunity can such fluidity and care for the individual be reached. It is a well-known paradox that a certain order is necessary for the maximum of freedom in any society, which in itself is a good argument for planning on the socialist scale. Thus it is under a socialist régime, exercising complete control over the financial resources of the country, that a plan can be conceived wherein a child can be treated as important in himself, freed from the rigidity of haphazard systems, clogged by out-worn traditions and petty commercialized mentality, all of which now conspire to keep a child in the class that gave birth to him. Under socialism which can provide really adequate universal education, free from the strains that are put on the social services in time of capitalist depression, and a social environment in which that education may be put to good use, a child has some chance of finding himself born into a society that does not expect him to be 'either a little Liberal or else a little Conservative', nor even a little socialist, but simply a person with his own unique character to develop, and his own unique contribution to make to society.

The other conception that seems to me to be fundamental to all true education, is also latent in A. N. Whitehead's statement: that education is not a mere preparation for life, but is life itself. There is no artificial division between apprenticeship and mastery in the craft of living; we begin to live when we are conceived, not when we leave school, and we never cease to learn till we die. Many a speech-day bore has pronounced that education is never finished; few among the educational practitioners have fully realized the implications of the corollary, that education even in its earliest stages is life. No child should be denied the sympathy that believes him to be of importance in himself, not merely as a potential adult. This idea may be used as a touchstone with which to test the stock problems of education; its courageous application is necessary for the socialist who is aiming at giving the fulness of life to all citizens at all stages. It is also psychologically acceptable, for we have long ago dismissed the idea of the mind as an instrument that can be perfected before it is used; 'learning by doing' is not only desirable; it is unavoidable. The mind is always in activity, and though the teacher may have control over the restlessness of a child's body by means of some form of discipline, he can never bring the mind to passivity; he can only harness its activity to various projects. It follows that to attempt a wide divergence between school- and after-life, is to depend on an antithesis between two things that are not sharply divisible. Consequently the more nearly education approximates to the realities of life as it is lived outside the school, the stronger will be its appeal, the more satisfactory to the child's interests. Artificiality in education is always met, though usually unconsciously, with indifference or rebellion in the child, which is the reason why subjects that seem to have little connection with real life arouse so little enthusiasm, and why the old discipline, imposed from above and enforced by fear, has never been successful, for a discipline to be successful must be unobtrusive and unself-conscious. This incompatibility of moral code is also one of the greatest faults of the public schools; their standards of behaviour, good or bad, have little to do with contemporary morality.[1]

We can apply this conception of reality to one burning question, which we have not yet touched on, co-education. Mr. W. B. Curry, headmaster of Dartington Hall, a co-educational school, looks at this matter in this light: 'Children are not, after all, born with all the boys in some villages and all the girls in others. I would suggest, therefore, that the real burden of proof is upon those who believe in segregation.'[2] In the essay on Bedales, the pioneer English co-educational boarding-school, in the *Handbook* the headmaster states: 'If the life is to be at once complete in itself, and a pre-

---

[1] 'The standards of morality current in the outside world do not obtain in the public schools. Life there would not be tolerable if they did; it is difficult enough as things are, when there is a recognized code of warfare between old and young, played according to certain well-defined rules, so that lying, meanness, cheating and other ugly-sounding things are by mutual consent given quite harmless names'.—L. B. Pekin, *Progressive Schools*, p. 33.   [2] *The Modern Schools Handbook*, p. 62.

paration for life to be lived under normal conditions at a later time, it would lose greatly in our view if it were not to be shared by both sexes throughout the whole range of the school years.'[1] The writers on progressive schools which are not co-educational, either leave the question untackled, or defend segregation on the grounds of personal incapacity to deal with both sexes. Thus the headmistress of Maltman's Green says: 'To be quite consistent my school should, of course, be co-educational, but for many reasons—notably my own inability to carry out co-education as I feel it should be carried out, and the unsuitability of the house for the purpose—I knew that I could accomplish what I meant and wanted only if the school were confined to girls.'[2] There has never to my knowledge been any argument put forward in favour of segregation that can stand against this accusation of artificiality; children are going to live in factories, in homes, in shops and offices where men and women work together; they will be better prepared for such life by one that has given them every opportunity to understand the other sex. The fears of the puritanical are much exaggerated, and if anything, co-education is a safety-valve, working against the violent reactions consequent on the sudden discovery that the other sex exists and is attractive. The self-possession of the American adolescent provides a better basis for securing a sane and intelligent attitude to sex, than the nervous ignorance or secretive excitement of the normal product of the English segregated schools. Again, a fuller life with every opportunity of individual development can be given in a co-educational school, where a child learns by his relationship with the children of the other sex, and gathers a valuable variety

[1] *The Modern Schools Handbook*, p. 45.   [2] Ibid., p. 257.

of experience if he is taught by both men and women. It is to deny an individual an experience that is his right, to bring him up in a segregated school. The sex-taboo, that is, of course, an important reason for the continuation of this segregation, is somewhat outside this argument, though a society that has the courage to review its whole economic and social activity should also have the courage to face and dispel the clouds of irrationality that are gathered round the fact of sex. One aspect of it has some more immediate reference to socialist ideals. The subjection of women was in the past intimately connected with their lack of educational opportunity, professional training in particular being denied them. The socialist principle of equality cannot allow the last vestiges of that subjection to persist. Segregated schools emphasize that inequality between the sexes, whereas economic status should be judged without reference to sex. As one example, it is simpler to pay men and women on different rates of pay if they work in separate schools; whereas it is an obvious anomaly in co-education. Mixed schools would also help to eradicate the mentality that takes this inequality for granted; I suspect that one of the reasons for the progressive woman educationalist being unwilling to branch out into co-education, is that she has well-founded fears that men would not work under her. On all considerations, it seems inevitable that a progressive educational policy, such as a socialist state should adopt, will include co-education as psychologically and socially desirable. If all new state schools were co-educational, and the principle were carried through from the early stages of the present elementary schools, the remaining institutions would soon be brought into line.

The conceptions of fluidity and realism that I am advocating for socialist education as psychologically suitable, need courage to apply, and nowhere more so than in the spheres of discipline and school-management; but without these conceptions it is impossible to reduce them to their proper insignificance. The fact that discipline has always loomed so large on the teacher's horizon, is in itself a condemnation of many of our present methods, for a child does not go to school primarily to be disciplined or managed, but to develop and to learn; when we suggest that a child must be disciplined before it can be taught, we are guilty of yet another false division and one which has brought more heart-burning to the teacher and more suffering to the child than any other misconception in education. Rigidity has meant that we have remained under the spell of class-teaching, of the kind that endeavours to pour knowledge into the receptive minds of the children. Thus the class is thought of as an audience, often an unwilling one, which has to be cajoled or more frequently bullied into some show of attention. Even the martinet has always the problem of day-dreaming to combat, for though he may have subdued his class to the semblance of a collection of statues, the body may obey, while the mind is refreshing itself by flights into romance.

There are roughly three methods of obtaining attention or its semblance; it can be induced by fear, by sexual attraction, or by interest in the subject on hand. The use of fear presupposes a relation of ruler and ruled, and though that relation has been much modified of late, particularly in modern girls' schools, it underlies all our systems of school discipline. Psychologically there is nothing to be said for it whatsoever; it is ultimately useless. Mr. L. B. Pekin says: 'Punishment is the appeal to force and force produces unnatural growth; it is the appeal to fear and fear is the worst motive that can sway a child or any human being; it is the weapon of hatred, and out of hatred nothing good can finally come.'[1] Punishment imposed by democratic society seems to be an evil necessity; that imposed by an autocracy or tyranny is degrading, and what is more, it does not work, if the object of such punishment is deterrence and not the pleasure of the autocrat. It continues to be practised in schools because we, teachers and autocrats, lack the courage to shed an artificial dignity and to probe into our own secret motives. A scientific, psychological approach to this problem would reveal many hidden gratifications and enjoyments. 'Repression is however too popular to disappear suddenly since the people who approve it are not likely to be easily convinced. Repression affords too much gratification to the person who imposes it for this to occur, being a form of domination and self-display that being carried out for ostensibly moral reasons, has behind it a great weight of public approval, however useless it has proved in practice.'[2] The weapons of repression vary from corporal punishment to the bad mark that carries with it no further penalty. The first, which the psychologist has shown to be so closely linked with sexual perversion and repression, is a remnant of sheer barbarism in our schools, which most continental and American schools have removed long since.[3] The second is frequently

[1] *Progressive Schools*, 1934, p. 84.
[2] *Psycho-analysis in the Class-room*, G. H. Green, 1922, Chap. 4.
[3] The Russians have a characteristically whole-hearted attitude to this matter: 'In the U.S.S.R. even the parental slapping of disobedient children is not only a serious moral delinquency, but actually a criminal offence.'—*Soviet Communism*, S. and B. Webb, p. 1047. Though I have in Rostov seen an Armenian woman use

nothing but a poor joke, but, nevertheless, vastly preferable to the first, as its consequences are usually little more than amusement or indifference. The plain speaking, that can be a form of cruelty and which is practised in most girls' schools, presupposes a relationship where one party to the conversation has a right to be as rude as possible, and the other has none; one of the rules of that game is that the child does not answer back. The imposition of extra work as punishment kills all interest in the subject thus admitted to be unpleasant, and makes the application of the third motive well-nigh impossible. And a more useless way of wasting one's time than in writing 'lines' it is difficult to imagine.

The method of sexual attraction is a matter that psychology alone can elucidate and has little connection with the difference between socialist and capitalist education; though a point in favour of a freer atmosphere in school life is that it often makes this method unnecessary, for one of the few things that we know about it is that it is fraught with dangers for the unwary. The third method, the discipline provided by the subject-matter, has one great advantage in that it correlates the training of character with the acquisition of knowledge, so that it is unnecessary to attempt to discipline the child before he can learn. He is disciplined through learning, and all the old aids to order and quiet, from birch-rods to bad marks, become unnecessary. In the class-room the game of giving the teacher the maximum amount of annoyance with the minimum inconvenience to himself, loses most of its fascination for the child; he is too busy thinking about something else. A discipline that is latent in the subject-matter is not an open

this method to impress her son with the danger of playing in the middle of the road.

invitation to rebellion, such as is provided by that dependent on the will of the teacher, an antagonist with chinks in his armour, or to use a more modern metaphor, gaps in his navy. Psychologically this method has proved highly successful, and the casual observer will bear witness to the fact that there is no attention so concentrated as that of a child absorbed in some pleasurable activity. A child will take infinite pains, will master uninteresting subject-matters, and undertake tasks so formidable as to appal the adult, to arrive at a desired end. Such a discipline has a stronger hold than any other.

Which method is socialist education to adopt? There can be only one answer when it is fully realized that a discipline based on fear must be imposed from above; a socialist state should be a democratic state, where the ruled are also the rulers, where the state has no welfare apart from that of its citizens, where the discipline does not appear to be imposed by any power that is impervious to the claims of the individual. Therefore, if we are to breed citizens who are not afraid to rule themselves and to accept the discipline of active participation in creative labour, fear must be banished from the schools; and with fear go hatred and cruelty. Hatred is dissolved when punishment is not meted out by an individual: 'If Johnny hits Bobby the latter is free to express his hate of Johnny, but if Bobby is hit by father he cannot possibly express his hate of father. So when a jury in Summerhill fines Willie, age eleven, for puncturing Mabel's bike maliciously, Willie is free to hate the whole jury. But the queer thing is that he doesn't. When children make their own laws they do not resent the consequences if they break their own laws.'[1] Disobedience

[1] *The Modern Schools Handbook*, A. S. Neill on Summerhill, p. 124.

and inattention in schools are usually ultimately due to boredom; a discipline that results from interest in a project is positive, and does away with the state of mental and emotional undernourishment that is the cause of anti-social behaviour. Similarly crime in society grows out of poverty, unemployment, and bad social environment; a state which can provide work with a real importance to society for all its citizens, will go a long way towards the reduction of crime. In the same way a school that can satisfy the particular interests of the children and focus their attention through some work that appeals positively to them, will have solved its major disciplinary problem. What remains of crime when this form of discipline is applied in school and state will probably be due to pathological causes and should be treated as a doctor would prescribe for a sick man.

We have been discussing the problem of discipline from the particular aspect of attention, with reference to the individual and his peculiar interests. A school is, however, a community and the management of individuals in their relations with others is a further aspect of discipline. Schools and society generally should aim at allowing the maximum of freedom to the individual, including the freedom to learn by his mistakes, that is compatible with the security of the other members of the community. In some instances now the claims of the community are pressed too far; on the other hand, some individuals are allowed too much liberty at the expense of others. To-day in some schools it seems to me that the community claims too great a uniformity; it has been said somewhat sweepingly that 'the whole of our education has hitherto aimed at suppressing the heretical tendency in common folk'.[1] For instance, in

[1] *Leisure in the Modern World,* by Delisle Burns, p. 33.

AIMS AND METHODS OF SOCIALIST EDUCATION 221

elementary schools and in the first stages of secondary education, all children in a class must learn the same thing at the same time. Most secondary schools demand that' a uniform should be worn. Mr. Pekin quotes an amusing extract from a *Daily Telegraph* supplement on the public schools, showing how a school community can enforce a rigid caste system by differences of dress, allowing the individual no freedom of choice in this matter: 'Two-yearers wear all their coat-buttons but one undone and may turn their collars up. Three-yearers undo all their coat-buttons and wear stiff collars of a turn-down type, silk scarves and coloured socks.'[1] A collection of people may very well look better in the mass if they are all dressed alike, but this seems to me a case where the little good of communal uniformity might be sacrificed to the greater benefit of the individual; it is of no great seriousness what a community looks like, but it is a good thing that the individual should learn by experiment to combine good taste and comfort in dress.

The rival claims of individual freedom and communal order seem to be reflected in two distinct educational movements, a combination of which is possible and may provide the maximum of these two desirable qualities that can be obtained simultaneously in a school; they are the various schemes for individual work, such as the Dalton Plan and the Project Method, and self-government. The idea behind these new methods of presenting subject-matters to children, mostly emanating from America, is that no individual can be expected to acquire new knowledge at exactly the same pace as and from the identical viewpoint of any other; yet on this supposition is based our present insistence on class

[1] *Progressive Schools*, pp. 30-1.

teaching. The Dalton Plan therefore makes to the child assignments of work in various subjects, to be completed in a certain time, a week, a month, or a term. In the school there are subject-rooms, replacing form-rooms, where the child can find the materials requisite for working on each subject, and a specialist teacher whose help he can command if necessary. The advantages of this scheme are that the child can work at his own pace, and for any length of time he desires at one subject, thus avoiding the main objections to class teaching, the uneven mental standards of the individuals composing the class, and the scrappiness of the teaching, divided arbitrarily into fixed periods of time, so that at the ringing of a bell, for instance, English stops and Geometry begins. In this way the clever waste a good deal of their time and the dull feel perpetually rushed and bothered, while interest cannot be sustained and has to be re-created every fresh lesson. These are educational reasons for the adoption of the Dalton Plan, and as such have recommended themselves to many progressive teachers. But the most interesting social aspect of such an educational method is the insistence on the individuality of each child who is considered as having his specific requirements with regard to pace and division of time between subjects.

The Project Method also stresses the individuality of the child, but mainly from the point of view of his interests; by this method, a child is given a project to work on, some concrete piece of work, usually historical in the first instance, round which any number of subjects are interwoven, so that handicrafts, literature, geography, even languages and mathematics, are grouped about a central point of study, for as long as the project lasts. The educational value of this method is obviously the correlation of subject-matters, in such a way that it becomes clear to the child that one is necessary to the understanding of another. Psychologically the method lays stress on individuality, as the project may be set from any standpoint, particularly interesting to the individual. These two methods, in various combinations and modifications, will probably be adopted in the schools of the future, as it is impossible ultimately to escape the psychological truth that interest is essential to attention, and interest is an extremely individual thing. If courageously applied, these methods will be sufficient to ensure that the individuality of no child is sacrificed in the socialist school, and there is no reason whatsoever why socialist education should not adopt them, being unhampered by perverse economy, in the provision of adequate buildings for subject-rooms, and the necessary equipment. If the true educationalist can accept the socialist state as fair and just, he himself, being nearly always an individualist, caring more for the ultimate happiness of each child than for the general good of the school, will strive to see that the balance is not overweighted in favour of the community at the expense of the individual, and will be anxious to apply those methods of teaching which will encourage individuality; and as I have argued, there seem to be strong reasons why the progressive educationalist will be able to accept the socialist state.

The arguments for the adoption of these methods in the socialist schools seem at first to be somewhat dashed by the fact that the Russians, having used both methods in the Soviet schools in the first years of the revolution, have now abandoned them. In the first place the short time in which the Soviet state has existed is hardly sufficient in which to judge the efficiency of these methods, when attempted under such adverse conditions as obtained in the early revolutionary years. The attitude that considers an efficient standard of mere knowledge as the main object of education, I have already indicated as one explanation of this change of method. Soviet educational officials admitted to me in conversation that the present aim of Russian education was a certain standard of knowledge, a regrettable attitude, it seems to me, induced by fear of war and isolation. With regard to the failure of these methods to produce such an efficient standard of knowledge, Mrs. King, in her recent book on Russian education, *Changing Man*, quotes Epstein, the Vice-Commissar for education: 'The method may be suitable for a bourgeois country, but it is quite unsuitable for a country building Communism. It gave the children a superficial knowledge of a great many things, but no proper groundwork of the foundation of education' (pp. 22–3). It will be noted that the Project Method is judged by its ability to produce a standard of knowledge but not by any other criteria; that there is no attempt to assess the value of the method in itself and a rather facile assumption that the method rather than any other cause was the reason for the superficiality complained of. The reference to the suitability of the method to a bourgeois country is of little value, as in general the capitalist educational systems of Europe have maintained class-teaching and subject-divisions in their state schools. It must be remembered that the average class in Russian schools still contains forty children and Krupskaya admitted to Mrs. King: 'That at any rate part cause of the failure may have been the inexperience and lack of training of the teachers' (p. 22). To me there seems no doubt that these transitional conditions of overcrowded classes and inexperienced teachers are chiefly responsible for the failure of these methods in the Russian schools. They do depend for efficient working on a generous quota of well-trained staff, so that a child may have the undivided attention of a specialist in any subject that is claiming his interest at any moment. It is obviously easier for a comparatively ignorant teacher to deliver a lecture at a fixed time on a given subject, a lecture that can be carefully prepared, than to answer questions and give advice on the spur of the moment on a variety of matters. I look forward to the time when, having considerably reduced the size of their classes and obtained a high standard of efficiency among the teachers, the Russians will reconsider the desirability of these methods.

The individual at school and in the wider society cannot, however, escape community life, and it is for the socialist to consider what type of social administration is most suitable for school communities. He has decided the forms of society generally on the basis of economic utility and certain wider ideals; he can apply those ideas to the internal government of schools. It is not a question of infusing the schools with a community spirit; they cannot avoid being communities, but the machinery of their government moulds the community and the attitude of the children towards the administration of wider social forms. With regard to the actual teaching, it is obvious that a certain amount of collective work is necessary; the teaching of languages, where the pronunciation is affected, depends on constant reference to and contact with the spoken word; the problem is to discover the best way to conduct such class-work, while obviating the worst deficiencies of the usual forms of class-teaching. The Project Method provides a solution when applied to group or classwork. A project may be completed by one person or several, but if many take part in it, each individual brings his own particular contribution, and everyone is not expected to do the same thing at the same time. Thus, for instance, in producing a play, the general project is fulfilled by the fusion of various different kinds of work; the actors, the producers, the propertymen, the costumiers, the needlewomen, and electrical engineers, and many more are all essential to the final result. Incidentally children may learn a foreign language by the dramatic method, and voice-production is an obvious adjunct. In this way group work can be conducted without making a class of children a merely passive audience.

This type of work, which is constructive and positive, satisfies the instincts of group feeling, which are now chiefly relegated to the games field. Such community spirit is parallel to that which the socialist wishes to evoke in the building of his new society, where each individual seems satisfied with the knowledge that his work is an essential though possibly small part of a vast enterprise, and that the final product can be improved by his own efforts. It is this type of community spirit which does not frustrate personal freedom and effort, but is one of the means of individual self-realization; it is one that impresses visitors to Russia, where, whatever the faults of the whole system, one feels the contact of countless energies let loose from repression and negative discontent. This is the practical value of co-operation, that it eliminates much of the waste of time and energy that is involved in the usual type of competitive class-teaching. A judicious combination of individual assignments and group projects, a combination which would vary with each child, would provide a balance of independent and communal work. In the time set aside for individual studies, a child would, of course, always be free to do such work as could later be incorporated into the group project.

There must also be the possibility of working in groups even without a project; schools will continue to have various societies, debating, musical, scientific, and even mathematical, for there are some people who find the acquirement and practice of a skill sufficiently interesting without some ulterior motive; Caliban's solvers obviously find mathematics an amusement. With a sufficient number of staff and adequate buildings there should be no difficulty in giving each child the opportunity to learn what appeals to him, by himself or with others; in this way a child, fundamentally interested in his work, could experience the delight of giving his share to the general well-being of a society, a delight which the socialist feels to be sufficiently strong to make the main motive force in a nation kept together by countless individuals doing different jobs. It is a particularly strong power when it is linked with interest in the work itself.

There is thus the possibility of great individual freedom in this type of school society, if sufficiently ordered to be efficient, and that such methods can be efficient has been proved by the products of the progressive schools, which are not a collection of ignoramuses as their critics would sometimes like us to believe. There is one point in connection with individual freedom that should be discussed; is the child to be free to attend lessons or not? Following the comparison with socialist society in wider fields, it would appear that socialism cannot allow idleness: 'The idler will be treated not only as a rogue and a vagabond, but as an embezzler of the national funds, the meanest sort of thief.'[1] Idleness is one of the liberties that socialism will destroy, as Shaw has pointed out, because the liberty to be idle, with money in your pocket, is always achieved at other people's expense. Must we apply this idea to the child? I should say not, and plead that the inconsistency must be overlooked in view of the different psychological stages of the child and the adult. It must be remembered that idleness is unnatural, and that even the so-called idle rich are all busy spending money on activities that kill time for them; they do not sit with folded hands doing nothing, but work hard amusing themselves. The state, in putting an end to that type of existence, will be merely insisting on a change of activity, from one that is harmful to one that is beneficial to others. A child is not naturally idle, and usually only misses lessons where he has the liberty to do so, when he has formerly suffered from boredom and compulsion in school. Even then he is usefully employed in ridding himself of repressions that otherwise would have affected his adult outlook. Children who have not known compulsion are more easily led to direct their activities towards what are regarded as the more normal fields of education; they are naturally eager for some activity. Thus we arrive at the paradoxical situation that where there is freedom to be idle as far as the ordinary round of school work is concerned, it is rarely exercised, but compulsion gives a distaste for work and an itch to be free from the prescribed activities. This freedom is possible in schools, as a change in activity and abstention from the usual forms of work will not be immediately socially dangerous as in the wider adult community; of course the results of 'slacking' in the routine

[1] *The Intelligent Woman's Guide to Socialism and Capitalism*, by G. Bernard Shaw, p. 400.

manual labour of a boarding community, such as bed-making or washing-up, can be made obvious to any child without punishment or compulsion, by the natural effects of his idleness in the form of tumbled beds and dirty dishes.

Such an atmosphere of freedom, which is more likely to impress the child with the inevitable consequences of anti-social behaviour, will arrive most surely at giving the young man or woman, ready to begin work in the larger community of the state, a sense of the individual and social value of labour. Those who wish to compel are nearly always afraid of the transference of the evil tendencies in human nature, which have been greatly increased and provoked by the compulsion itself, to the new state of affairs where compulsion is lifted. Freedom, however, is not merely the absence of compulsion but something more positive; though that absence in itself will allow of the development of a mentality that can find more satisfaction in the use of opportunities than in mere idleness. In discussing this question of freedom as it occurs in the U.S.S.R., the Webbs give a point of view that from its psychological aspect is applicable to education: 'Those whose intellectual training has been unconsciously based on the hypothesis of a static universe almost inevitably think of freedom as the absence of restraint; those who assume that every part of the universe (including minds) is always in motion are apt to think of freedom as the presence of opportunity to act as they desire.'[1] This attitude to freedom must be encouraged if the future

---

[1] *Soviet Communism*, p. 1033. The quotation also shows the link between this conception of liberty and that of fluidity that I have claimed elsewhere as necessary to the socialist state, cf. Pt. 1, pp. 64-6.

citizens are to live in a society that refuses idleness as the right of any of its members.

Is competition wholly bad and is it going to disappear altogether from these new schools? The old forms of competitive examinations, marks, and prizes do produce activity from some individuals. That competition is efficient as a motive force to a certain extent cannot be denied, nor that there are dangers in depending too uncritically on the spirit of co-operation. That co-operation is preferable morally is accepted by anyone who prefers love to hate; the man you work with in real sympathy is your brother; the man you work against is your enemy. It is also generally more economical to make use of everybody's work fitted into a pattern, than, as so often happens in a competition, to use the best or even merely the cheapest labour, while the efforts of the rest are scrapped. But men and women, and children particularly, do find a satisfaction in beating their neighbours in a race, as well as in working with them in a common activity; the older type of educationalist had some justification for his dependence on competition though he drove it to death. In relegating the competitive motive to the second place, there is no need to aim at its complete suppression; the Russians have a very practical solution to the problem in Soviet society, whereby competition is made a group matter; socialist competition means that type that occurs between two groups, two factories, farms, or schools, for instance, to see who can first complete their portion of a planned co-operative enterprise. 'Everyone is familiar with the desire "to do the other fellow down", in games and sport, in solving cross-word puzzles, in aerial flights, and automobile records of speed. What is original and so far as we know, unprecedented, is the transfer, in the U.S.S.R., of the sporting instinct to the everyday operations of industrial and agricultural production.'[1] Another aspect of this type of group competition is that it appears to dissolve feelings of resentment at defeat. We all know that the captains shake hands when it is all over; in Russia the winning factory goes so far as to send its experts to the assistance of the defeated. Group competition, or emulation as the Webbs prefer to call it, is easily applicable to schools[2] and should be sufficient to satisfy normal competitive yearnings. Thus, for instance, I know of a school which was divided into two groups to compete in weeding two pieces of lawn; the rivalry was intense but never once obscured the satisfaction in having got rid of the weeds by communal effort. Projects, dramatic and otherwise, are obvious material for group competition.

If co-operation is to be the main motive of activity in socialist schools, we must consider certain dangers in that motive, for, like every other good thing, it is not wholly good and may be applied to bad ends. The dangers are at once apparent when it is remembered that the fascist state is a corporate one, which is proof enough that the spirit of co-operation can be used for widely different ends. What better example is there of co-operation than a battleship or a well-disciplined army? The capitalist can use the co-operative spirit and the socialist the competitive. These are ultimately motives, not aims; the ends which they are used to achieve

---

[1] *Soviet Communism*, S. and B. Webb, p. 735.

[2] 'One group within the class will challenge another to carry out certain duties or to undertake the achievement of certain tasks. The competition may be between classes or between schools. There have been occasions when all the schools of one district have challenged the schools of another district.'—*Changing Man*, Beatrice King, p. 93.

decide their ultimate value. Mr. Harold Stovin, a young man who appears to be having a reaction against the very new, and whose criticism of the progressive schools I have already quoted, in an interestingly aggressive book called *Totem: the Exploitation of Youth*, has been at pains to show the dangers of co-operation when it is linked with too facile a sentimentality. His book is a study of various youth movements in England to-day, the Y.M.C.A., Boys' Clubs and Scouts, and others, which he considers are attempting to give to the working-class adolescent what the public schools give to their pupils. For instance, he quotes the following passage from Basil Henriques in *Club Leadership*: 'It (the club) must do for him what the public school has done for the privileged boy.' Mr. Stovin comments that the same insistence on 'clanishness', on the glory of the particular institution, is present in both public school and boys' club; the pith of the aim of these clubs, 'as of the Public School system is the creation of "character"—which is to be interpreted, loyalty to the tribal code—through *esprit de corps*' (op. cit., p. 46). He has a footnote at this point on Dr. Norwood's book, *The English Tradition of Education*, which looked at morphologically, he finds 'instructive and self-deceptive in a very marked degree'. In other parts of the book we find these clubs, with their use of magic and tribal myth, compared to the continental Youth Movements, out of which grew fascism in Italy and Germany, where it is maintained by these same methods of psychological appeal that Mr. Stovin has called 'totem'. In Chapter Two he has some interesting quotations from the literature of the English group movements and the fascist organizations, showing surprising parallel states of mind and psychological methods.

It cannot be denied—and it is a disturbing thought—that the psychological attitude of our public schools and the fascist states have some remarkable similarities, involving as they do the reverence for the Leader, the abstraction of the group spirit, or the *esprit de corps*, the honour of the school or the prestige of the nation, all depending on certain manifestations of the co-operative appeal. There is sufficient similarity to make Mr. Pekin's words worth weighty consideration: 'When one considers the general trend of Air Force policy during the last few years and the increasing fascination of the police (official lecturers have recently been touring the public schools with the idea of luring "gentlemen's sons" into its ranks—or rather into its positions of command) does one need to be of a very suspicious nature to suppose that authority may be quietly preparing to resist progressive social change by force?'[1] The enthusiastic admirer of the U.S.S.R. who visits Lenin's tomb with a glow of satisfaction may ask himself some serious questions as to his own attitude.[2] Presumably he will answer those questions by reference to the ideals of Soviet Russia, as compared to those of

---

[1] *Progressive Schools*, L. B. Pekin, p. 102.
[2] Mr. Stovin will doubtless also have culled material for his thesis from commentators on Soviet Russia. I make him a present of the following instances from the Webbs' *Soviet Communism*, if he has not already discovered them. No less a person than Krupskaya is quoted in an address to Comsomol workers among Pioneers, the communist children's organization. 'Their disdain for bourgeois child movements, especially the Boy Scouts, causes many Pioneer leaders to miss much that is instructive in their approach to the child' (p. 405, footnote). The Scouts are one of Mr. Stovin's pet abominations.

The laws and customs of the Pioneers include the following:
'The Pioneer is faithful to the cause of the workman class and the precepts of Ilych.
'The Pioneer is industrious and persevering, knows how to

present-day Germany or Italy, implying that magic is necessary to human beings, still essentially primitive, but that it becomes virtually harmless when the prestige of a nation is made to depend on the development within it of social justice, and not on foreign conquest and victory in war. Nevertheless, the socialist will do well to ensure that the motives of co-operation that he depends on will be attached to some enterprise that calls for intellectual hard work as well as sincere feeling. Competition at its worst becomes associated with hard-headed indifference to humanitarian considerations, and the self-deception that refuses to apply the morality of one sphere of life to any other; we are all familiar, from fiction or real life, with the business man with a wide divergence between the morality of his public and private life. Co-operation at its worst descends into mawkish sentimentality and facile emotions at the beck and call of every muddled-headed enthusiast or unscrupulous propagandist. When a nation goes to war, the necessary fever is produced by an appeal to co-operation: 'Brothers, to arms' and 'Unity is strength' are the battle-cries. What, after all, is the reason for the sustained success of the so-called National Government in acquiring the confidence of the people, but a clever application of this same co-operative spirit, or why bother to preserve the fiction of all-party government?

There seems to be one safeguard possible, the infusion of sound logic into all enterprises dependent on the

work collectively under all and any conditions, and finds a way out in all circumstances.

'The Pioneer does not swear, smoke, or drink' (p. 403).

These are remarkably like the incantations that Mr. Stovin quotes from the literature of the organizations that he has under review.

co-operative motive. Intellectual honesty would not allow the business man to justify himself by any sophistry, if he failed to live up to his private standards of morality in his commercial transactions. Constructive and critical reason would make plain the poverty of achievement that stands in the names of the various fascist régimes and our own National Government, and also the almost complete lack of concrete aim within the societies that Mr. Stovin trounces. In schools the problem may be solved by making sure that group work is concerned with something really worth doing. The barrenness of the usual team-spirit, its inability to develop into anything that might be termed real understanding of one's fellows, is chiefly due to the fact that, through the medium of team-games, which in most schools provide the sole means of evoking the co-operative motive force, it is allowed to fasten on such nebulous creations of the mind as the honour of the school or the house; no one has yet managed to define this honour with any intellectual clarity; in fact, as a conception that can in any way be related to common sense it was exploded long ago by no less a person than Sir John Falstaff. In Soviet Russia their myth, the worship of Lenin, has never reached dangerous magnitude, because their major efforts are directed towards building a new state of society, an enterprise that requires careful planning, expert knowledge, and patient thought. In schools the co-operation that is evoked by the communal construction of a swimming-pool or the production of a play or a geographical survey of the environs, is kept clean of magic and cheap sentimentality by the fact that it is obvious and, indeed, satisfying that everything has been achieved by human effort guided by human reason. It is not necessary to abolish team-games and athletics altogether, but only to 'debunk' them from the misty realms of 'honour', where they are a form of worship of the gods that are known as 'the school' and 'the house'.

Co-operation can arise out of the necessities of work in society; it becomes also a necessary concomitant to the smooth working of a social organization. In an imperfect world it is apparently not sufficient to group people together in common effort to complete a piece of work; laws to maintain the security of life and property must also be evolved, and, least desirable of all, punishment to uphold those laws. The aim of society should be as far as possible to eliminate the repressive tendencies of law and justice. It seems ideally conceived, as if economic equality combined with a democratic political system, will do much to remove the opportunities of tyranny and injustice that are within our modern legal systems. Socialism is pledged to economic equality and has its best opportunity of giving expression to its ideals in a political democracy, where each citizen sharing in the government, is ultimately responsible for the laws of his country. The odium of meting out punishment is also spread over as large a number as possible, in order that no individual thus penalized should feel resentment towards any other individual. If we apply the principle that the school should approximate as closely as possible to the pattern of life outside it, there can be no doubt as to the form of government that will prevail in the socialist schools; it must be democratic. Government there must be, for while the individual should have the choice of the subjects and hours of his work, society will have to restrain him if his behaviour results in any harm or inconvenience to any other individuals.

Democracy applied to school-management, or self-government as it is usually called, has a great deal in its favour from many points of view. In the first place it uses the co-operative spirit for purposes that can also be served by the intellect, and that we have already seen to be a desirable mixture. It is this side of school-life that emphasizes the communal spirit, making plain to children that co-operation is an absolute necessity in some form for the smooth running of society, if the rights of the individual to choose his own work and recreation are not to be trespassed upon. Those rights are most clearly recognized in the Dalton and Project Methods, and are by no means incompatible with self-government. Secondly, democracy in a school lends reality to the conception of government; the job of ruling themselves will teach children more than all the civics in the world; for 'to the young child whose mind is just opening to the movement and wonders of the world, the 'abstraction of the nation does not exist'.[1] The child will find it far easier to think logically about the nation and its needs if he has come across the practical difficulties of government at school. But— and this needs saying with emphasis—the democracy must be real; there must be no suggestion of play, no feeling that the staff can step in and alter the decisions of the community if their judgment disagrees with that of the children. Even where the contemporary schools have in force the system of prefects, a form of oligarchy, as in the public schools, there is this fatal atmosphere of play, of apprenticeship about the authority of the older boy, an atmosphere that breeds irresponsibility. Mr. Bernard Darwin, thinking this to be a merit of these schools, makes this point very well: 'It

[1] *The Nation at School*, F. S. Marvin, 1933, Chap. 18.

is to be remembered that all school-boy authorities from the captain of the school downwards are in a sense only playing at being rulers, although the game is a serious one. They hold their authority only on sufferance and there is a master to undo or over-ride their mistakes and to deprive them of office if they make too many.'[1] There can be no educational value in such authority, which is dangled before the young as a toy and, anyway, is only lent them. Real democracy means that the school council, which makes the laws and punishes offenders, is all-powerful, for its term of office, though it may be criticized openly and fearlessly. That council must be elected by an equal vote from all members of the community, staff and children, old and young; on the council, a staff vote should count as much as, but no more than, a child's vote. The staff will come under the same laws as the children and must treat them as seriously.[2] Will this mean riot, irresponsibility, disrespect or the appearance of any other

---

[1] *The English Public Schools*, p. 58.

[2] There seems to me to be a certain latent muddle-headedness in Mrs. King's comments on this problem in connection with the Russian schools in her book, *Changing Man*. She discusses the latest restriction by the Soviet government of self-government; such a statement that 'the ultimate responsibility for self-government rests with the teacher, and finally with the Head' (p. 100), seems to me to reveal an inherent falsity in the system she is describing, just such an element of irresponsibility as I am here condemning, although the resultant compromise may of course work to a certain extent. Mrs. King thinks it possible that the present Russian admixture of 'disciplined and regulated class teaching with the great variety and freedom offered by the arts opportunities in out-of-school activities for creative self-expression will make the almost perfect education' (p. 121). Such inconsistency in education will, I believe, always have some unfortunate result, in this case, of course, an attitude of boredom and intolerance towards 'school-work' as differentiated from more pleasurable activities.

bogey, that so frightens the school teacher now? Mr. Pekin says that self-government 'would mean the growth of a new attitude to government, which regards it not as something externally and arbitrarily imposed, but as created by the governed themselves according to their knowledge of their own needs and as therefore worthy of loyal support'.[1] That feeling of responsibility has been the aim of all disciplinary methods, but is very rarely achieved. In the more common girls' day-school, where the authority of the staff is ultimately absolute, it is usual for the form to elect its own leader; it is extremely rare for the form to feel any respect for the authority of that leader, who, in an atmosphere of latent antagonism between staff and pupils, will nearly always side with her fellows, a fact on which the rest of the form has usually learned to count. The authority of prefects is also usually in need of underpinning by that of the staff. The mixture of two forms of discipline induces an elaborate self-deception that girls' schools seem to specialize in. Self-government needs a new orientation of mind and cannot be successful unless applied whole-heartedly; the democracy must be complete and utterly serious. At present, the game of defying an authority that is an absurdity, is much more amusing than the game of playing at democracy; the petty officials of a tyranny have always been the objects of the intense scorn and hatred of the populace.

Psychologically will it work? There are some even among the progressive educationalists who consider that self-government puts too great a strain on the individual child, especially at the early stages of education. This does not seem to be the case where it has

[1] *Progressive Schools*, L. B. Pekin, Chap. 4.

been tried; the child can easily bear a collective responsibility, whereas an individual one, such as is involved in the office of form-leader or prefect, would worry him or make him precocious. Nor need any of the problems that arise for his consideration be beyond his powers, as long as they are not related too soon to wider theoretical issues of morality or politics, as they will all be closely connected with his own life and his immediate needs and ideas. We do not debar a man from the political vote because he has not studied political economy; we depend on his judgment of his own requirements. Why debar a child from his share of school government on the plea that he is too young to understand such things? If the atmosphere of the proceedings is serious, self-government will not mean chaos. On the whole a child resents assaults on his property as much as, if not more so, than an adult; bullying is usually a matter of individual maladjustment, and in the mass children have a strict sense of justice; to-day nothing arouses more enmity against a teacher than 'favouritism'. But the greatest revolution that such a system demands, is in the attitude of the teacher to the child, and vice versa. A new humility is necessary in this sphere; we school-marms and pedagogues must cease to be demi-gods. We are no better in ourselves than many of the children we teach. That we know more, even that we are sometimes in greater control of ourselves, is due to our age. Meanwhile we have probably lost something in spontaneity, energy, and generosity. Is there anything that is disgraceful or unseemly in being the equal of a child?. I might quote the Gospels at this point, but no one takes them seriously these days. As for teaching, as Xenophon said: 'How shall a man learn except from one who be his friend?'

and of what value is the friendship in which one party demands the constant recognition of his supposed superiority? Self-government, with its necessary condition that the teacher lose an artificial dignity, to ask for a new one dependent on his merits alone, is the only form of discipline that will fit into a school that is based on sympathy and mutual understanding, and not on fear and hatred. But this last change is perhaps the most difficult to achieve of all the reforms I have been advocating; it is easier to build fifty new schools, to evolve a totally new curriculum and time-table with new methods of teaching, than to eradicate the tone of command from the voice of a schoolmistress, or to drag a schoolmaster from his pedestal of superiority. All we can do is to find comfort in the idea that in a society where unemployment is unknown, no one need become a teacher for any reason but love of children (love of teaching is no qualification), and that love breeds humility.

Discipline should, however, always remain subsidiary to the other activities of the school, and the best training of character is gained in the process of mastering a subject-matter. We have discussed methods of teaching and school management; the matter of education now remains. The idea that every man and woman should be engaged in some activity which is ultimately useful to society, and does not exploit the labours of their fellows, has given rise to the most common misconception of socialist educational theory, that is, the notion that a socialist school will provide nothing but what is known as vocational training. This is an ancient squabble, and any attitude towards it is greatly conditioned by the social environment to which the critic is accustomed. The humane or liberal type of education usually opposed to vocational training, was bred out of a social system that despised manual labour.[1] The ancient Greeks brought liberal education to a fine art, and it was Aristotle who said: 'To seek utility everywhere is by no means the way of free men with a sense of their own dignity.' It was these same Greeks who made possible the existence of a leisured class by the system of slavery. Matthew Arnold, that fervent admirer of the Greek conception of the humanities, said: 'The study of letters is the study of the operation of human force, of human freedom and activity; the study of nature is the study of non-human forces, of human limitation and passivity.' Part of the reason why science has been received so slowly into the curricula of the traditional schools, is the fact that letters have always been thought a more fitting study for a patrician education. One of the results of the introduction of socialism, which refuses the liberty of selfish idleness to its citizens, will be the disappearance of a leisured class: 'The sharp division between work and leisure breaks down when there is no class in a community which can be called a working class, as contrasted with a leisured class, because all men have both.'[2] The ideology of the socialist state will be in direct opposition to that which bred

---

[1] It is probably true that this notion of a liberal education is more an ideal engendered in the nineteenth century to justify the existing curricula in the public schools, than an actual inheritance from older forms of English education. 'Originally, as Lord Eustace Percy has pointed out, the medieval grammar school was the means by which an ecclesiastical governing class recruited administrators and lawyers to carry on the work of church and secular government' (*Technical Education*, by Barbara Drake and Tobias Weaver, N.F.R.B., p. 18). For this particular practical end, of course, a largely classical curriculum was essential in the Middle Ages.

[2] *Leisure in the Modern World*, by Delisle Burns.

the concept of a liberal education; work of any kind will not be considered a disgrace, not even manual labour. In fact, the socialist has good reason to believe, as the Russians do, that work is salvation, and that the meanest manual task may provide a fulfilment of individuality, if the task is necessary to the general social well-being. The manual labourer in Soviet Russia has arrived at a new dignity, since he feels himself to be more than a mere drudge. Socialism will welcome workers of all kinds as valuable members of society, and definitely will not want a special training for its ornaments; ornament that is not an integral part of the whole is frequently bad. But the contemporary state schools, under the influence of the nineteenth-century public-school tradition, are still giving their pupils an imitation liberal education, though they will have little chance of being idle unless they are unemployed, and the dole does not provide a standard of life conducive to the enjoyment of the humanities. To-day manual labour is despised; the training in physical skill in creation, the teaching of craftmanship is hardly existent in the public schools,[1] and is only allowed a second place in many state schools on sufferance. Moreover, the system of fagging, common in most public schools, perpetuates this notion that it is a privilege to be relieved of the necessity of making your own bed or washing up, that certain forms of labour are socially inferior. 'This fagging system creates the very snobbery which manual labour sensibly undertaken should eradicate; the junior feels he is the inferior of the prefects for whom he works and looks forward to being rid of the jobs he is at present forced to do; while the prefect regards ordinary simple

[1] Cf. *Progressive Schools*, L. B. Pekin, p. 117.

manual tasks as menial and degrading to his proud position.'[1]

Psychologically regarded, this attitude of contempt for labour is ludicrous, for it is an accepted fact that a great satisfaction can be obtained by the successful completion of work, manual or intellectual. The human mind cannot be vacant, nor the body totally inert. Delisle Burns quotes an amusing passage from *A Writer's Notes on his Trade*, by C. E. Montague: 'So powerful is the innate craving for labour that it may take all the massed resources of a great public school and of a famous and ancient university to make a boy believe that real work is a thing to flee from, like want or disease, and that doing it and "having a good time" are states naturally and inimitably opposed to one another.' The progressive schools, realizing the child's natural propensity to some creative activity, have seen a definite educational value in physical labour, so much so that crafts form a large part of their curricula, such as wood- and metal-work, mechanics and various types of construction, and for girls practical domestic work. Some of the schools represented in the *Handbook* run a farm also, so that the children may have the opportunity to work on it, while others have gained immediate and long-distance advantages in the construction by the pupils of swimming-pools, levelled ground for playing-fields, and even additional buildings. This idea of the value of manual labour in education is most profoundly stated by Dewey, a great educationalist, and has been put into practice by the Soviet state, so that we have ample opportunity to assess its degree of importance. The Montessori method of giving children various materials to handle had proved satis-

[1] *Progressive Schools*, L. B. Pekin, p. 119.

factory in many ways, when Dewey criticized it as providing the child with substances which had already passed through the mill of adult mentality, whereas he believed, applying the principle that school life should approximate as closely as possible to the life of society outside the school, that all material handled by children should be raw material, such as the adult has to deal with, in industry and agriculture. The division between vocational and liberal education was one of the cleavages that Dewey wished to see closed by a new synthesis. 'Both practically and philosophically the key to the present educational situation lies in a gradual reconstruction of school materials and methods so as to utilize forms of occupation typifying social calling and to bring out their intellectual and moral content.'[1] This was not from any over-emphasis on utility, but as a reform needed for the ultimate ends of education itself, for Dewey said in the same book: 'The dominant vocation of all human beings at all times is living, intellectual, and moral growth.' The Project Method is only another way of making the child handle real material, and its educational value is that it emphasizes the practical connections and uses of the more abstract sciences, and relates artistic sensitivity to the acquirement and practice of skills. There is this considerable consensus of opinion in educational thinking in favour of labour, practical and manual; it is acquiring a dignity from being considered educationally valuable, but it will probably be impossible to make full use of this new method, in reorganizing education, until a more equable society has removed the social stigma that now attaches to manual labour. When it is no longer despicable to mend a road, weave cloth, or wash up dishes, then we

[1] *Democracy and Education*, by John Dewey.

may see the abstract sciences claiming more general respect than they now receive, because of their ultimate practical utility, and these manual tasks in return being lightened of much of their irksomeness.

In the Russian schools the educationalists have lately evolved the method of 'polytechnikization'. This means that all teaching, particularly that of science, starts from a practical basis and uses as its illustrations various facts drawn from the conditions of contemporary production and distribution. Schools were formerly attached to various productive institutions, neighbouring factories, bakeries, engineering shops, and so on, but recently it seems that this connection between everyday life and scientific theory is made clear mainly in the workshops of the school itself. Now this method is not followed for the purpose of feeding a rapacious and tyrannous society with the fuel of specialized workmen that it requires, but in accordance with educational principles. 'They are not seeking to direct the pupils' attention to particular occupations, or to persuade them to choose such occupations when they leave school, or even to create in them any special fitness for these occupations. . . . What is quite sincerely intended by the polytechnical school is the very opposite of training in any particular vocation or craftmanship; in fact, an improvement in the intellectual equipment of *all* the pupils throughout the land, irrespective of the particular occupations they will severally choose.'[1] The education of Soviet Russia is thus based on a wise principle, to develop initiative and intellectual awareness in its citizens, qualities that its social system can afford to encourage. Vocational education or specialized training begins at eighteen, and the Russians are aware

[1] *Soviet Communism*, S. and B. Webb, p. 900.

that work that has been chosen freely has a good chance of being enjoyed and therefore well performed, and that you cannot develop qualities of enterprise and social loyalty by sausage-machine methods of apprenticeship. These Russian schools are putting into practice Dewey's theory of the educational value of the use of raw materials. Pinkevitch quotes Lenin on the subject: 'Communism would wage a struggle for the abolition of the division of labour and for the bringing up, education, and training of harmoniously developed human beings, capable of doing everything.'[1] He also definitely refutes the idea that Soviet education is concerned merely with the training of skilled workmen: 'The whole spirit of the Soviet polytechnical schools is diametrically opposed to the mere teaching of trades.'[2] Visitors bear witness to the vitality and energy of the product of the Russian schools, when our main problem remains the conquest of apathy and the defeat of the idea that school work is necessarily boring.

We may therefore decide the attitude of the new education in the socialist state of England towards labour. First an equable society will remove the stigma on manual labour, and make it a possibility that the best in education shall include this practical orientation, whereas now the social superiority of academic learning makes even the socialist disclaim practical training as inferior to an education often barren of interest and excitement to the normal child; everybody wanting to

[1] *Science and Education in the U.S.S.R.*, Pinkevitch, p. 29.
[2] Ibid., p. 31. Krupskaya, speaking in 1930 at a conference on 'The Reconstruction of the National Economy and Polytechnized Education,' is quoted by Beatrice King in *Changing Man* (p. 59) to the same effect: 'The aim of polytechnikization was the all-round education of a highly developed worker, who could at the same time be worker and master of industry.'

climb feels the need of a liberal education as the mark of social standing. Secondly, there will be no special schools for training various kinds of workmen apart from the usual state schools; it must be axiomatic that every child in the socialist state must have a general education, though one of the methods of that general education may well be through practical and manual work. Vocational training will be undertaken after the school years in connection with the universities, though courses providing such training may differ according to subject-matter, from purely academic study to part-time work in offices or factories.[1] It may happen that a child shows a definite bent before the age of eighteen, in which case he will take some share in an adult enterprise while still at school. One of the advantages of the socialist state is that it will be possible to bring the child into close contact with institutions and factories outside the school, without his being exploited by employers wanting cheap labour. In fact, I should like to see the school having such close relations with the larger community of the surrounding town, that it offers some communal service to its well-being, which might vary from road-sweeping to the provision of concerts and plays. In doing this the school will be

---

[1] Of the various institutions in England to-day, coming under the designation of technical education, many can be scrapped. Part-time courses for adults will come under the administration of the local universities, along with all other continuation classes. Part-time junior work will be automatically abolished with the creation of universal free secondary education. Junior full-time technical schools can easily be absorbed into the new state system, as their bias to manual creative labour in the curriculum makes them usually sound. They may even be models for the normal secondary school of the future, with reference to one side of their work, at any rate.—Cf. *Technical Education*, by Barbara Drake and Tobias Weaver, N.F.R.B., p. 8.

looking after the interests of the individual who needs an atmosphere of vigorous social life for the realization of some sides of his personality.[1] When labour has been freed from its connections with exploitation and social inferiority, educationalists can obtain the maximum value from it, with no fear of prejudicing a child's chance of rising in the world or of supplanting educational ideals by economic necessity. As Tawney says, the socialist state 'instead of valuing schools because they produce better workmen for factories, . . . will value factories partly because they produce the wealth which may make possible better schools'.[2] In this matter, as in many others, it is only when the state has its economic house in order that education can be considered on its own merits. 'Just as the man who is constantly toiling for bread is debarred from purely cultural pursuits, so the nation whose economic position is unsound can spare its children neither the money nor the time for any education beyond the most elementary.'[3]

If education makes any pretence at being more than the preparation for some employment, then it must make provision for the enjoyment of the leisure hours of the future citizens. It is unfortunately necessary for people to be trained to use their leisure, at least so it appears from the present perpetual demand from child

[1] This form of school social service has been widely developed in the U.S.S.R.

'One very widespread form of "socially useful work" is the children's participation in different campaigns which are carried on in the Soviet Union. For example, village school children between the ages of ten and twelve might assist in a milking contest by measuring the amount of milk drawn from the cows.'
—*Science and Education in the U.S.S.R.*, Pinkevitch, p. 36.

[2] *Education, The Socialist Policy*, R. H. Tawney, 1924, p. 6.

[3] *Procrustes, The Future of Education*, Alderton Pink, p. 43.

and adult, 'What shall I do?' The problem is all the more urgent as the socialist state would probably see a great reduction in the hours of labour, through the scientific application of machinery to industry. It also seems probable that, however much the socialist state may invest manual labour with dignity, the work of the majority of people engaged in industry will become increasingly monotonous and dull. 'For a vast number of men and women, work is failing to give a meaning to life. In consequence, if leisure is to become the valuable thing we hope it will be, it must be filled with something as serious as work formerly was.'[1] It may be some time before the economic life of the country can depend on an hour or two's labour a day from each citizen, but it is sensible to look forward to a period when the economic problem will sink back to its rightful place of unimportance, leaving the major part of an individual's time for purposes other than the merely economically productive. What those purposes will be can hardly be conjectured at this stage, but that need not deter us from training minds to meet many eventualities. At the moment we have the ridiculous situation that we put children into dull routine work, having given them a faint glimpse of liberal education, in which the delights of culture are divorced from all reality. 'We still complacently take boys from working-class homes, give them a "liberal" education, and then turn them adrift to become clerks or grocers' assistants, laying the flattering unction to our soul, as we say farewell, that they will add their figures or cut their rashers all the better for having tasted the sweets of poetry or wrestled with the problems of geometry.'[2] Now the solution is not to deny poetry

[1] *A New World in the Making*, Johannes Novrup (Denmark).
[2] *Procrustes*, Alderton Pink, pp. 39–40.

and geometry to grocers' assistants; though education must be rooted in contemporary ideology, it should also have an eye to the future. 'Education should produce, not new toilers in the old mill, but men and women too good for the shabby gentilities and ill-rewarded labours of existing society.'[1] Socialist education must aim at developing, not the type of mind that can see no further than its immediate surroundings, but one that can range for its pleasure over wider fields. That this will produce some discontent in the transition is not to be denied; poetry is no salve for the sores of unemployment, nor a liberal education much comfort to the slum-dweller; but it is a divine discontent and even politically dangerous. That is one of the reasons why the socialist urges educational progress and why his opponents have ever been unwilling to concede more than the scraps of learning to the working-class child. It is not merely that education as it is to-day may with luck teach you to think; it may also arouse emotions that would otherwise remain dormant; it may harness sensations to ideals and faiths, rather than allow them to evaporate in the misty romances of films and novels at their worst. It may against great odds do these things to-day; in a socialist state there must be no doubt about it; it must.

What constitutes training for a good use of leisure? One profound aspect of this subject is almost beyond the influence of a social system: 'One may reform the police-system or improve the drainage for the sake of others; one may eat a good dinner for self-realization, but one does not "live" *for* anything at all. One just lives. The perception of that fact and of its importance may very well come from doing nothing.'[2] That is a profoundly

[1] *Leisure in the Modern World*, Delisle Burns.   [2] Ibid., p. 206.

true statement and the socialist state can provide the leisure, but possibly not the type of mind that can do nothing profitably. Yet there is perhaps a certain connection between the modern wild-goose chase for adventure, the desire for 'something to happen', the craving for events and amusements to mark the passage of time, and the type of society that has turned the gift of leisure into the curse of unemployment, and has refused to the leisured rich the satisfaction of hard work at a favourite pursuit, if it does not happen to be socially correct. If that is so, then a society that relieves its members from economic insecurity may allow a man to do nothing without being haunted by the idea that he is wasting his time and possibly starving his wife and family. The socialist state will be able to provide other aids to the good use of leisure. The general cultural level of such a township as I have envisaged, directed from the university, should be much higher than it is at present. Thus, for instance, socialist town-planning and the lack of competitive production and distribution, may allow a town to be a fine and noble environment, a series of related and dignified buildings, unmarred by screaming advertisements. Again, the type of constructive energy that I should like to feel running through all socialist activity, an atmosphere of initiative and enthusiasm, in which every person takes his share in the common creation, will provide endless opportunities for the individual to find a method of self-expression. Without prejudicing national endeavour in the making of films and the presentation of plays, which when freed from commercial pressure should reach a high level of artistic merit, there should be every encouragement to the individual to participate in local artistic activity. God forbid that we should multiply the number of amateur theatrical societies, those breeding-grounds of spite and bad art, escape worlds where dissatisfied wives and husbands can at least pretend to be married to someone else. But in a small town the fifth-rate travelling company would be replaced by local people, using all the technique and equipment that to-day are the prerogative of the professional. Local films and orchestras might also flourish and reach a high standard of performance.

Schools might take a large part in these activities, and every child should have the opportunity to discover any artistic talent he possesses and also of hearing good music and plays, seeing good films, and generally appreciating a varied range of artistic performance. It would, I believe, be a psychological improvement to put all artistic subject-matter outside the normal school curriculum altogether. Let there be no set teaching of English literature, for example, until a pupil with a special interest in it has reached the stage of specialization. Thus we may avoid the fantastic absurdity of the English examination, wherein the examiner requires the child to appreciate (that is, have an emotional experience concerning) a given poem at a given time, or is reduced to the fatuity of asking for 'a description of three poems in this anthology dealing with birds'. A library should do for literature what a studio can do for art, allow an individual to discover for himself the golden realms of poetry and the delights of prose. Only so will it be possible to make certain that he enjoys his reading and that is the one essential. His interest may be awakened by the enthusiasm of the librarian who is a specialist in the subject, and also by various societies in and out of school; a poetry-reading society, for instance, might exist in the school whose members would have the bond merely of common enjoyment. Such a society should be affiliated to its adult counterpart outside the school, so that a child who has discovered in himself an artistic talent or enthusiasm may naturally come into the right group when he leaves school, and will already have worked with adults who take his interest seriously while still within the school society.

I have stressed the artistic subjects at this point, in order that no accusation may be made that I have reduced the socialist school to a scientific workshop and nothing more; there must, of course, be every opportunity for the individual to find his own personal delight in any direction he chooses. He may want to garden, to collect specimens, to tinker with bits of iron and all sorts of oddments evolving some startling invention. A child delights in collecting things; let him be given the opportunity to collect things more exciting and more educative than cigarette cards, makes of cars or silver paper. If a child can have found scope for his enthusiasm while still at school—and a child without some enthusiasm, be it only a day-dream, is almost a contradiction in terms—he will bid fair to carry that enthusiasm into his adult life, and the modern attitude of mind that expects all enjoyment and amusement to come to it without any effort on its part, will be partly overcome. To preserve that enthusiasm into adult life two things are necessary: it must be allowed to be spontaneous, never killed by routine or fixed hours of study. All such enthusiasms should find expression in hobbies, by which I do not mean an activity that is not taken seriously, but simply one that is taken up at will and freely chosen.[1] The various school societies, that

[1] One of the most satisfactory aspects of Russian education to-day is the attention paid to what they call 'cultural' work.

I have referred to should always be the natural result of a demand on the children's part, never instituted by adults. In the same way, though the training of the emotions is a much-neglected and very important aspect of education, and even though for very young children some definite training in sensitivity in the appreciation of the differences between colour, texture, and sound, may be possible, at the adolescent stage such training should be unobstrusive and brought in by the back door. Thus I look with suspicion on some of the early morning gatherings even as practised by progressive schools, where music is played or poetry read, for if the individual is out of tune with the prevailing mood, boredom and irritation must result, and these are as blight and disease to the true artistic pleasure. Let music be played every day in the school, but let the performers be in a room apart where the audience can gather if it wishes. A child may consequently listen to music at school or in the town; if he develops from curiosity to real enjoyment his own interest will lead him to discover from fellow enthusiasts and books all he really needs to know of the facts concerning his subject.

The second necessity for preserving enthusiasm is that the child shall feel his interest to be of real importance. There must be no indulgence on the part of the adult; if he is not prepared to share an enthusiasm on equal terms with a child, let him keep out of his way.

In circles held in schools, but out of school hours, in the children's sections of the clubs belonging to factories, farms, and other institutions, in the serious use of the theatre and the cinema to meet the special needs of children, the Soviet is aiming at just such provision of opportunities of self-fulfilment and creative expression as I am here advocating.—Cf. *Changing Man*, by Beatrice King, Chap. 6.

Only by genuine enthusiasm on the part of the adult will the child be preserved from putting away enthusiasm with other childish things. If he is collecting specimens he should have part of the school museum to fill and all materials for classifying and arranging his collections; if a job can be found for him at the town museum so much the better. If he aspires to be a gardener, he should work under the school groundsmen or in the public parks. Let the budding musician play to the school and in the town orchestra when his performance is adequate. The problem of leisure will be on the way to solution if every individual has managed to carry with him a child-like enthusiasm through life; the variety of interests possible is all to the good of society which needs both potato-growers and philosophers. A social system that generates enthusiasm, and also allows its citizens the pure enjoyment that often lies in doing nothing after social obligations are fulfilled, will get its full return in a culture invigorated by countless individual creations and participations, and a multitude of socially desirable achievements. This idea is, of course, only another application of the two principles with which I began this chapter, that education should be fluid, making possible the absorption of new ideas and developments and allowing for the particular bent of each individual child; and that it should in all phases have links in organization and spirit with the life outside the school.[1]

[1] This atmosphere of enthusiasm and unsophisticated energy is to my feeling Soviet Russia's major achievement. The Webbs quote a passage that puts into words that feeling as adequately as any I know.

'This quality of exuberance the Russians share, but they work while they study and study while they work, uniting theory and practice not in minor jobs whose outcome is private profit, but in

In attempting this description of the spirit in which I believe socialist education should be undertaken, I have deliberately laid stress on the development of the individual and his claims to consideration. Where I have argued for communal types of educational method or organization, I have done so because I believe the majority of individuals need the opportunity of community life and service to arrive at self-realization, because in fact community life and individual development are not incompatible; indeed, the latter is frequently given strength and width by the former. Sir Percy Nunn, who typifies the extremely individualistic educationalist, considers it an erroneous thought 'that social conduct involves the sacrifice of individuality, not its enrichment, that it means self-surrender, not self-fulfilment'.[1] Delisle Burns says that 'the supposed lack of individuality in modern conditions is an illusion of superior persons. In all societies the common element in the minds of its members is very large; and certainly modern conditions have enlarged this common element. But it is an illusion to suppose that the more common life there is, the less individuality there is. The whole thing grows; as common life grows, so individuality grows, because there is no fixed limit to human capa-

---

a vast social upbringing. . . . They are enjoying life while they are changing it. . . . There shines from their eyes a concentrated and eager intensity such as I have never seen before outside a religious revival or a strike meeting. . . .

'Their ruggedness has been filled with the greatest purpose that can enter into man.'—*Soviet Communism*, p. 407. Quoted from *Soviet Russia—Land of Youth*, by Harry Ward, in *The Nation*, New York, 1932.

The passage explains that enthusiasm as springing from those principles of fluidity and realism that I have been advocating in education.

[1] *Education, its Data and First Principles*, Percy Nunn, Chap. 15.

S

cities'.[1] I have said that socialist education should aim at being educational rather than primarily socialist. I have emphasized this aspect because I wish to conciliate the intense individualism of many educationalists, who are alarmed by certain aspects of the socialist doctrine. It will be as well to deal with the problem separately, summing up various arguments already put forward.

It is safer to make certain admissions at once, when considering what share the state will take in education and how far it will deny the individual certain liberties, educational among others. Everyone is bound to admit that the state will put some restriction on individual activity; every society of any kind whatsoever has always done so. Secondly, socialist education will be socialist, just as education in England to-day is capitalist. I have been at pains to show that an educational system must be coloured by the wider social forms around it, and I have suggested that a really satisfactory education makes the relation between the school and society as close as possible. When the social system is just and equable this is clearly an advantage. Thirdly, I allow the point to any unfriendly critic, that in Russia, the only place where socialist education can be observed at work, there has been deliberate and prolonged propaganda in the schools in favour of the existing type of social system. The programme of the Communist Party of the Soviet Union defines the function of the school as follows: In the period of the dictatorship of the proletariat, i.e., the period of preparation of the conditions required for the full realization of communism, the school should not merely be the vehicle of the principles of communism generally, but also a means of conveying the organizing, educating, ideological influence of the

[1] *Leisure in the Modern World*, Dehsle Burns, p. 28.

proletariat to the semi-proletarian and non-proletarian layers of the population, with the object of bringing up a generation capable of establishing communism.'[1]

To take the last point first—we need not evade the issue by saying that what happens in Russia need not happen here; critics and admirers of the socialist theories have an equal right to refer to Russia as providing the only possible illustration of socialism at work. There is, however, an obvious mitigation of the more intense propaganda in the schools in recent years, owing partly to an increased feeling of economic security and partly to common sense.[2] One has some sympathy with the father who 'in a meeting of the Central Executive Committee of the U.S.S.R., rose to complain that his own children, though eager and bright, could not spell, were weak in their arithmetic, and knew more about the bad conditions of labour in capitalist countries than about the geography of the U.S.S.R.'[3] There appear to arise occasionally in the world's history times when the normal balance between the good of the community and the freedom of the individual, that exists at that particular historical stage, becomes dislocated. As the result of licence allowed to some individuals to destroy the liberties of others, society has its revenge, and for some time will impose its good on the wills of its members as an object of more importance than their individual happiness; that is, in familiar terms, there will be a

---

[1] *Science and Education in the U.S.S.R.*, Pinkevitch, p. 27.
[2] 'There have been far-reaching changes in the teaching of social science, the aim being to eliminate the narrow, prejudiced outlook, the very marked political propaganda which would on occasion gloss over inaccuracies of fact when they did not fit in with the theory. The efforts to a more tolerant, wider, and less biased outlook were generally evident.'—*Changing Man*, by Beatrice King, p. 163.   [3] *Soviet Communism*, S. and B. Webb, p. 897.

revolution. No one pretends that a revolution is a pleasant or valuable thing in itself; it is an evil springing out of tyranny, and if out of the revolution is born something of value, like the socialist state, then the revolution that imposes that type of society on individuals is possibly a means that is justified by the end. In any case the former tyranny makes it inevitable, and the period of reaction against that tyranny will witness the suppression of individual freedom for the purpose of preserving that form of society. The ultimate good of individuals which consists in the preservation of that society will take precedence over their more immediate good; and it is only in times of such dislocation that the immediate and ultimate benefits are incompatible. Consequently in Russia, until the fears of armed intervention from abroad and of insecurity at home have disappeared, we may expect some propaganda in the schools which is a time-honoured means of retaining the forms of society free from modification. In England, if socialism is heralded in by revolution and violence and the new state has to face a ring of enemies, then we may also expect intensive socialist propaganda in the schools. It is one of the prices that the capitalist will have to pay, if he refuses to forgo his power except at the point of the revolver.

By propaganda in this sense I mean the definite statement that one state of society is better than another, with constant emphasis on ideas, events, and persons that are connected with that form of society and the omission of full particulars of the case for the other types. The violence of one's dislike for this procedure depends naturally on one's political opinions; I find it vastly more exasperating to witness a glorification of an English monarch or naval hero, to observe history being manipulated to the honour of Wellington or Victoria, for instance, than to that of Lenin or Stalin. Similarly the educational tyranny of the fascist states is peculiarly abhorrent to the socialist; the picture of Hitler or Mussolini on the walls of a school will make him rabid in his denunciation of fascism, though Lenin's portrait displayed in a crèche will do nothing worse than cause him amusement. The ideals of Soviet Russia impress me as valuable and exalted, and those of imperialist nineteenth-century England do not, and consequently propaganda in their favour is particularly irritating to me. I am aware that for the anti-socialist the opposite is true; these prejudices are bound to appear. Therefore I can only make the plea, which will be entirely unsatisfactory to the confirmed supporter of capitalism, that direct socialist propaganda will be a very minor evil to the converted, who it is hoped will be the majority, and though I should be strongly against its use where it is possible to avoid it, I should never give up hope of socialist education if I found that in its first stages it resorted to direct propaganda, provided that fundamental reforms were also carried through. Thus I consider other aspects of Russian education to be very much more important than this matter of propaganda. I would go so far as to say that, if the new socialist state has to struggle for existence, the good of the individual, in being allowed as impartial an introduction to the question of the socialist-capitalist struggle as is humanly possible, would quite rightly be made subordinate to the greater good offered him by the preservation of a just and equable society around him.

If, however, we discount the possibility of violence, and presuppose that the transition to socialism occurs without too great a dislocation, then there is very little to be said for direct propaganda. Ultimately the safety of human civilization depends on the ability of human beings to make independent decisions, and that in its turn depends on the development of the scientific attitude of mind reviewing all the evidence before making a judgment. If we imagine a time when sufficient of the world is under socialist control to ensure that socialism will run its natural course of life, there should then be no blatant propaganda in the schools. To return to the second admission, we shall find the seeming paradox that, while socialist schools are not concerned with making socialists in the way that the Jesuits wish to make Roman Catholics, education in these schools will have to be socialist. If we mean by 'propaganda' any influence whatsoever of the social system on its members, then propaganda there must be; and I have argued for a complete acceptance of this fact, by advocating much closer links with other institutions that reflect the social system.[1] I have argued for this partly because it is wise to accept the inevitable and partly because I believe the socialist state would make that inevitability an educational advantage; psychologists have recommended it on other grounds. But a confirmed capitalist in a socialist society would presumably wish to find a school for his children as far removed from surrounding social realities as possible,

[1] In Russia the direct propaganda is inextricably mixed with this more general influence of society. Witness this set of themes for children in pre-school institutions, for example: 'Participation in celebrations of the November Revolution; organization of "economic corner"; participation in general work of organizing for winter sports; Lenin Commemoration Days; participation of children in the Red Army celebrations; spring-work, organization of open-air playground; organization of vegetable-gardens and flower-beds.'—*Science and Education in the U.S.S.R.*, Pinkevitch, p. 50.

just as to-day the socialist parent prefers to remove his child from the capitalist mentality that is latent in all schools established by the state. The socialist reply to this demand brings us back to the consideration of the first admission, that society will always limit the freedom of the individual, and this liberty to pick a non-state school for one's children is one that the socialist state will destroy. Consequently it may appear that there will be less educational freedom under socialism than under capitalism. I deny the quantitative criticism; there will be infinitely more liberty in other directions but there will be a shift in freedom undoubtedly. What may be freedom to the parent is slavery to the child. What state allows the parent the freedom to kill its child with impunity? I would contemplate undisturbed the denial of the parent's freedom to remove the child from the state school, because by attending that school, if it at all comes up to my expectations, the child will be acquiring vast possibilities of development, in fact, the freedom to reach to the height of its powers. That higher freedom depends on the spirit in education, ultimately on the quality and amount of attention given to each child in his training. Society must impose restrictions on some individuals to achieve that freedom in education; socialism, for reasons already given, seems to me to be the social system most likely to provide that freedom for the individual, the freedom to abstract the essence of community-life while preserving his own intellectual integrity, the freedom to be a social being, deriving from society all the immense benefits springing from communal creation and service, and at the same time using his own capacities for reasoned and balanced judgment on every action of his own and of society. As a socialist should never need to fear real intellectual criticism, we may end this argument on liberty and control by a comment on the scientific spirit which I hope socialist schools will make it their business to develop. But if the reader considers that the liberties that I have suggested as arising out of the organization and spirit of socialist education do not outweigh the liberties of the average child to-day (and I mean child and not parent) then I have no other argument to put forward; to the educationalist everything is subordinate to this and I believe that ultimately an educationalist who has the welfare of children at heart must accept the society that can make such changes possible. If, however, he is a member of the old school of educational practice and sincerely believes in luxury and licence for himself and hardship and repression for the child, he is not likely to have read so far with patience, and I shall have no compunction in destroying his liberty to give his child an unbalanced, harmful training, that can hardly go by the name of education at all; he is one of the minority of individuals who must suffer a curtailment of liberty in order that the balance may be adjusted.

It may possibly be true to say that the paradox, that the only constant thing in the universe is change, is an idea the implications of which must shortly be realized by the mass of people, or the attempt to preserve unchanged a structure that has rotted will bring disaster onto civilization. It is the task of a new education to create a new citizen, one who will be able to contemplate unabashed a wide field of thought, and both envisage and direct change in his environment. The direction of that change must finally be understood by all citizens in the state, if we are to live democratically, and to create the means to that understanding is, after the development of the individual, the most important function of education. 'The problem of education under the influence of the democratic ideal is not how to produce copies of an ancient pattern, but how to produce the common man alive at all points, vigorous in his interests, capable of co-operating with his fellows in the control of public affairs and the services required by a civilization such as never existed before.'[1] When Lenin made his famous statement that without literacy there can be no politics, only rumours, scandalmongery, and prejudices, he meant what has been often said before, but rarely acted upon, that real democracy presupposes real education. The task of socialist education is not merely to make the plain man understand the workings of society around him, but to make him contemplate intelligently changes in that society. What is the state of mind most conducive to acceptance of change? A faith is a grand but narrow conception, a spear-head that concentrates a man's thrust into a weapon terrible and rapier-keen. The great things of the world have been wrought by the concentrated force of men who have believed themselves to be entirely and eternally right; they have been willing to die and what is more to kill for their beliefs, and they have earned the devotion and the hatred of their fellows. There is the opposite mentality that believes that there is some latent good in all systems, in all ideas, in all faiths, and that intelligence will not always allow a man to abandon himself to one guiding idea: 'Orthodoxy is the grave of the intelligence no matter what orthodoxy it may be. And in this respect the orthodoxy of the radical is no better than that of the reactionary.'[2] It is well for the society that can inspire the logician with enthusiasm

[1] *Democracy*, by Delisle Burns, p. 173.
[2] *Education and the Social Order*, Bertrand Russell, Chap. 1.

for a cause, but apart from this question of enthusiasm, intellectual integrity, and scepticism are essential to civilization and alone can adequately conduct society through great changes. It seems, therefore, that it is impossible to allow the teaching of any orthodoxy in schools, if the highest possible use is to be made of the powers of logic and intellectual criticism. There seems to be no possible reason for not developing those powers to their fullest; the mentality that disregards those powers is that of the superstitious and the fearful, the fundamentalist, and the fascist. In the socialist schools there will be no teaching of 'truth', but only the presentation of opinions; the teacher must deny himself the satisfaction of one of the major desires of mankind, the wish to convert. No principle, no idea, no opinion must be presented as having more than human support, though it may be pointed out for the sake of convenience that certain ideas are accepted by the majority on account of their utility, such as 'two and two make four'. We must cultivate a morality that admires mental honesty and we must get rid of the notion that integrity has connections only with money. Self-knowledge should be a necessary qualification of a teacher: 'Intellectual honesty consists in recognizing when our views are coloured by our wishes, in distinguishing clearly between judgments of fact and judgments of value.'[1] To deny a child knowledge is starvation of the mind; to present it with only part of the relevant facts is dishonest.[2]

[1] *A New World in the Making*, N.E.F., E. Claperede (Switzerland), p. 19.
[2] 'The teacher should be infused with the scientific spirit and possessed of a world view rather than dominated by a political party or economic class. Propaganda by a teacher, be it nationalist or anti-nationalist, communistic or capitalistic, any prejudiced,

There are two criticisms of this attitude which it seems necessary to answer; in the first place that the scientific impartiality here approved is not humanly possible. In criticizing the capitalist bias in present education, I have argued that such impartiality is unobtainable and I have admitted that the prevalent form of society is bound to have a strong influence on its citizens. Society itself, however, should, to be healthy, become imbued with the acceptance of change as natural, so that the influence of environment should not always be in favour of the preservation of the *status quo* in every detail. But the inevitable bias towards the existing modes of living is a further argument for a conscious, deliberate effort to create a scientific impartiality within the school itself. This may be encouraged by two methods, but never by imposing the task of impartiality on the teacher alone, though the present educational tradition would attempt it. His best work can be done with enthusiasm for a subject viewed from his own particular standpoint. But even his training in logic, modified though it must be by that enthusiasm, should enable him to recognize an opinion as an opinion, not a divinely revealed truth, and it should be expressed as such; any enthusiast that is not a complete fanatic is able to give some credit to the opposite point of view. The children should come in contact with members of the staff who disagree and be present at arguments where the opponents are matched in knowledge and expressiveness. For even under a democratic system of school government, the extra years and intellectual experience of the

one-sided attempt to influence children towards his own viewpoint, or the official one, is a violation of that freedom of thinking which is essential for social growth.'—*A New World in the Making*, N.E.F., C. Washbourne (U.S.A.), p. 81.

teacher give him too great an advantage if the controversy is always between himself and the children. Every unofficial organization and society that grew up in a school could be used to advantage to destroy the pedestals onto which the child has unconsciously lifted the teacher and his opinions.

Secondly, the various methods of teaching that have been advocated for the socialist schools, which consist in the discovery of the fact by the child himself, will ensure that a great many ideas and opinions will be received by the child not from persons but from books. Although individual bias is present in any book, it is not so persuasive as that which comes direct from a person, and there is more chance of a child reading different points of view within a short time than of its hearing them personally expressed, for not even a socialist school will be able to provide as many history or science teachers, for instance, as there are books on these subjects in the school library. If any idea is to be impressed on children by direct methods, it is the idea that nothing is certain, that it is the duty of every individual to doubt every proposition that is put to him, to test every thing by his own intelligence, and only when accepted by his reason as well as his desires, to act on a judgment. Indeed, such is the persuasiveness of print and personality, that it may be advisable to use some form of inoculation, such as is advocated by some progressive educationalists to-day, alarmed by the dictatorship of the Press and the nationalist tendencies of modern education. Both these evils we may hope to see lessened by a true democracy; nevertheless, for years to come, exercises in intellectual doubt, in the recognition of the motives behind public pronouncements, in comparison of Press reports, may provide a practical method of destroying the present easy acceptance of any seemingly official declaration, without out criticism or comment. In short, we cannot attain to impartiality in teaching or judgment, but we need not therefore despair of dissolving the worst excesses of partial and dogmatic human nature.

A further criticism of this seientific state of mind is more serious. According to this argument the future citizen, the product of a new truly democratic education, has to be a man or woman trained in the intellectual processes that produce self-criticism and cool judgment. Is he, therefore, to lose his faith, his burning energy, his capacity to move mountains? Are honest doubt and intellectual integrity incompatible with zeal and fervour? This is a question that is almost impossible to answer, for history gives us no example of a society that has been based on a truly democratic education. It would be a major tragedy if the clear light of self-criticism were to dissolve such faith as is building modern Russia, the intense excitement that welds a nation into one mighty and complicated instrument for the betterment of society, to raise its masses from poverty and ignorance. Yet the perils of modern society are in one sense due to the fact that we cannot be certain that human beings will be capable of making sound judgments on national and international affairs at moments of crisis; there would be no more war and no more exploitation if men could read and listen with constant watchfulness and personal reservations. It seems, however, from a review of broad world changes that the scientific frame of mind does not necessarily grow in a different soil from enthusiasm and religious fervour. In fact, a time of intense excitement in all phases of life, like the Renaissance, breeds as much interest in science and abstract thought as in art, which is the commonest expression, with the possible exception of religion, of emotional enthusiasm. An age in English history and literature, much admired to-day for its sweet reasonableness, the eighteenth century, shows a dearth of creative excitement, due, I feel, to a lack of interest in the new, of a sense of discovery. Their one great poet, Blake, has been considered the antithesis of all the eighteenth century stood for, clarity, logic, and coherence; yet in his poetry there is logic of fresh approach and devastating effect, exploring fields of experience that had elsewhere become conventionalized and dull, so devastating that those of conventional outlook prefer to dismiss his writings as the ravings of a madman.

> If he had been Antichrist, Creeping Jesus,
> He'd have done anything to please us:
> Gone sneaking into the Synagogues
> And not used the Elders and Priests like Dogs.[1]

Who amongst all the thinkers of this time ever said anything so bitingly reasonable about the Christian religion?

This excursion into the realms of literature is made to prove my point, that the great romantics, the great enthusiasts, are not incapable of thinking logically; in fact, the sense of discovery, the vision of the new in the old, which is the spur to the poet, is also an essential to the scientist. A scientist is nothing if he is unimaginative. In Russia to-day we have the nearest approach the world has known to socialism in action, and one of its most pleasing aspects is its combination of intense enthusiasm disciplined by religious fervour with the intellectual soundness of the Marxist dogma. As an

[1] *Everlasting Gospel*, Nonesuch edition, p. 135.

example, education itself has progressed as the result of one of those campaigns that the Russians can make significant to the millions of their citizens, with the consequence that illiteracy is rapidly disappearing. The numbers of those taking advantage of the measures for the abolition of illiteracy increased from 732,100 in 1927–8 to roughly 20,000,000 in 1932.[1] On the other hand, along with this attempt at universalism in education has gone much hard thought and study on all aspects of the educational problem. The plans themselves are gigantic intellectual achievements and are carried through with a prolonged excitement that in the capitalist world is only paralleled by the interest in sport.

Let us say finally that we cannot ever get beyond the springs of action that lie in the emotional nature of man; his instinctive reactions will always remain the basis of all achievement. While nothing can or should be done to remove that source of energy, much can be obtained by the direction of the instincts by the intelligence. Civilization has been from one point of view the history of the sublimation of man's instinctive nature; there are many who feel that its continued existence depends on further sublimation. The intellect cannot kill emotional excitement; psychologically it depends on it for existence; it may even give enthusiasm a new life by breaking the bounds of contemporary knowledge. Reason seems to become a dead thing only when it is restricted to the narrow limits of 'schools of thought', making endless annotations to a once vivid but long

[1] Beatrice King in *Changing Man* (p. 269) gives the following figures:
Illiteracy. Percentage of Population: 1913, 78 %; 1927–8, 44 %; 1934–5, 8 %.

since petrified idea. It is possible to get excited over a reasonable proposition. In answering the critics of the co-operative spirit as dangerously sentimental, I pointed out that the harnessing of that spirit to an intellectually acceptable idea was the way to ensure that it will not be exploited for merely sentimental reasons or more dangerous national ends. There is the opposite truth that an idea to arouse wide-spread enthusiasm should be in line with the general tendency of contemporary thought. Intellectual controversies of past generations seem to us absurd, but were in their own day vivid and interesting. The well-known tale of the controversy that, at a time of narrow vision and small-mindedness, raged round the problem of how many angels could stand on a pin-point, seems to us almost too ludicrous to be true; men fought and martyred, however, for ideas that needed far greater qualities of logic and the controversy was no less intense in thought than in war; the Puritans of seventeenth-century England were hard thinkers. To-day we can breed an enthusiasm in incubators, feed it on magic, and deny it all logical exercise. But I know of no enthusiasm among any of the groups that manufacture this product, from Buchmanites to fascists, that can achieve an article of such lasting quality as that made in the Russian factories, where enthusiasms centre round a series of logical reductions from hard fact made by some of the most unsentimental thinkers of all time, Marx, Engels, and Lenin. It is perhaps one of the major arguments in favour of socialism that it can be called a faith and at the same time is attractive to people of high intellectual standard. We need not, I think, be afraid of killing the springs of zeal by training the children of the future in logic; in fact, it has been said with possible truth that if everyone could take a course in economics the world would be socialist very quickly.

In conclusion, I make the claim that the introduction of 'socialism would mean considerable improvement in the quality and quantity of education. The evils of capitalism deny to many children the possibility of benefiting by the little education that is now allowed them. It has been pointed out again and again that slum conditions and unemployment make education a farce. Socialism can remove that obstacle to true education by intelligent economic control; what is more, it can provide a society that can encourage those things of value that are outside the economic sphere, a society whose birth from our present system alone can justify the barbarities that capitalism perpetrates. It was the conviction of Sanderson of Oundle, a great educationalist, and of his admiring biographer, Mr. H. G. Wells, 'that the present common life of men, at once dull and disorderly, competitive, uncreative, cruelly stupid and stupidly cruel, unless it be regarded as a necessary phase in the development of a nobler existence, is a thing not worth having'.[1] That nobler existence is possible under socialism, where economic sanity will free education from financial pressure, where a spirit may be abroad among men which will allow each individual to know the satisfaction of creation in company with his fellows, the pleasures of using a highly-trained intellect, where a man may criticize with some hope of creating what is better; a state of society where there is some possibility of reconciliation between the good of the individual and that of the community, where a man may develop his powers of thought to the utmost and

[1] *Sanderson of Oundle. The Story of a Great Schoolmaster*, H. G. Wells, 1924.

exercise his abilities fully, without the fear of cheating his fellows out of their right to work for their living, by doing so. To the economist the possibility of producing the maximum amount of material necessary to a high standard of life for all men, is attractive. It is a tragic waste to destroy wealth of any kind, and the critic of capitalism may well be driven to exasperation at the sight of burning wheat and rotting fish. Yet there is no waste so tragic as that of human material, such waste as is found in the under-nourished child, toiling in factories or hotels or workshops for a pittance that has to help keep a large family; or the waste of a fine brain, cramped and ossified by the rigidity of outlook and social dictatorship of a bad traditional school. No system of society has to-day justified its existence until every child within it is unwasted; that is to say, is given the opportunity of full physical, mental, and emotional development. By the fact of wasted human material alone, capitalism stands condemned; we are supremely justified in substituting socialism, if, along with more material advantages, it holds promise of a rich harvest of intelligent and competent human beings. To find and expound reasons for believing that it does hold such promise has been my object in writing this book.

INDEX

Adams, Sir John—
  Educational Theories, 58
  The Teacher's Many Parts, 84–6
Adult education, 48, 52–6, 166
Alderton Pink, *Procrustes, The Future of Education*, 190–1, 249–50
American schools, 104, 108
Apprenticeship, 158 fn., 247–8
Armistice Day, 89–90
Arnold, Matthew, 67–8, 242
Arnold, Thomas, 66–8, 74, 88, 186
Arts, the, teaching of, 100, 252–6
Athletics, 95–6, 235–6

Barnardo's Homes, 93
Beacon Hill, 203
Bedales, 44, 213
Bell, 27
Bembridge, 203
Bias in education, 58–102, 267–9
Birkbeck College, 52–3
Blake, William, 88, 270
Board of Education, 29, 167–70
Borstal, 51
Brendon, *Britain and Her Neighbours*, 78
British Broadcasting Corporation, 19, 92
British and Foreign Schools Society, 27
British Medical Association's scales of nutrition, 151–2
Bryant, Sophie, *Moral and Religious Education*, 62
Buchmanism, 8

Building grants, 34, 135–7
Burns, Delisle—
  Democracy, 192, 265
  Leisure in the Modern World, 97–8, 220, 242, 244, 251, 258–9

Cambridge, 45–7, 69, 188–9, 193–6
Capitalism and culture, 17–19, 121–3
Chaning, Pearce, *Chiron: The Education of a Citizen of the World*, 101, 183–4
Charity, 93–4
Chartist movement, the, 53
Circular 1421, 29
Circular 1444, 41 fn., 136, 173 fn.
Citrine, Sir Walter, 184 fn.
Civics, 60–2
Clarke, F., *Essays in the Politics of Education*, 60
Classics, cf. also Latin, 67–9
Co-education, 107–8, 213–15
Community, the, 6–11, 220–1, 225–6
Competition, 111–14, 202–4, 230–1, 234
Co-operation, 202–4, 230–6
Corporal punishment, 100, 217
Crafts, 70, 244
Curricula, 37–8, 67–71
Curry, W., 201–5, 213

Dalton Plan, 221–5, 237
Dartington Hall, 197, 202–3, 213
Darwin, Bernard, *The English Public School*, 183–5, 238

Dewey, John, 244–5, 247
  Democracy and Education, 245
Discipline, 100–1, 111, 213, 216–20, 238–9, 241
Drake, Barbara, and Weaver, Tobias, *Technical Education*, 45, 165–6 fn., 190 fn., 248 fn.

Eden, Anthony, 8
Education—
  and capitalism, 11, 20, 103, 128, 274
  and culture, 11, 121–3, 252–5
  and leisure, 249–56
  and religion, 27, 87–9, 178–81
  and socialism, 8, 11–12, 56–7, 127–9, 207, 273
  and the state, 58, 169–70
Elementary education, the history of, 26–8
Empire Day, 90–1
Employment Bill, 55
Employment, juvenile, 152–3
English literature, the teaching of, 122–3, 253
Equality of sex, 105–8, 214–15
Equipment of schools, 81–4, 137, 161
Eton, 84, 185
Examinations, 114–20
Expenditure in education, 104 fn., 155–6
Experiment in education, 109, 198–201

Fagging, 101, 243–4
Family, the, 145, 163–4
Farm schools, 176
Fascism, 6, 19, 72, 122, 261
Fawcett, E. N., and Kitchen, M. le S., *The World To-day*, Vol. 8, 81–3
Firth, C., *History, Senior Course*, Book 3, 80

Fisher Education Bill, 28
Fluidity in education, 208–12, 256
Freedom in education, 227–30, 263–4
Froebel, 40–1

General Schools Certificate Examination, 49, 76, 115–16, 119–20
Girls' Public Day School Trust, 43
Girls' schools, 42–3, 106–7
Grand National Consolidated Union, 53
Gray, J. L., and Moshinsky, P., Investigation into inequality of opportunity among London schoolchildren, 20–1 fn., 23–5, 39 fn.
Green, G. H., *Psycho-analysis in the Class-room*, 217

Hadow Report, 29–30, 131–2
Health visitors, 145–6
Higher Schools Certificate Examination, 49, 115–16
History, teaching of, 71–2, 75–81
Hitler, 7, 261
Hodgekin, 53
Hore-Belisha, 7
Horrabin, W. and F., *Working-class Education*, 27 fn., 53–4

Illiteracy, 12, 271
Individualism, 6–8, 210–11, 221–3, 257–8
Industrial Revolution, 27, 77, 132–3 fn.
Inequality in education, 20–57, 103
Inspection, 168–9
Internationalism, 204

Kaiser Wilhelm 2nd, 60
King, B., *Changing Man*, 43 fn., 46–7 fn., 142–3 fn., 200 fn., 224, 231 fn., 238 fn., 247 fn., 254–5 fn., 259 fn., 271 fn.
King-Hall, Stephen, 92
Kinglake, *Eothen*, 68
Kingsley, 53
Krupskaya, 224, 234 fn., 247 fn.

Labour and Education, 129–30, 136, 158 fn.
Labour Party, The, 16–17, 57, 127–8
Lankester, 27
Latin, the teaching of, cf. also Classics, 33, 210
Lawrence, D. H., 19
Lawrence, T. E., 8
League of Nations, 91
League of Nations Union, 93–5
Leavis and Thompson, *Culture and Environment*, 18
Leavis, Mrs., *Fiction and the Reading Public*, 18
Lenin, 64, 78, 80, 247, 261, 265, 272
Liberal education, 67, 241–3
Local authorities, 136, 147, 173–5
London County Council, 71, 175
London Labour Party, 71
London Working Men's College, 53–4
Lowe's system of Payment by Results, 28
Lynd, R. and S., *Middletown*, 18, 122

Maintenance grants, 134–5
Malnutrition, 147, 150–4
Marvin, F. S., *The Nation at School*, 109–10, 115, 119, 237

Marxist theory, 11–14, 56, 75, 76, 78, 81, 88 fn., 89, 272
Maurice, 53
McMillan, Margaret, 40, 201
McNally, C. E., *Public Ill Health*, 147–8, 151–3
Mechanics' Institutes, 52
Medical inspection and treatment in schools, 145–55
Milk Marketing Board, 155
Miller, *Beginner's History of England*, 78
Modern Schools Handbook, 182, 197, 202–4, 210 fn., 213–14, 219, 244
Montague, C. E., *A Writer's Notes on his Trade*, 244
Montessori, 40–1, 244–5
Moshinsky, cf. Gray.

National Council of Labour Colleges, 56–7
National Government—
 first, 29, 31, 36, 55, 135–6, 141
 second, 28, 129–30, 134 fn., 173, 235
National Society for the Education of the poor in the principles of the Church of England, 27
National Union of Teachers, 86, 172
Neill, A. S., 109, 201, 210, 219
New Fabian Research Bureau, 127
Newbolt, Sir Henry, 91, 96
New Statesman and Nation, 35 fn., 78, 87, 183 fn., 188 fn., 196 fn.
New World in the Making, A.
New Education Fellowship, 65, 202–4, 250, 266, 266–7 fn.
Norwood, Dr. Cyril, *English Tradition in Education*, 12, 97, 110, 232

Nunn, Sir Percy, *Education, Its Data and First Principles*, 113, 257.
Nursery schools, 39–41
  Consultative Committee to Board of Education, on, 40

Officers' Training Corps, 96–9
Oman, Sir Charles, *A Junior History of England*, 77–8
Orr, Sir John, 153
Over-crowded classes, 35, 138–9
Oxford, 46–7, 69, 120, 188–9, 193–6

Pekin, L. B.—
  Progressive Schools, 66, 213 fn., 216–17, 221, 233, 239, 243–4
  Public Schools, 99 fn., 99–101
Percy, Lord Eustace, 242 fn.
Pickard-Cambridge, Dr. A. W., Presidential Address to the Educational Section of the British Association, 117
Pindar, A., 85 fn.
Pinevitch—
  The New Education in Soviet Russia, 16
  Science and Education in the U.S.S.R., 112 fn., 208 fn., 247, 249 fn., 258–9, 262 fn.
Planning in education, 169–72, 174–5, 177
Plebs' League, 56
Ploughshare, The, June–July, 1936, 104 fn.
Polytechnikization, 246–7
Prayers in schools, 87–9
Prefects, 100–1, 238–9
Private schools, 44, 48, 181
Privy Council Committee, 1839, 28
Prize-givings, 89–90
"Problem child," The, 51

Progressive schools, 182, 196–206
Project Method, The, 221–7, 237, 245
Propaganda, 59–61, 66, 71–83, 258–62
Provision of Meals Act, 150
Psychology, 25, 106, 111, 146
Public schools, 99–102, 109–10, 182–8, 213

Raymont, *Modern Educational Aims and Methods*, 117
Reality in education, 212–13, 256
Research, 190–4
Robinson, C. A., *A History of England. The Nineteenth Century and After*, 79
Romilly, G. and E., *Out of Bounds*, 83, 98–9
Roosevelt, 7
Rowse, Dr., 33
Rugg, H., quoted from *A New World in the Making*, 204
Rural education, 175–7
Ruskin, 53, 112
Russell, Bertrand, 109, 144, 201
  Education and the Social Order, 65, 265
Russell, Dora, 201, 203
Russia, 12, 72, 145, 226, 233–6, 256–7 fn., 269–72
  the Church in, 178
  conditions of work for teachers in, 142–3 fn.
  culture in, 123 fn., 193
  education in, 157, 162, 200 fn., 208, 223–5, 246–7, 254–5 fn., 258–61, 262 fn.
  equality of sex in, 43
  manual labour in, 243
  planning in, 174
  the Press in, 18

Russia—*contd.*
  socialist competition in, 112, 230–1
  tradition in, 64

St. Christopher's, Letchworth, 197–203
Sanderson of Oundle, 70, 273
Scholarship ladder, the, 22, 50, 103, 118–19
School-leaving age, the, 22–6, 28, 129–35
School societies, 253–5
Scientific attitude, the, 262, 265–73
Self-government, 237–41
Shakespeare, 122
Shaw, G. B., *The Intelligent Woman's Guide to Socialism and Capitalism*, 228
Showan, *Citizenship and the School*, 61
Socialist, The, 131, 133 fn., 153 fn.
Socialist schools, 159–62
Society for the Promotion of the Christian Religion, 27
Southgate, G. W., *A Text Book of Modern English History*, 81–2
Soviet Russia, cf. Russia.
Spaull, Hebe, *World Problems of To-day*, 87–8 fn.
Specialization of schools, 161
Stalky and Co., 59, 96
Starr, Mark, *Lies and Hate in Education*, 81, 85, 91, 181 fn.
Stovin, Harold—
  Education in the Wasteland, from *Growing Opinions*, 205–6
  Totem, 232–3, 233–4 fn., 235
Summerhill, 197, 219

Tawney, R. H., 127
  Education, The Socialist Policy, 105, 249
  The School-leaving Age and Juvenile Unemployment, 131
Teachers, 13–14, 140, 171–2, 240–1
  conditions of work for, 141–4
  training of, 35–7
  uncertificated, 36, 139
Technical education, 44–5, 248 fn.
Text-books, 76–83
Thompson, cf. Leavis
Tickner, F. W., *The Headway Histories*, Junior Series, Book 4, 82
Tom Brown's Schooldays, 68
Trimmer, Mrs., 27

Unemployment, 132–3
Universities, 45–8, 165–7, 188–90
University Extension Movement, 55

Vocational training, 241, 245–9

Weaver, cf. Drake
Webb, S. and B., *Soviet Communism*, 18, 22–3, 84, 157–8, 162 fn., 217 fn., 229–31, 233–4 fn., 246, 256–7 fn., 259
Wells, H. G., *Sanderson of Oundle, The Story of a Great Schoolmaster*, 273
Whitehead, A. N., *The Aims of Education*, 116–17, 194–5, 209, 212
Whitridge, A., *Life of Thomas Arnold*, 66

Wilde, Oscar—
  The Importance of Being Earnest, 15 fn.
  The Soul of Man under Socialism, 201–2
Wilson, Dover, *The Schools of England*, 23
Wilson, Woodrow, 60

Workers' Educational Association, 53, 55, 57
Wynn Williams, E., *The Kingsway Histories*, Book 4, 72

Yoxall, A., *New Guide Histories, Intermediate*, 80

Printed in Great Britain by
UNWIN BROTHERS LIMITED, LONDON AND WOKING